# Communities of Potential

# COMMUNITIES OF POTENTIAL
## SOCIAL ASSEMBLAGES IN THAILAND AND BEYOND

Edited by
### Shigeharu Tanabe

The Regional Center for Social Science
and Sustainable Development
Chiang Mai University

ISBN: 978-616-215-117-0
© 2016 Silkworm Books
All rights reserved

First published in 2016 by
Silkworm Books
104/5 Chiang Mai–Hot Road, M. 7, T. Suthep, Chiang Mai 50200 Thailand
P.O.Box 296 Phrasingh Post Office Chiang Mai 50000
info@silkwormbooks.com
www.silkwormbooks.com

Cover: Wat Manichan, Buri Ram Province
Photo by Mr. Pattaya Chandakool, Artnana Studio (www.artnana.com)

Typeset in Minion Pro 10 pt. by Silk Type

# CONTENTS

# ACKNOWLEDGMENTS

This book originates from the international research project "Community Movements in Mainland South East Asia" organized by Shigeharu Tanabe under the scheme of a JSPS (Japan Society for Promotion of Science) Overseas Research Project for 2011–13 (Project No. 23401050). All the papers contained in this book are derived from that project and its related seminars held in March 2013 at the Faculty of Social Sciences of Chiang Mai University and in March 2014 at Lanna Resort in Chiang Mai. Besides the authors in this volume, we also thank Motoji Matsuda and Surasom Krisanajutha for their participation in this project.

We wish to express our gratitude and appreciation to Chayan Vaddhanaphuti, who acted as a discussant at the two seminars and kindly wrote the preface to this volume. Our gratitude goes to Amporn Jirattikorn, Aranya Siriphon, Phra Maha Boonchuay Sirintharo, Chantana Wun'Gaew, Paul Cohen, Motoji Matsuda, Nalinee Tantuwanich, Pensupa Sukkata Jai Inn, and Ryo Takagi for their invaluable comments on the papers submitted to the above two seminars and other occasions. I am grateful to the Center for Ethnic Studies and Development, and the Regional Center for Social Science and Sustainable Development, Chiang Mai University, for subsidizing part of publishing cost. Finally, my sincere thanks is due to Joel Akins at Silkworm Books for his substantial and meticulous work.

**Shigeharu Tanabe**
April 2015

# PREFACE

Community has been a research focus among anthropologists and sociologists in Thai society for more than six decades. Different perspectives toward community have generated many lively debates among scholars and development practitioners. Like those in different parts of the world, communities in Thailand have faced many challenges as they have been incorporated into the market economy as well as subjugated under the politico-administrative integration of the state. The major concern has been how these communities have changed over time, how they react to external forces—particularly during the age of globalization—and how social relations within a community have altered, or have been estranged, as a result of its articulation with the outside world. Community cannot be construed just as consisting of a group of households sharing a physical space together. It is a social entity with problems and potentials. An analytical assessment of community in the context of constant change is always needed, and the concept of "social assemblage," which runs through the articles in this edited volume, should be helpful as a heuristic device in understanding the social nature of community.

The Center for Ethnic Studies and Development (CESD) under the Faculty of Social Sciences is proud to be part of the efforts led by Professor Shigeharu Tanabe in trying to understand different types of potential and some of the complex problems of communities in Thailand and beyond in coping with social and political changes. We are thankful for his intellectual leadership in guiding and supporting junior Thai and non-Thai scholars in their quest to analyze the newly emerging community movements which aim to improve and transform life circumstances of community members through their participation in and construction of new communities. Our appreciation also goes to all the contributors of this volume.

**Chayan Vaddhanaphuti**
Center for Ethnic Studies and Development
Chiang Mai University

# INTRODUCTION
## Communities of Potential

SHIGEHARU TANABE

The main objective of this book is to reveal prominent features of newly emerging communities and their movements in mainland Southeast Asia, focusing on cases in Thailand and Cambodia. In particular, we pay close attention to the potential imagination and practice of individuals involved in their enterprises, as well as relational and organizational aspects of their community movements. Individual chapters in this volume focus on a wide range of movements, such as religion, development projects, nongovernmental organizations (NGOs), alternative medicine, local museums, and marginalized peoples on the border. All chapters investigate ways by which people intend to improve or transform part of their life circumstances through participation in and construction of new communities. The book also attempts to elucidate the processes in which these communities are constructed as multiple and heterogeneous individuals and groups, leading to new kinds of alliance and united through their peculiar values and ethics.

In newly emerging communities and their movements, we can no longer apply classic theories of community and communality that have often assumed integrity and tradition in the shaping of the core identity of its members.[1] Yet we still often find a certain kind of alliance or communality in most, including a variety of networks developed through the Internet and social media, despite its content being historically transformed. Within these movements, the roles and functions of individuals and component parts are greater if compared with any other instances in the preceding eras. We therefore suppose that their alliance is formed upon certain autonomy and freedom, which make these movements more flexible in their composition and more open to the outside. These features seem to be fairly different from those of social movements in general before the early 2000s.

Another salient feature we should notice, of course, is the persistent development and transformation of such movements under the current globalizing milieus. It is widely acknowledged that many community movements, rural or urban, take manifold or multilayered forms, often consisting of heterogeneous interpersonal networks and institutional organizations. Many movements could not exist and sustain themselves without connection and engagement with diverse forces located in politics, the economy, religion, or media, such as local or international organizations and government institutions. Having recognized the configurations of these external forces and their features in the same way that many anthropological and sociological studies have characterized current community movements and social movements in general, this book posits various ways in which people develop their transformative potential to construct their lives to deal with rapid and fundamental changes. In this regard, we pay close attention to complex forms of assemblage which enable individuals to actualize their potential and exercise their agency in and out of the community concerned.

The book consists of three parts. Part 1 reveals major features of community movements in which multiplicities of individuals and component parts form assemblages to pursue common or varied goals through different approaches. The chapters focus on instances of religious and folk-medicine movements in northern Thailand and NGO movements in Cambodia. Part 2 investigates community movements in marginality that exist as spaces between an experiential condition of togetherness, or in contrast, where reflexivity is salient, leading to the construction of alternative communities. These contrasting features are examined in the cases of marginal Muslim communities, a novel spirit cult, a Buddhist educational movement, and local museum movements. Finally, part 3 focuses on personal experiences and ways of constructing embodied subjectivity, drawing on the cases of Buddhist women's movements, Buddhist monk networks for community development, and a training program of detoxification practices.

In order to offer an appropriate conceptual framework for all these instances of new community movements in Thailand and Cambodia, this introduction provides a theoretical and ethnographic background to the sections that follow.

## Dynamics of the Assemblage

It is important to bear in mind the context of the recent emergence of community movements: recent transformation of nation-states, increased uncertainty of social life, growth of contingency, and the rise of neoliberalism, all of which impose market principles on almost every aspect of human practices. Under such fluidity, uncertainty, and commodification of social life, many contemporary community movements take on a complex form of "assemblage" (*agencement*), a concept posited by Gilles Deleuze and Félix Guattari in A *Thousand Plateaus* (1987) and in other works.[2] It is a dynamic and contingent configuration that emerges through articulation of diverse forces involved in global and local changes. An assemblage consists of a configuration of heterogeneous forces, institutions, individuals, groups, things, and nature where its constituent parts have significant roles and retain a certain autonomy. Furthermore, these individuals and constituent parts, instead of being a unified totality, contain the "virtual" (*le virtuel*) potential or capacity therein. Thus, community movements could be described and analyzed in terms of such conditions of assemblage, focusing on the ways by which people pursue changes and transformations of their own lives.

Regarding this attempt let me first consider the Deleuzean concept of the virtual in order to account for potentials underlying community movements. In doing so, we must be aware that the virtual, as in Henri Bergson's ontology, is not opposed to the real but to the actual. The virtual is a multiplicity, a fluid mass of power such as melody, memory, or life, which is actualized (not realized) in a visible form by a process of *differenciation* (difference in itself) (Deleuze 1988, 97; Patton 2000, 36). As Paul Patton summarizes, a process of actualization involves differences between the virtual point of departure and the actual outcome, and differences between the lines along which actualization can take place. For example, life may

3

be actualized as human, plant, or animal, or anything else. For Deleuze, all things in a world are the expression of virtual or potential multiplicities (Patton 2000, 36–37).

As such, an assemblage is fertile soil for actualization of one's potential or capacity, which otherwise remains untapped or underdeveloped. As Manuel DeLanda[3] (2002, 47) and Arturo Escobar and Michal Osterweil (2010, 190) suggest, such actualization involves transformative processes: the actualization of the virtual entails the transformation of "intensive differences" into readily visible "extensive differences" through historical processes, which involve interacting parts and emerging wholes called assemblages. In other words, the differences, in the Deleuzian sense, display the full potential of material and energy for "self-organization" leading to heterogeneous assemblages (Escobar and Osterweil 2010, 190).[4] In social-scientific terms, the significance of interacting individuals and parts within an assemblage come from the negation of the modernist conceptions of totality and essence. Escobar and Osterweil (2010, 191) thus assert that assemblage theory differentiates itself from classic theories that rely on concepts of organic totality, such as system or structure, and essence, such as ethnicity, culture, or class identity, which assume the existence of seamless webs or wholes like a nation-state or global capitalism.

Then how are individuals and parts combined or united within an assemblage? Fortunately, in his dialogue with Claire Parnet held in the late 1970s, Deleuze clarifies the emerging self-organizational features of an assemblage in an almost anthropological fashion. He contends that an assemblage is a multiplicity, made up of many heterogeneous components, groups, or individuals that set up liaisons, alliances, or networks among themselves across different ages, sexes, sites, spaces, states, natural environments, and so forth. If there is any unity of the assemblage, it is only a unity derived from "co-functioning" based on "symbiosis" or "sympathy" (Deleuze and Parnet 1989, 69). Deleuze asserts further that

> Sympathy is not a vague feeling of respect or of spiritual participation: on the contrary, it is the exertion or the penetration of bodies, hatred or love. (Deleuze and Parnet 1989, 52)

Another relational aspect of individuals and component parts is concerned with their exteriority. As DeLanda and others have emphasized, the reason why individuals and parts have a certain autonomy can be explained by the fact that they are self-subsistent and are articulated by the "exteriority of relations." They can be detached or made a part of another assemblage. Thus, the exteriority provides individuals and parts a certain autonomy in the way they relate to each other. Therefore, the whole of an assemblage cannot be explained by the properties of components but by the actual exercise of the potentials or capacities of autonomous components through actualization of the virtual (DeLanda 2006, 11; see also Escobar and Osterwel 2010, 191).

Such relations of exteriority in assemblage theory can provide a framework to account for such "intermediate entities" as interpersonal networks and institutional organizations—social movements, governments, nation-states, cities, and so forth (DeLanda 2006, 5–6). This indicates that most social movements we encounter in the contemporary world are a mixture of hierarchies and self-organizations. One such instance in Thailand is the relationship between the networks of HIV/AIDS self-help groups as "self-organization" and the dominant institutions and networks within the public health system of the state. These multiple networks of self-organization and dominant institutions formed complex power relations in the late 1990s (Tanabe 2008b, 189). We can also observe similar relationships between government institutions and people's organizations in recent forest conservation policies and community forest movements as depicted in many parts of Thailand, and in Indonesian case studies analyzed by Tania Li (2007).

Concerning the relational aspects of community movements, we have to examine how the individuals and component parts come to join the community or its movement made up of an assemblage. We have found in many recent ethnographic cases that an encounter with others in an event can be a significant occasion to enter relations within an assemblage. Recent ethnographies on social and community movements have paid much attention to encounters as events that lead to further steps toward transformation of the participants (see Escobar 2008; Leyva Solano and Gunderson 2011; Deleuze 1995, 176). One point is that a chance encounter often occurs as a vital opportunity to participate in a community or its movement. Yet classic sociological and anthropological theories favoring the "interiority" of relations explain the logically necessary relations making an individual join the community or movement as an organismic whole. On the contrary, it would be rather pertinent to assert that component parts or individuals set up alliances or unity in almost "contingently obligatory" fashion, having little to do with the predicted organismic wholes (see DeLanda 2006, 11).

## Assemblages in Community Movements

Everyone recognizes that the classic image of a community is one that shares collectivity, political integrity, and cultural homogeneity within its closed boundaries. Social movements and labor movements before the late 1960s were also constructed through homogeneous class identity under the leadership of communists, social democrats, or trade unions. After the decline of these classic types of social movements, around the 1970s, we witnessed the rise of so-called new social movements in Europe, the United States, Japan, and other industrialized countries, and later in many parts of Southeast Asia including Thailand and Cambodia. Alberto Melucci, one of the prominent sociologists working on the "new social movements," asserts that participation in these movements is based mainly on individuated personal life and not on a presupposed monolithic unity like class identity or "communitarian community." For Melucci, social movements such as feminism, ecological movements, gay/lesbian rights movements, and later antiglobalization movements have engendered in the process of their movements a "collective identity" central to their politics. This collective identity is, however, not a reified and monolithic one, but a process involving a self-reflexive and constructed manner (Melucci 1996, 76–77). In relation to Melucci's proposal, it is noted that the participants in contemporary community movements, as argued in this book, might share a common goal but not necessarily a single collective identity, as clearly exemplified by some cases discussed in part 3, titled "Experience and Alliance." Yet these community movements have shared certain features with the "new social movements," especially in their individually oriented motivation in participating in collective action.

In addition to the individuated motivation, assemblage provides a major feature to many community movements dealt with in this volume. It provides the participants in movements with a basis of articulation, cooperation, or solidarity with other forces and organizations. Let us pay attention to how people cooperate with or resist the forces and organizations, including international, transnational, or local organizations, governments and their agencies, and other NGOs that intervene in these movements. It then becomes clear that the major characteristics of the newly emerging communities, which include internal multiplicity and heterogeneity and the potential of individuals and parts, have all contributed to make these communities open, linking them with outside people, organizations, and institutions to form an assemblage. Such communities thus acquire the power and potential to create new practices through self-transformation and negotiation and cooperation with other people, organizations, and institutions.

As Kwanchewan Buadaeng demonstrates in chapter 2, in the pagoda construction project extending across the Thailand-Myanmar border, an assemblage has been formed to attain this religious enterprise among the agencies with multiple ethnic, educational, and occupational backgrounds, and with different goals. Nobuko Koya argues in chapter 3 that the development of the folk medicine revival movement in northern Thailand has progressed through an "intermediate entity" which has been constituted by the network of folk healers (*mo mueang*), medical institutions, government agencies, NGOs, Buddhist monks, and media in the nationwide upsurge of health-care concerns since the 1990s. As she demonstrates, folk healers have been able to actualize their own potential in multiple ways within the assemblage and gradually gain legitimacy as healers. Similarly, compositional features can be detected in other cases examined in this volume: the northern Thai network of development monks (chapter 10); the Muslim Da'wa movement in Mae Sot (chapter 5); and Cambodian NGO movements supporting a variety of victims, including minority groups, in the judicial process of the Khmer Rouge Tribunals (chapter 4). These are all recently developed community movements that have been organized in the form of assemblage or "embryonic assemblage," as Toshihiro Abe calls it in the case of Cambodian movements.

In recent arguments in geography, as Sallie Marston and others contend, "sites" can be reconceptualized as contexts for "event relations" and become an emergent property of its interacting human and non-human inhabitants (Marston et al. 2005, 425). Many community movements are often accompanied by new or renewed articulation, alliances, and relations of humans, things, nature, and other elements that result in emerging new sites. The local museum movements in Thailand described by Kyonosuke Hirai in chapter 8 provide a case in point: the villagers have encountered the renewed value of traditional handicrafts, tools, and so forth, with which they have sought to revive a lost communal ethos in the renewed meanings and context of the local museum movements during the late 1990s and early 2000s. In this sense, the local museums are sites of emergent property in which production of nostalgia proceeds.

In a quite different political context, that of the Khmer Rouge Tribunal in postwar Cambodia, Abe analyzes in chapter 4 the transformation of two NGO movements led by diaspora-returnees. These movements also created "event relations" or communicative spaces in which multiple minority groups were allowed to speak out as victims from their different historical experiences and from which they emerged with a shared sense of victimhood. Abe verifies that, as the gap between the elite returnees as leaders and the participating locals deepened, the latter began to identify the former as outsiders in the Cambodian social context. Finally, the two NGO-led movements thus either became institutionalized under government authority or collapsed, maintaining only sporadic action.

Such new or renewed relationships, including emerging "sites," could be called assemblage in the original Deleuzian sense, in which it signifies an ensemble or context of cofunctioning between humans, animals, plants, objects, tools, machines, and so forth (Deleuze and Parnet 1987, 69–70). Many instances of such assemblage are given in this book: in chapter 1, I give an account of the religious retreat of King's Mountain in northern Thailand, which has recently become a site of unconventional religious practices by hermits and yogis; Kwanchewan gives an instance in chapter 2 in which a Buddhist pagoda as a new religious site on the Thailand-Myanmar border has been constructed where multiple groups of actors have joined to accomplish their own religious and secular ends; and Ariya Svetamra describes in chapter 6 the revitalized spirit cult centered on the town spirit (*phi mueang*), in which many villagers have taken part to cope with anxiety, insecurity, and uncertainty in their lives in the transforming social and cultural context outside the city of Chiang Mai.

## *Communitas* and Reflexivity

Some communities and community movements emerge at the confluence of liminality and *communitas*. Victor Turner, drawing on Arnold van Gennep's concept of liminality, argues that liminal entities are neither here nor there; they are betwixt and between the positions assigned by law, custom, and ceremony (Turner 1969, 95). Based on this ritual context, he puts forward a major model of social relationship called *communitas* as an unstructured and relatively undifferentiated community emerging recognizably in the liminal period, as opposed to that of society as a structured hierarchical system (Turner 1969, 95–96). This indicates that certain community movements share such features of *communitas*, which arises from marginality of a larger structure under the current political, economic, and cultural contexts. Marginality could be one of the conditions from which an assemblage of individuals or component parts arises.

At the margins or borders of a modern larger system such as capitalism, nation-states, or dominant religions, we have witnessed the rise of many community movements as "antistructure"; that is, they get rid of such systems to allow different forms of social relations to materialize through a feeling of *communitas* (see Turner 1977, 47). In this sense, *communitas* has the potential of binding and articulating individuals and component parts within an assemblage (see Delanty 2003, 46). As Deleuze indicates, cofunctioning or alliance in community movements never takes the form of filiations, but rather of contagions, epidemics, or the wind, as shown by the practices of magicians (Deleuze and Parnet 1987, 69). As such, the relational aspect of an assemblage is based on affect or "affectual *communitas*" (Turner 1977, 48). Turner, thus, argues for the potential derived from *communitas* by partly drawing on Bergson's *élan vital*, or evolutionary life-force, which has not yet been actualized and is fixed in structure:

*Communitas* breaks in through the interstices of structure, in liminality; at the edges of structure, in marginality; and from beneath structure, in inferiority. It is almost everywhere held to be sacred or "holy," possibly because it transgresses or dissolves the norms that govern structured and institutionalized relationships and is accompanied by experiences of unprecedented potency. (Turner 1969, 128)

Ryoko Nishii offers in chapter 5 an ethnographic instance of a Muslim community as *communitas* in Mae Sot on the Thailand-Myanmar border. With the increased inflow of migrant Burmese into Mae Sot in the 2010s, the Muslim community has become heterogeneous and the Muslim assemblage has since been articulated with Thai-Muslim and Burmese-Muslim subgroups. One of the prominent features of this Muslim community is the Da'wa movement, involving many Burmese Muslims and also a few Thai. In Da'wa, they experience a periodic retreat from ordinary daily life by traveling together to many mosques to devote themselves to religious learning and activities. The liminal state, or space between, is experienced by the people who participate in the Da'wa movement and the *communitas*, and its "symbiotic" or "sympathetic" relationships are then developed among them. As Malee Sitthikriengkrai demonstrates in chapter 11, experiences within the detoxification training program as a "community of practice" also engender an intense *communitas* or antistructure even though it lasts for a limited time within the movement (see Hetherington 1998, 97).

We have also come across the recent resurgence of spirit cults in many parts of Thailand indicating the appearance of *communitas* among groups of small peasantry and townsfolk who are marginalized from the flux of rapid capitalist development (see Tanabe 2013, 180–81). We should take into consideration that long, sustained marginalization engenders deterritorialization stemming from seemingly insurmountable flux and opens up a niche for survival. Ariya (chapter 6) describes such a newly emerged *communitas* of a spirit cult in a peripheral district town of northern Thailand, centered on a young male spirit medium who has finished studying medical science at university. King's Mountain (chapter 1) is also a typical site of *communitas*, in which hermits and yogis have developed their particular style of practices of *dhamma*.

In these community movements, we can detect *communitas* in marginality appearing on the borders between the nation-states, between the sangha and laypersons, and through interstices of capitalist development in rural and urban lives of Thailand.

Another noteworthy feature of community movements in marginality dealt with in this volume involves their reflexivity, which relates to their dissent or resistance and sometimes leads to imagining and constructing alternative communities (see Tanabe 2008a, 11–12). Scott Lash distinguishes reflexive communities and their movements from "traditional communities" founded on supposedly shared meanings and embedded practices. He pointed out, in the early 1990s, the main features of these reflexive communities, and these still seem applicable to contemporary cases. Lash contends that people are not born or thrown into communities but instead make choices to join certain communities and that they may be widely stretched over abstract space through networks such as the Internet and other media. Thus, these communities, whose tools and products tend to be abstract and cultural rather than material, consciously pose themselves the problem of their own creation and constant reinvention much more notably than do traditional communities (Lash 1994, 161). Therefore, as Melucci (1996, 76) contends, contemporary movements become ever more conspicuously the product of conscious action and the outcome of self-reflection.

Kanoksak Kaewthep examines, in chapter 7, such reflexivity in Santi Asoke, a Buddhist group rejected by the Thai sangha and an increasingly marginalized movement in Thailand. He reveals an intense alternative mode of socialization in the case of the Samma Sikkha schools of the Santi Asoke. These schools have maintained an alternative community with apprenticeships built on the idea of "learning while working," which has reflexively developed for promoting a sense of spiritual and mutual sharing and the preservation of community life in Buddhist terms. The local museum movements analyzed by Hirai in chapter 8 represent another example of a reflexive project. The reflexivity of the local museum movements involves dynamic interactions within the assemblage, which consists of villagers, monks, educated persons, local governments, academics, and outside donors. In such a composition, multiple and competing concepts and discourses on community and tradition are entangled among the variety of individuals and component parts who assign different meanings to the museums. In such reflexive practices of the Santi Asoke and the local museum movements, we thus need to draw our attention to the fact that multiple or unique imaginations and meanings about their own community are overtly manifested rather than preserving a state of *communitas* as observable in the cases cited above.

## Experience and Alliance

The chapters in this book reveal, from different angles, that for the new communities and their movements to be active and sustainable, certain conditions must be in place, such as internal multiplicity, heterogeneity, and individual potentials on the one hand, and cofunctioning, alliance, or communality on the other. In many cases, alliance derives not from traditional values and normative structures but from the "desire"[5] of participants and their social action to allow new practices and ethics to materialize through constructing a new community or reflexively problematizing their existing community. Most community movements, approaching the sphere of values and ethics, raise a fundamental question of how individuals and groups can maintain their lives in changing political, economic, and cultural contexts. This question should be considered in relation to a certain kind of alliance, affinity, and imagination that emerges from the social practices among multiple and heterogeneous individuals and groups.

Mayumi Okabe considers in chapter 10 the ways in which development monks have engaged in community development activities through the Community Development Monks' Network in Northern Thailand. She doesn't account for the movement and its network through a unified definition of development monks, which risks representing a static and reified notion of collective identity. Rather, these monks always try to construct their alliance with other multiple forces through continuous discussions of their experiences on a variety of occasions in the movement, which leads to finding oneself in terms of one's relationship to another. Thus, as Kevin McDonald put forward, grammars of movement could be better understood in terms of cultural pragmatics and personal experience rather than collective identity as argued by Melucci and others (McDonald 2006, 4; also see Touraine 2002; Melucci 1996, 76).[6] As such, we would further say that the contemporary community movement grows its alliance as a process, which derives from personal experience rather than filiation that shapes collective identity.

As I have argued before, if chance encounters often become moments to participate in many social movements, they also provide occasions in which participants can find themselves through their experience within the movement as communicative space (McDonald 2004, 586). Apinya Feungfusakul argues in chapter 9 that a variety of female Buddhist practitioners in contemporary Thailand develop their own religious communities and communicative spaces, which, in turn, shape their sense of self. In her study of identity politics and religious form, Apinya examines three communities of Buddhist women in which different religious spaces have been developed: a communal sanctuary for *bhikkhuni* (fully ordained nun in yellow robe observing 311 precepts); a *mae chi* (nun in white robe observing eight precepts) within the community of forest monks in northeastern Thailand; and the community of a lay practitioners focusing on sexuality and gender issues, violence, and so forth. In these cases of Buddhist women's achievements, we verify their embodied subjectivity and the related sense of self, cultivated through Buddhist practices.

In this regard, McDonald offers an instance of constructing embodied subjectivity in the process of recent re-Islamization spreading over many parts of the world. In what he calls the Islamic piety movement, individual participants are neither expressing an identity nor constructing a constituency but are involved in forms of embodied makings of the self, and, according to his observation, their understanding of language is not framed in terms of the primacy of the symbol, but sound, hearing, and the related ethic are more important for their understanding (McDonald 2006, 214). He thus concludes, in contrast with Jürgen Habermas, that the forms of practice and communication in these Islamic movements are more embodied and sensual than deliberative and representational (McDonald 2006, 4). In this volume, the the Islamic Da'wa movement examined by Nishii (chapter 5), the renewed spirit cult investigated by Ariya (chapter 6), and the detoxification program analyzed by Malee (chapter 11), to varying degrees all share "sympathetic" and embodied communication.

Constructing embodied subjectivity is also at stake in the case of the detoxification program investigated by Malee in chapter 11. Her descriptions and analyses of the detoxification training session provide a clearer picture of the participants' relation to self, in which they constitute and recognize themselves as "subject," as pursued by Michel Foucault in the late twentieth century.[7] It is extremely interesting to notice that the processes of constituting their embodied selves through detoxification practices also cultivate friendship and an "affinity group" in which the participants are concerned about each other. Such a site engenders *communitas*, as I touched upon earlier, and also actualizes the potential of individuals, leading them to gain a new understanding of knowledge on the body and health.

What we have pursued in this volume is not community as underlying reality, structure, or essence but community as a process. Community is always constructed and sustained through action, struggle, resistance, and movement; and it is also demolished by disasters, wars, and a variety of human practices. As Gerard Delanty (2003, 123) puts it, "it is a processal concept of community in which community is defined and constructed in social action rather than residing in values and normative structures." This definition indicates that it is a process of achieving, and, therefore, it always has a "cognitive capacity" for imagining and engaging in a new community and society, as Benedict Anderson inspired us to see a long time ago (see Delanty 2003, 124). In this sense, community is a process of and a product of imagining and reflexive practices of the people who intend to expand and revitalize their lives and their spaces (see Tanabe 2008a).

Following the preceding arguments, we might be inclined to find two models of community movements: the *communitas* model and the reflexivity model. The former seems to fit the King's Mountain retreat, the religious assemblages across the Thailand-Myanmar border, the Da'wa movement, the renewed spirit cult, and the detoxification training program. The second model, on the other hand, fits the folk-medicine revival movement, the Cambodian NGO movements, the Santi Asoke schools, the local museum movements, the female Buddhist movements, and the development-monks movement. We had better say, however, that both the *communitas* and reflexivity models are, basically, ideal types and any of these cases contain, in reality, features of both, to varying degrees. In addition, these ideal features might disappear as the activities of movement are routinized or formally institutionalized with the lapse of time, as often observable in many movements. This inclination is observable especially in the assemblage consisting of "intermediate entities," articulated with homogenizing forces such as the nation-state and other modern institutions and systems of knowledge.

Finally, a fundamental theoretical point we suggest in this book is the cofunctioning complexity consisting of multiple and heterogeneous components that actively engenders practices to actualize their potential. Assemblage and its associated components and alliance could be viewed as the outcome of an alternative order or another kind of "order-world," which is perhaps hidden or suppressed by the structurally constructed order within the modern order.[8] The community movements dealt with in this book reveal only a glimpse of such alternative order though its full picture is yet to appear. Bearing this in mind, our attempts in this book, I hope, contribute in some way to unfolding a new terrain of research on community and community movements that is beginning to spread out before us.

## NOTES

1. Neither do we see community movements only as a phenomenon particular to contemporary civil society. Rather, we regard such movements as a wider research subject in social sciences across premodern, modern, and postmodern cultural and social settings.

2. In addition to *A Thousand Plateaus*, Deleuze concisely elaborates on the concept of assemblage in his dialogues with Claire Parnet (1987, 69–76). In these dialogues, Deleuze develops a variety of aspects of the concept of assemblage, ranging from assemblages of man-animal-manufactured object, regimes of utterances, territory, and deterritorialization, and the transformative potential of "becoming" (*devenir*). For "becoming" in anthropological analysis, also see Biehl and Locke (2010) and Tanabe (2013; 2015).

3. An application of the concept of assemblage to social movements owes much to DeLanda (2002; 2006; 2010) who has developed a different and stronger version of "realist social ontology" by elaborating on the original Deleuzian ideas (Deleuze and Parnet 1987; Deleuze and Guattari 1994).

4. Marylin Strathern's argument about "unmediated relations" and "enchainment" in relation to gift economy also seems to account for articulatory relations of components and individuals within an assemblage (Strathern 1988, 178–79; Jensen and Rödje 2010, 23–24).

5. Paul Patton argues, "The component of the Deleuzian concept of desire which corresponds to Spinoza's affect or Nietzsche's feeling of power is the concept of intensity" (Patton 2000, 75).

6. For McDonald's "experience movement," see McDonald (2006, 223–26).

7. For the directly relevant arguments concerning this point, see Foucault (1987, 5; 1997, 290–91) and Hall (1996, 12–13).

8. In *A Thousand Plateaus*, Deleuze and Guattari propose an alternative order called rhizome, defined by multiplicities, regulations, and movements completely different from the order modeled on a tree and its roots in modernity. Their efforts are intended to reveal the continuity and movements of such alternative orders appearing across different spheres (Deleuze and Guattari 1987, 21).

REFERENCES

Biehl, João, and Peter Locke. 2010. "Deleuze and the Anthropology of Becoming." *Current Anthropology* 51(3): 317–51.

DeLanda, Manuel. 2002. *Intensive Science and Virtual Philosophy*. New York: Continuum.

————. 2006. *A New Philosophy of Society: Assemblage Theory and Social Complexity*. London: Continuum.

————. 2010. *Deleuze: History and Science*. New York: Antropos Press.

Delanty, Gerard. 2003. *Community*. London: Routledge.

Deleuze, Gilles. (1966) 1988. *Bergsonism*. Translated by Hugh Tomlinson and Barbara Habberjam. New York: Zone Books.

————. (1990) 1995. *Negotiations, 1972–1990*. Translated by Martin Joughin. New York: Columbia University Press.

Deleuze, Gilles, and Félix Guattari. (1980) 1987. *A Thousands Plateaus: Capitalism and Schizophrenia*. Translated by Brian Massumi. Minneapolis: University of Minnesota Press.

————. (1991) 1994. *What is Philosophy?* Translated by Graham Burchell and Hugh Tomlinson. New York: Columbia University Press.

Deleuze, Gilles, and Claire Parnet. (1977) 1987. *Dialogues*. Translated by Hugh Tomlinson and Barbara Habberjam. New York: Columbia University Press.

Escobar, Arturo. 2008. *Territories of Difference: Place, Movements, Life,* Redes. Durham: Duke University Press.

Escobar, Arturo, and Michal Osterweil. 2010. "Social Movements and the Politics of the Virtual: Deleuzian Strategies." In *Deleuzian Intersections: Science, Technology, Anthropology*, edited by Casper Bruun Jensen and Kjetil Rödje. New York: Berghahn Books.

Foucault, Michel. (1984) 1985. *The History of Sexuality, Vol.2: The Use of Pleasure*. Translated by Robert Hurley. Harmondsworth: Penguin.

———. (1984) 1997. "The Ethics of the Concern of the Self as a Practice of Freedom." In *Ethics: Subjectivity and Truth, Essential Works of Foucault 1954–1984, Volume One*, edited by Paul Rabinow, translated by Robert Hurley et al. New York: The New Press.

Hall, Stuart. 1996. "Introduction: Who Needs 'Identity'?" In *Questions of Cultural Identity*, edited by Stuart Hall and Paul du Gay. London: Sage Publications.

Hetherington, Kevin. 1998. *Expressions of Identity: Space, Performance, Politics*. London: Sage.

Jensen, Casper Bruun, and Kjetil Rödje. 2010. "Introduction." In *Deleuzian Intersections: Science, Technology, Anthropology*, edited by Casper Bruun Jensen and Kjetil Rödje. New York: Berghahn Books.

Lash, Scott. 1994. "Reflexivity and its Doubles: Structures, Aesthetics, Community." In *Reflexive Modernization: Politics, Tradition and Aesthetics in the Modern Social Order* by Ulrich Beck, Anthony Giddens, and Scott Lash. Cambridge: Polity Press.

Leyva Solano, Xochitl, and Christopher Gunderson. 2011. "The Tapestry of New-Zapatismo: Origins and Development." In *The Movements of Movements: Struggles for Other Worlds*, edited by Jai Sen and Peter Waterman. New Delhi: OpenWord. Available online at http://www.rauhanpuolustajat.org/tiedostot/5XLS&CG-The_Tapestry_of_Neo-Zapatismo.pdf#search='Leyva+Solano%2C+Xochitl+and+Christopher+Gunderson'.

Li, Tania Murray. 2007. "Practices of Assemblage and Community Forest Management." *Economy and Society* 36(2): 263–93.

Marston, Sallie A., John Paul Jones III, and Keith Woodward. 2005. "Human Geography without Scale." *Transactions of the Institute of British Geography* (NS) 30(4): 416–32.

McDonald, Kevin. 2004. "Oneself as Another: From Social Movement to Experience Movement." *Current Sociology* 52(4): 575–93.

———. 2006. *Global Movements: Action and Culture*. Oxford: Blackwell.

Melucci, Alberto. 1996. *Challenging Codes: Collective Action in the Information Age*. Cambridge: Cambridge University Press.

Patton, Paul. 2000. *Deleuze and the Political*. London: Routledge.

Strathern, Marilyn. 1988. *The Gender of the Gift: Problems with Women and Problems with Society in Melanesia*. Berkeley: University of California Press.

Tanabe, Shigeharu. 2008a. "Introduction: Imagined and Imagining Communities." In *Imagining Communities in Thailand: Ethnographic Approaches*, edited by Shigeharu Tanabe. Chiang Mai: Mekong Press.

———. 2008b. "Suffering, Community, and Self-Government: HIV/AIDS Self-Help Groups in Northern Thailand." In *Imagining Communities in Thailand: Ethnographic Approaches*, edited by Shigeharu Tanabe. Chiang Mai: Mekong Press.

———. 2013. "Spirit Mediumship and Affective Contact in Northern Thailand." In *Duai Rak: Essays on Thailand's Economy and Society for Professor Chatthip Nartsupha at 72*, edited by Pasuk Phongpaichit and Chris Baker. Bangkok: Sangsan.

———. 2016. "Resistance through Meditation: Hermits of King's Mountain in Northern Thailand." In *Scholarship and Engagement in Mainland Southeast Asia*, edited by Oscar Salemink, 115–37. Chiang Mai: Silkworm Books.

Touraine, Alain. 2002. From Understanding Society to Discovering the Subject. *Anthropological Theory* 2(4): 387–98.

Turner, Victor. 1969. *The Ritual Process: Structure and Anti-Structure*. London: Routledge and Kegan Paul.

———. 1977. "Frame, Flow, and Reflection: Ritual and Drama as Public Liminality." In *Performance in Postmodern Culture*, edited by Michel Benamou and Charles Caramello. Madison, WI: University of Wisconsin–Milwaukee / Coda Press.

# PART I

# ASSEMBLAGES IN COMMUNITY MOVEMENTS

# HERMITS OF KING'S MOUNTAIN
## A Buddhist Utopian Movement in Northern Thailand

SHIGEHARU TANABE

Maybe the target nowadays is not to discover what we are, but to refuse what we are. We have to imagine and to build up what we could be to get rid of this kind of political "double bind," which is the simultaneous individualization and totalization of modern power structures.

—Michel Foucault (1982, 216)

## Introduction

In 1986, I wrote an ethnography of a peasant leader called Pan, who lived in Mae Wang District (then San Pa Tong District), Chiang Mai Province, in northern Thailand. The study focused on the construction of a utopian village community called Ban Mai Sawan (New Heavenly Village) during the 1970s, and also on the dhammic practices he carried out at Doi Saphanyu—a forest retreat—during the 1980s (Tanabe 2004). During both these periods, he focused on meditation while wearing the yellow robes of a novice, and occasionally worked as a peasant leader (clad in black) on irrigation management activities. In 1997, he moved to a hilly area called Khao Phra Racha, or "King's Mountain," located nine kilometers northwest of Ban Kat, and began to establish a forest retreat which ran a number of projects aimed at constructing Buddhist and Hindu statues, *chedi*s, a *wihan* (*vihara*), and also residences. Even before that point—since the early 1990s—he was already a hermit (*ruesi*), wearing white robes and focusing on dhammic practices. As a result, his role as a local leader had diminished considerably.

My ethnography in the 1980s described how a utopian site had been established while Pan practiced his *dhamma*, transforming it into political power which he used to govern the community. Nearly thirty years later, however, what I came across at King's Mountain was a significant level of zeal among the people there, including Pan, his disciples, and the yogis (*mae pha khao*, or female ascetics), in terms of their desire to transform themselves into "something else." As a result, this utopian movement now seems to have developed into one of "becoming"—becoming somebody or something else (see Tanabe 2013b, 182)—rather than a movement set up merely to construct new social relations.

This chapter explores the ways in which a variety of actors within Pan's movement have pursued freedom and transformation within their lives by refusing to accept their present state of being. In order to help readers understand this movement, the chapter will also shed light on the ways in which this transformation has become possible in terms of social arrangements and relations. To this end, I will first examine the more recent phases of Pan's utopian project, those that have taken shape since it moved to the King's Mountain in the late 1990s. Second, I intend to describe how a variety of actors, such as hermits and yogis, are able to pursue their own "becoming" through liminal practices in this utopian space. Finally, I approach this utopian community movement as an assemblage, one consisting of multiple and heterogeneous individuals and groups and that helps members actualize their own potential or capacity to become "others," both inside and outside of the King's Mountain community.

## King's Mountain: A Utopian Topography

The spatial arrangement of monuments and residences in the project area of about 250,000 square meters is rather incongruous when compared with ordinary Buddhist sites. Coming into the compound through the tall, "surrealistic" gate made of wood and stone, one first comes across the homes of Pan and his fellow hermits, around which are a pasture containing horses, cows, and buffaloes. Up a slope is a Buddha statue with many small statues of Mae Phosop (the rice goddess) and Ganesha around it, while to the north of the Buddha statue are the residences and workplaces of yogis allied with the male hermits. On top of the hill is Chedi Sri Lanna (Chedi for Heroes) which is under construction, a pagoda with Indra at the top, in memory of the Lanna kingdom's historical heroes, over a *wihan* underneath. To the west of the *chedi* are many buildings containing statues of the Buddha, Khuba Sriwichai, and Hindu deities, and a pond dedicated to Mae Thorani (the earth goddess). At the end of the compound is a ruined hermitage—formerly Pan's residence—called Phalam Phala Phaya Thammikarat (Pavilion of Thammikarat), named after a millenarian righteous king. Here, Pan and others are currently developing a project to construct the Chedi Chet Thawip, also called "Chedi for Heroines," in memory of historical heroines (see map 1).

None of these monuments has been constructed under a single, rational master plan; instead they are the product of a series of visions (*nimit*) Pen has had while meditating over the past two decades. In recent years, the visual images appearing in Pan's visions have increasingly centered on Phra Sri Ariya Mettrai (or Phra Sri Ariya Mettaya), a Buddha of the future who emanates lovingkindness (*metta*). Therefore, the latest monument is a huge reclining Phra Sri Ariya Mettrai, constructed in 2012 on the southern side of the hill. Many small statues representing Mae Phosop surround this reclining Buddha.

Within the rather incongruous spatial arrangement of the King's Mountain hermitage, one can see combinations of somewhat enigmatic male/female and orthodox/heterodox representations. On the one hand there are male *chedi*, traditional male Buddha statues, and statues of the venerated teacher Khuba Sriwichai, of Indra, and of other Hindu deities, while on the other there are female figures such as Mae Phosop, Mae Thorani, and Bodhisattva Kuan Im. Perhaps the pasture adds to the strangeness of these monuments and statues—a curious juxtaposition between humans and domestic animals. There is also a project in progress to construct a walled palace for cows and buffaloes (*wang wiang ua khwai*) at Ban Mai Sawan, which is six kilometers southeast of King's Mountain, at which people will be invited to show their gratitude to the cows and buffaloes for their hard labor.

MAP 1. Plan of King's Mountain (Khao Phra Racha), 2015

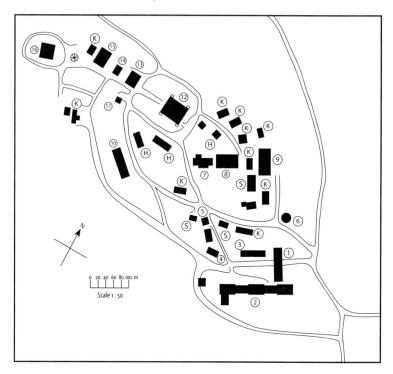

1  Gate
2  Main hermitage
3  Sacred log
4  Stable and pasture
5  King Phra Naresuan statue
6  Mae Kuan Im statue
7  Buddha statue with Mae Phosop
   (Rice Goddess)
8  Nunnery (Chao Regina and female
   acsetics)
9  Workshop
10 Reclining Buddha Phra Sri Ariya
   Mettrai
11 Khuba Sriwichai statue
12 Chedi Sri Lanna (Chedi for Heroes)
13 Office of King's Mountain

14 Pond of Mae Thorani (Earth
   Goddess)
15 Wihan (Vihara)
16 Pavilion of King Thammikarat
   (ruin), site for Chedi Chet Thawip
   (Chedi for Heroines)

H  Hermit statue
K  Hermitage
S  Shop

The combination of these monuments, statues, and animals seems to engender spaces for "alternative ordering" to take place, to borrow Kevin Hetherington's (1998, 132) term, or for Michel Foucault's "heterotopia" to be represented. Foucault suggests that heterotopias have a function in relation to all the space that remains:

> Either their role is to create a space of illusion . . . [o]r else, on the contrary, their role is to create that is other, another real space, as perfect, as meticulous, as well arranged as ours is messy, ill constructed, and jumbled. This latter type would be the heterotopia, not of illusion, but of compensation. (Foucault 1986, 27)

In accordance with Foucault, the King's Mountain hermitage falls into the latter category; acting as an alternative real space that displays Pan's Buddhist utopian ideals, those taken from his visions. At the same time, the hermitage also operates based on multiple alliances and relationships recently developed with other institutions, practitioners, and visitors, as shall be discussed later.

## Marginal Practices at King's Mountain

### The birth of *Ruesi* Pan

In the early days at Ban Mai Sawan and Doi Saphanyu, Pan was deeply involved with two seemingly opposing practices: local irrigation management activities with nearby farmers, and the practice of *dhamma,* as a Buddhist novice. This double identity—which meant Pan occupied a marginal position outside the monastic order—continued until the early 1990s. At the time he felt that secular and Buddhist practices did not contradict each other because activities such as irrigation and conflict resolution represented a form of justice, something always determined by *dhamma.* However, in the mid-1990s Pan finally became a hermit, wearing a white robe, in order to seek greater freedom to practice *dhamma.*

By the mid-1990s, Pan was already well known for his charisma—and his esoteric spells, cures, and divinations—among monks and novices, and also villagers in Mae Wang and San Pa Tong Districts in Chiang Mai as well as Pasang District in Lamphun and beyond. Since that time he has attracted a large number of disciples from many areas of northern, northeastern, and central Thailand. Since moving to King's Mountain, many Buddhist monks, as well as hermits, yogis, and even spirit mediums, have visited him to honor him and to practice divination, chant spells (*khatha*), and write esoteric verses (such as *yan*, or in Pali, *yantra*).

Together with these practitioners, Pan now receives a large number of lay visitors and clients, often with their partners, every morning and afternoon. These people visit Pan in order to ask for esoteric verses to be written on to paper, cloth, or foil, or inscribed on candles (*yan thian*) and amulets (*phra khrueang*), and treated with holy water or other sacred objects, as this represents good fortune. Others visit to have their illnesses cured, and for these people he chants Buddhist spells (*khatha*) and sometimes rubs their skin using a type of stone (*lek lai*) renowned for its healing properties.

## Who are the hermits?

The practices carried out by the hermits at King's Mountain are different to those institutionally organized and discursively structured within the Buddhist order. As has appeared in myths, legends, and paintings in northern Thailand, such ascetic conduct and lifestyle can be seen as marginal, in the sense that they normally live in the forest, away from the secular center of society and even apart from Buddhist institutions (see Tambiah 1984, 295–96). In a wider sense, the key practices performed by the hermits are similar to those of Buddhist monks seeking *dhamma* through meditation at forest retreats and other hermitages in Thailand, Laos, Myanmar, and Sri Lanka (see Carrithers 1983; Tambiah 1984). As previously mentioned, Pan was not fully ordained as a monk (*tu*) but remained a novice (*pha*), observing only ten precepts. In later years he chose to become a hermit in order to pursue a more flexible and ascetic lifestyle, one detached from the Buddhist monastic order.

As Pan has said, "hermits live in freedom, and are not governed by any dominating rules and precepts (*phra winai*)." According to Pan, in order to maintain this level of freedom when pursuing *dhamma*, he and his fellow hermits have to continually maintain discipline, rigorously governing their immediate surroundings and their conduct. To maintain such discipline, the hermits, both men and women, need to have strong self-discipline, as those "outside" the Buddhist order. It has to be borne in mind, however, that hermits at King's Mountain are not completely isolated but maintain contact with people outside and have social lives. Therefore, it can be discerned, in line with the thoughts of Victor Turner, that their social status is liminal; that is, they are detached from any arrangement of positions or statuses, engendering new experiences by turning toward and facing others in society (Turner 1967, 126–27).

## *Nimit* as a source of conduct

It is worth mentioning that at King's Mountain, use of the imagination and the development of imaginative ideas are encouraged, including flashes of inspiration during meditation and even dreams. These occurrences are often discussed among the hermits, including Pan.[1] What are called *nimit* (based on Pali *nimitta*, a sign or omen), visions or signs preceding an event, especially those appearing at certain stages of *chan* (*jhāna*) consciousness or "absorption" during meditation, are highly significant. According to Buddhaghosa, a fifth-century Sri Lankan meditation master, at an advanced level of *chan* consciousness during meditation, the clarity of perception gives rise to *nimit* such as flashes of bright light and other illuminations, as well as joyous, devotional feelings and acute levels of faith (Buddhaghosa 1991, XX, par. 105–30). Buddhaghosa also said that *chan* consciousness engenders a variety of visions that may represent a pseudo-nirvana, meaning that the person meditating needs to ascend further to reach the summit, true Nirvana (*nipphan/nibbana*, or enlightenment) and a state of "signless liberation" (*animitta-vimokkha*) (Buddhaghosa 1991, XXI, par. 67–73; Tambiah 1984, 43–44).

In contrast, in the Lanna Buddhist tradition and especially that embodied by the *khuba*s (venerable teachers), *nimit* has long represented an important element of planning the construction and renovation of Buddhist monasteries and monuments, since the Khuba Sriwichai/Khuba Khao Pi tradition developed during the twentieth century (Cohen 2000, 2001; Kwanchewan 1988; Tanabe 2004, 195–97). As part of this tradition, a *khuba* and his followers recognize the visual images and affects attached to a khuba's *nimit,* and these act as a trigger for the establishment of *phuttha thet* (*buddhadesa*, or a "Buddha-land"), a utopian Buddhist cosmology within this world (Tanabe 2012, 107–8). It can, therefore, be assumed that the *khuba* tradition places a greater emphasis on *nimit,* the result of an embodiment of Buddha or dhammic qualities through meditation, as carried out by *khuba.*[2] While in Doi Saphanyu, Pan too has often talked of *nimit* as referring to a Buddhist cosmology, and since the late 1990s has planned and constructed many Buddhist monuments inspired by his own *nimit,* in order to create his own utopian topography at King's Mountain.

## Practices of other hermits

In the hermitage there are, in addition to Pan, normally three to five male resident hermits. During my fieldwork between 2012 and early 2014, I generally met with four resident hermits: White, a Tai Yai (Shan) in his early thirties from northern Myanmar; Smart, a thirty-three year old from Chiang Mai; Book, a thirty-one-year-old Khon Mueang (or northern Thai) and a recent arrival at King's Mountain (and who, during my fieldwork, in December 2013, was ordained as a monk [*tu*] at Wat Don Chan monastery in Chiang Mai); and Hot, a forty-seven year old who more recently joined the community, having been a monk in Lampang and later in Hot District, Chiang Mai. When Pan is away, visitors and clients visit him on Pan's behalf to ask for divination, to have their fortunes told and their illnesses cured, and in search of amulets and other magical objects.

These hermits, from diverse backgrounds and with a variety of experiences, come to King's Mountain to conceptualize their lives and make a break with their past. They devote themselves to a variety of Buddhist meditation practices, such as concentration meditation (*samatha*) and walking meditation (*chong krom*), which they believe will help them perform deeds worthy of merit. Hot, an eager practitioner, trained for many years in Lampang and was admitted more than once to a psychiatric hospital in Chiang Mai. Hot told me, "A hermit's motivations (*kham khwan*) usually emerge through his or her flashes of inspiration, those that appear at various levels of *chan* consciousness while meditating." His target is to follow Khuba Sriwichai, Khuba Khao Pi, and Queen Chamathewi and to construct a Buddhist monastery. At King's Mountain, all his practices merge together, to follow the paths of his great predecessors and as prophesied in his visions.

It is worth focusing on Hot's meditation practices, as he focuses on a change in mental state during meditation.[3] On this he told me, "The major sign that one is a hermit while practicing meditation is that as a man one can become a woman, and as a woman one can become a man." A number of times while Hot chanted and gave blessings to visitors, I noticed his voice change suddenly to a high-pitched female one.[4] Hot admitted that "while giving a blessing, I feel as though I am possessed by a deity (*thep*), and this deity controls my body, causing my voice to change and my body to shake uncontrollably." Indeed, this "becoming" looks very much like a possession one might observe in the case of spirit worship (Tanabe 2013b, 182–84).

## Insanity and "becoming"

While such manifestations of "becoming" may occur among spirit mediums, more moderate versions may be frequently observed among the male hermits at King's Mountain. At this point, it has to be noted that many of the hermits at King's Mountain, including some yogis, experience bouts of insanity, depression, stress, and various mental illnesses before joining the hermitage. Book suffered insanity prior to joining the hermitage and was hospitalized twice, while some younger hermits who have experienced life inside a psychiatric hospital occasionally join the hermitage, working in the rice fields and doing chores alongside Pan.[5]

All these hermits, including those who have suffered from mental illness, are in the process of transforming themselves into something new at King's Mountain. Book recalled that the encounters he has had with different people from a variety of backgrounds at King's Mountain have given him a sense of release and of having settled with the past. Hot has been able to rid himself of the suffering he experienced due to his visions and is now able to control them on a day-to-day basis. Even having been discharged from hospital, while practicing walking meditation he could not stem the flow of auditory hallucinations and visions he suffered, and he had to cope with them for quite a long period of time. Shortly after joining the King's Mountain hermitage, his visions stabilized and he was even able to utilize them as part of his divinatory and fortunetelling (*du chata chiwit* and *poet kam*) practices, when giving spells (*khatha*), and when curing visitors and patients.

What we can discern from these stories is that those staying at the hermitage have been able to summon their inner strength in order to "become a hermit." They have been able to maintain their passions for becoming not part of the majority, but as hermits part of the "minority," outside any established social institutions such as a Buddhist monastery or hospital. As a result, for them being a hermit does not represent just a state of being; it is more than that,[6] as it means they continuously maintain their own liminality as hermits and remain part of a collective *communitas* or utopian communality.

## "Embodying the teacher": Becoming a hermit

One occasion during which the intensity of this *communitas* at the hermitage is increased is the Brahmin rite of *khrop khu* (meaning "embodying the teacher," or literally, "covering with the teacher"), which is held on Pan's birthday during February each year. On this day, a *khu*, or teacher, represents a deity—a source of power and knowledge. Before the rite is carried out, at midnight, Buddhist monks are invited to chant an "extending lifespan" (*suep chata khon*) sutra for Pan for a few hours. In the morning, Pan and his disciples hold that Brahmin rite which can be seen among performing artists, spirit mediums, traditional healers, and artisans in northern Thailand.[7] Before the ritual starts, Pan prepares sacred water called *nam o phra in*, which literally means "Indra's reed water" and contains reeds, honey, coconut juice, and magical stones (*lek lai*). The hermits and other disciples then get together at Pan's residence and he passes the drink among them.

After this, each hermit will take hold of a *pho kae* mask (mask of the old father) from the altar, and hold it in front of Pan (the "old father" or *pho kae* is a teacher or hermit, and is also seen as a deity).[8] While chanting a spell, Pan puts the mask on each hermit's head, at which point he shouts twice, "*Saksit pakasit, saksit pakasit!* (Sacred decree, sacred decree!), adding, "may the power of *pho kae* help you successfully become a hermit," after which the hermit's entire body trembles with excitement as if his body has been occupied by the *pho kae* or teacher. According to Pan, in this way the power of the teacher is transmitted to the disciple's body, in order that he or she may become a hermit. The rite is thus performed to enhance the level of intensity felt during the "becoming" process.[9]

## Yogis and their practices

Yogis (*mae pha khao*; female ascetics) have also represented a key presence at the King's Mountain hermitage since it was established. Throughout 2013 there were five resident yogis at the hermitage and around three to five temporary members. These yogis are sometimes referred to as "female hermits" or *ruesi maeying*. Chao Regina, a female spirit medium, set up the first nunnery at the hermitage, on a hillside near the Buddha statue in 2004. Before arriving at King's Mountain, Chao Regina had been ordained as a yogi at Wat Doi Saphanyu, meeting Pan there in 1991. In the late 1980s she was afflicted by a serious and unknown illness over a long period, and was finally possessed by a spirit called Chao Pu during one Thai New Year festival (Songkran). At the time she felt her entire body come under the control of a strong force which ordered her to recite sutras and worship the Buddha. After that she became a spirit medium and started a small cult at her house in San Pa Tong District in Chiang Mai Province, finally arriving at Wat Doi Saphanyu to practice *dhamma* in 1991.

Since arriving at King's Mountain in 2004, Chao Regina has worked as a spirit medium, most of the time possessed by King Phra Naresuan (who ruled between 1590 and 1605 AD) of the late Ayutthaya period. Phra Naresuan has been widely worshiped as a national hero in Thailand since the 1990s, and is believed to have passed through the area around King's Mountain during his campaign against Burma (Myanmar). As well as possessing Chao Regina, Phra Naresuan is quite a prominent figure among the people in the area, and a large statue of him was erected near King's Mountain in the late 1990s based on donations from a yogi in Bangkok.

As well as being a spirit medium, Chao Regina is a specialist in crafting *baisi* ornaments, which are made of woven banana leaves and cooked rice, with an egg placed on top, and which are used as offerings to deities and the Buddha (*buang suang thewa but*). With her yogi colleagues, she makes these ornaments for Buddhist monasteries and ritual specialists, for use with a variety of rituals. She also reads "divine prescriptions" (*ongkan*) for Hindu deities at such rituals, held both at King's Mountain and outside. In addition, Chao Regina and her colleagues produce votive Buddha tablets, plus small stucco statues of the Buddha, Phra Naresuan, and others, which are made in a small factory attached to the nunnery.

Chao Regina looks after all the yogis, who chant sutras every evening (*suat mon yen*) plus make *baisi* offerings and craft stucco tablets and statues during the day. The female yogis' activities differ from those of the male hermits, who concentrate on meditation, though chanting sutras and making *baisi* are key dhammic practices. As the yogis are sometimes called "female hermits," they enjoy a calm and ascetic life in the nunnery, in parallel with their male counterparts.

Most of the female yogis, as with the male hermits, have experienced a variety of problems throughout their lives, including mental illness, and arrive at King's Mountain having suffered much hardship and suffering. When compared to their male counterparts, the female yogis are rather isolated and associate less with people outside the retreat. One of the exceptions to this is Chao Regina, who as an active spirit medium with her own cult attracts a considerable number of clients. Most yogis practice *dhamma* with an unshakeable determination, in order to accumulate merit. Some are very passionate about their own liminality in a "folded space" (see Hetherington 1998, 126) as yogis, while others remain more as sojourners on a journey back to everyday life. However, all the yogis at King's Mountain wish to create alternatives to their previous lives and step into a preliminary state of "becoming."

## Assemblage of the Utopian Community Movement

### The advent of Phra Sri Ariya Mettrai

One of the most prominent features of King's Mountain is its organizational aspects. The retreat represents an articulation of multiple bodily and practical spheres, such as the male and female, hermit and yogi, hermitage and nunnery, meditation and sutra-chanting spheres. In Deleuzian terms, this kind of articulation is called an assemblage,[10] yet for such multiple spheres to fully function within an assemblage, one must wait for a certain event to take place.

Pan told me that before he moved to King's Mountain, Phra Sri Ariya had already moved to this world, in 1993.[11] According to Pan, this means that Buddhist morality has sovereignty, and that this world is beginning to fill with "noble people" (*ariyachon*). He also said that we already live in an age of freedom—the age of Phra Sri Ariya—but that we have to actively and subjectively understand *dhamma* in order to construct peace in the world, by promoting solidarity and mutual understanding and accepting the wide variety of ideas people have. This age of Phra Sri Ariya is still ongoing; he has only recently entered everyone's minds, and so we may have to wait another five hundred years before his coming is fully realized. However, Pan also said that this five-hundred-year wait might be cut to fifty or five years, or even five hours, if people are able to fully realize their Buddhist morality.

The advent of the age of Phra Sri Ariya is "an event," in the sense that, at least for the people of King's Mountain, it is an opportunity to participate in a new world. "Events" amid the flux of capitalism, however small and inconspicuous, can end up eluding control and domination or engendering "new space-times" in this world, to use Deleuzean terms (Deleuze 1995, 176). For the hermits and yogis of King's Mountain, Phra Sri Ariya's coming is an event that will bring to humans the significance of lovingkindness (*metta*), which has long been undervalued within the capitalist system. His lovingkindness, rather than his intelligence (*sati panya*), is an invaluable human potentiality that should, according to Pan, constitute an important element among communities and political leadership circles within the contemporary world.

Linked to the advent of Phra Sri Ariya, Buddhist millennialism may be attributed to the *khuba* tradition of Sriwichai and Khao Pi, which Pan is often associated with. However, Pan's form of millennialism may be distinguished from the passive acceptance of the arrival of a miraculous golden age, as seen in the sporadic Buddhist and other millenarian-linked revolts among minorities and local peasantries in the borderlands of mainland Southeast Asia (see Scott 2009). Pan's "millennialism," together with that of Sriwichai and Khao Pi is, as Paul Cohen puts it, "essentially a voluntaristic philosophy of moral generation" or an "active utopianism" (Cohen 1984, 207; 2001, 234; cf. Tanabe 2004, 221–24).

In this regard, we should further note that Pan's "active utopianism" was spatially organized after his first project was initiated at Ban Mai Sawan in the 1970s. From this, moral generation was expected to occur in individuals' minds through proverbs, and communal relationships thereafter nurtured and enhanced by extralegal "village laws" (*kot mu*) and village administrative committees. All these features were expected to work within the spatial framework of the village during the early days of Ban Mai Sawan. As with many of its utopian predecessors in sixteenth-century Europe, the underlying problem is that, as David Harvey puts it, "to materialize a space is to engage with closure (however temporary) which is an authoritarian act" (Harvey 2000, 183). In fact, authoritarian coercion, though in contradiction of Pan's utopian ideals, could sometimes be observed in the early days of Ban Mai Sawan (Tanabe 2004, 226–28).

## Assemblage of hermits and yogis

The perennial problem of "closure" that underpinned Pan's spatial utopianism, mainly in the 1970s and 1980s, seems to have been largely resolved since his move to King's Mountain. In his new location, Pan has been able to explore a wide range of human resource issues, including the potentiality of femininity. While male domination was quite strong in the utopian communities and forest retreats of former times, Pan now openly expresses the historical significance and emancipating role of femininity when faced with human and communal problems and conflicts over the years.

Due to the incongruity of the spatial arrangements at King's Mountain, there is an enigmatic disorder to the place: labyrinths containing Buddhist and Hindu statues, male and female monuments, and many statues of the earth and rice goddesses, arranged in clusters. As mentioned at the start of this chapter, this incongruity represents a resistance against and transgression of the current Buddhist symbolic and institutional order. Out of this incongruity of material and symbolic arrangements emerges an alternative mode of collective life, a utopian community which places a considerable emphasis on femininity.

Chao Regina and her nunnery acknowledge the significance of femininity within the practice of *dhamma*, and they sit among the resident male hermits and the Buddhist monks who frequently visit the hermitage. While practicing *dhamma* in the nunnery with a number of yogis, Chao Regina formulated a plan, together with Pan, to construct a female *chedi* (Chedi Chet Thawip, or "Chedi of the Seven Continents") dedicated to historical heroines, including Chao Suphan Kanlaya—Phra Naresuan's elder sister—and Chao Dara Ratsami, who was a princess of the Chiang

Mai court and later became a wife of King Rama V within the Bangkok dynasty. In order to implement this large-scale project,[12] Chao Regina sought donations, while still being responsible for managing the nunnery and looking after the increasing number of visitors to the mountain.

Despite such collaborations between the hermitage and the nunnery, neither exists under any single monastic order. From an organizational viewpoint, the hermitage and the nunnery are independent parts, separate from one another, even though they are both spatially located at King's Mountain.[13] As I shall show later, Pan's hermitage has strong connections with other monasteries associated with the *khuba* tradition or with Buddhist revivalism in northern Thailand (which has occurred since the early twentieth century),[14] and Chao Regina's nunnery has well-established relations with other kinds of monasteries famous for their exorcism rituals and other esoteric practices. There is, therefore, an emergent whole or assemblage in which the two retain a symbiosis and relative autonomy at the same time, meaning they can be detached from the assemblage and, if they want, maintain relations with other assemblages also (see DeLanda 2006a, 253). Pan's activities at King's Mountain have thus come to be articulated as an assemblage, one which consists of Pan and his hermitage, and of Chao Regina and her nunnery.

As Deleuze and Guattari put forward, such an assemblage can create the conditions for "becoming" hermits, yogis, or even animals—something totally different from other monastic institutions:

> These multiplicities with heterogeneous terms, co-functioning by contagion, enter certain *assemblages*; it is there that human beings effect their becomings-animal. But we should not confuse these dark assemblages, which stir what is deepest within us, with organizations such as the institution of the family and the State apparatus (Deleuze and Guattari 1986, 242, emphasis in original).

This articulation of the two parts engenders an alternative mode of collective life, one detached from the male-centric Buddhist order and one not realized previously in Pan's utopian community. Yet this emergent assemblage engenders the potentials or the "virtual" elements of each part and individual; the potentials of each are brought out from the mutual trust, respect, and hospitality that exist in relation to the practice of *dhamma*. The yogis often praise the hermits' meditation practices and the accompanying visions, while the hermits admire the yogis for their determination, spells (*khatha*), and oracles. On a daily basis, encounters with the yogis and their support and care reduces the sufferings and mental stresses experienced by some of the younger hermits. Such relationships between hermits and yogis are not confined to already-determined gender roles, as can often be observed in Buddhist monasteries, which may accept yogis or female ascetics but place their life practices in an inferior position, being strictly controlled by the male monks. In contrast, the articulation experienced within the assemblage at King's Mountain helps to produce new forms of relations and associated powers.

It is within this assemblage that different and multiple kinds of practitioners interact with one another; within the assemblage the potential or capacity of each individual and group can be actualized as one encounters and interacts with another (see DeLanda 2006b, 11). This symbiosis, as an assemblage, enables us to answer a question pertaining to the "politics of the virtual": how community, community movements, and gender relations can be enhanced based on their imaginations and desires (see Escobar and Osterweil 2010, 205–7).

## The *khuba* tradition and esoteric practices

Another feature of the King's Mountain retreat has been the development of networks outside the utopian community. This connection with other institutions began with Wat Phra That Doi Suthep in Chiang Mai, prior to construction of the hermitage in 1997. Pan passed Wat Doi Saphanyu, which he constructed in the 1970s, on to the abbot of Wat Phra That Doi Suthep, a site often identified with Khuba Sriwichai. Wat Doi Saphanyu then became a meditation center with links to Wat Phra That Doi Suthep, as Pan moved to King's Mountain. In fact, the institutional relationship Pan has developed with Wat Phra That Doi Suthep has enhanced his position within the *khuba* tradition, though he remains a hermit. A long-standing link with Khuba Khao Pi at Wat Phra Phutthabat Pha Nam (Li District in Lamphun) and Khuba Wong at Wat Phra Bat Huai Tom (also in Li District) has also added to his reputation within that tradition.

In this way, Pan's network has fostered a Buddhist revivalism characterized by a belief in Phra Sri Ariya, the serious practice of meditation, and the continuous construction and renovation of monasteries in northern Thailand. However, since the 1990s Pan has also developed another kind of network, with monks who engage in magic (*saiyasat*), employ spells (*khatha*), perform exorcisms (*lai phi*), and observe other esoteric practices. Since the 1990s, esoteric practices such as chanting spells, sacralizing Buddhist medals and amulets, and exorcism have become increasingly prevalent among those regarded as *khuba* in northern Thailand. As a result of this development, Pan has been able to link networks of monks and lay practitioners together.

Wat Don Chan in Chiang Mai city is one such monastery, as it specializes in a variety of esoteric practices, as well as the production of magical objects. This monastery is also widely known for its school which specializes in educating orphans and poor children, including those from ethnic minorities.[15] Phra Anan is the abbot of this monastery, and his exorcism of malevolent spirits is widely believed to be effective in healing those who have symptoms of insanity, including psychosis and neurosis, in addition to acute spirit possession. Therefore, one can see many patients and sufferers of such conditions when visiting the monastery, some of whom also visit King's Mountain in search of cures or stay there as hermits. Some who recover then become Pan's disciples and are ordained at this monastery also.

Exorcism itself has never been directly associated with Pan and his practices, yet King's Mountain has developed linkages in this area with Wat Don Chan and also Wat Phra That Up Kaeo Chamathewi (in Hot District, Chiang Mai), adding to the *khuba* tradition and the conspicuous relationship Pan has with the more esoteric Buddhist practices. In fact, in 2013, Khuba Thong Suk at Wat Buak Khrok Noi in the city of Chiang Mai, a specialist at sacralizing objects, was invited to King's Mountain on the Thai king's birthday (December 5, 2013), at which time he delivered a sermon at the statue of Phra Sri Ariya. In his sermon, he placed considerable emphasis on the legacy left by northern Thai Buddhism, especially that derived from the *khuba* tradition.

# Conclusions

At King's Mountain, the relationships that developed between multiple, heterogeneous actors now constitute an internal assemblage, one linked with networks that extend into the outside world. This assemblage, combined with these external networks, has led the individuals and groups at King's Mountain to become "something else." Furthermore, the assemblage to be found at King's Mountain is a center of "becoming" in the sense that it has enabled participants and practitioners to actualize their capacities and potential, from what was previously "virtual," having never appeared before in concrete form.

This assemblage and its networks have inevitably brought about social processes within the spatially arranged utopian site. Within such an arrangement of assemblage and networks, magic and Buddhist revivalism, spirit possession and meditation, hermits and yogis, and the insane and the normal appear sometimes to be contradictory or congruent or both. It is within this diverse and enthusiastic congregation that an enduring movement has been able to emerge.

Regarding the key features of this movement, I have to return to Turner's ritual process, as this describes a transitional phase called *communitas*, which is the very negation of social structure. The implications of Turner's formulation are useful for my conception of the community movement at King's Mountain, as one feature of *communitas*, as a creative phase of antistructure, can be detected in most dhammic practices among the hermits and yogis there, and this has led to them "becoming." Their individual liminality and their congregation as a *communitas* represent a movement of "folded reality," as opposed to not only the existing Buddhist order but also, more significantly, the dominating system of capitalist relations. The hermits and yogis at King's Mountain are not merely complementary to Buddhist institutions; they and their assemblage and networks enhance the movement and sustain its continuity and power. Being a hermit itself is also a movement of deterritorialization, or "a flight" in Deleuzian terms, from the rushing flux of desires, and from capitalism and its associated institutions. King's Mountain, as such, represents a deterritorializing community movement, one boosted through an assemblage consisting of multiple actors and groups.

The King's Mountain retreat is situated within a web of multiple networks and capitalist flows. These networks, representing the *khuba* tradition and forming links with Wat Phra That Doi Suthep, Wat Phra Bat Pha Nam, and others, remain a source of inspiration for Pan, though distributing amulets and magical objects, undertaking divinations, and fortunetelling have facilitated the development of a strong fetishism and, at the same time, have commodified relations. King's Mountain is not merely a site of spatial practice but is part of a flow of social processes involving relevant actors, groups, and institutions, making the site an emergent property, or an assemblage. In line with the work of David Harvey, this chapter has helped shed light on the key features of contemporary utopian movements such as Pan's, in which spatial forms and social processes combine in a dialectical fashion (Harvey 2000, 195–96).

## NOTES

The fieldwork on which this chapter is based was conducted in Chiang Mai and Lamphun Provinces intermittently between August 2011 and February 2014. I am grateful to Professor Paul Cohen, Dr. Apinya Feungfusakul, and Dr. Paritta Chalermpow Koanatakool for their insightful comments on earlier versions of this chapter. My gratitude also goes to Mr. Witoon Buadang for his unwavering support during many parts of the fieldwork.

1. For instance, Hot, a resident hermit, spoke about his encounter with the Dalai Lama in a dream after meditating, during which they talked in Tibetan of together supporting the people of the world.

2. The meditation practices of the *khuba* tradition are related to Tantric Theravada, as described by Kate Crosby (2000, 141–42; 2013, 3–5, 154n26). I discuss elsewhere *nimit* and dreams among Khon Mueang spirit mediums (Tanabe 2013a, 166–74).

3. Hot here refers to the proficiency of acquiring *chan* consciousness among his colleagues; proficient meditators are able to attain *chan* very quickly, in a moment, for as Khon Mueang say, "An elephant folds down the ears, a snake flashes the tongue, or a bird drinks water"(*chang phap hu ngu laep lin nok kin nam*).

4. Hot mentioned that this is because he is possessed by Phra Phothisat Kuan Im (Bodhisattva Quan-im), a statue of whom stands near the gate of the King's Mountain retreat. Sometimes while giving a blessing, his voice becomes deep, like an old man's.

5. Pan asserts that laboring in a rice field is a good time to learn how cows and buffaloes work hard in place of humans. So, he sometimes "becomes" a buffalo and pulls the plough himself.

6. Deleuze and Guattari state that "in a becoming, one is deterritorialized. Even blacks, as the Black Panthers said, must become-black. Even women must become-women. Even Jews must become-Jewish (it certainly takes more than a state)" (Deleuze and Guattari 1986, 291).

7. The ritual of "embodying the teacher," as seen at King's Mountain, has not traditionally been practiced in northern Thailand. Possibly, Pan introduced it from a Brahmin officiant for a variety of stage performances (*lakhon*) in central Thailand. Yet, Pan obtained the *pho kae* mask himself, which is currently used in the ritual in Chiang Rai, northern Thailand. For stage performances and the teacher-worshiping rituals, and for the *pho kae* mask used in central Thailand, see Deborah Wong's detailed ethnography (Wong 2001, 9–15, 84–86).

8. Concerning the *pho kae* mask and its representations among the performers in central Thailand, see Wong (2001, 84–86).

9. As to the intensity of the "becoming" process among the spirit mediums of Chiang Mai, see Tanabe (2013b).

10. The ritual "embodying the teacher" represents an important aspect of assemblage, which in this case is made up of a mask and a human body. As explained in the introduction to this book, an assemblage consists not only of multiple groups or packs but also of a unity of cofunctioning between humans, spirits, objects, plants, animals, insects, and machines. For detailed arguments, see Deleuze and Parnet (1987, 69–70).

11. According to Pan, this did not appear as his *nimit*, but became evident in an inscription discovered at a cave in the area of Thaton, in Bago Division near Karen State in Myanmar.

12. It is estimated that the cost of this project will amount to about 100 million baht.

13. The groups consist of multiple individuals who are eager to become hermits or yogis, instead of joining the sangha majority. They have a fascination with the "pack" and with multiplicity (see Deleuze and Guattari 1986, 239–40).

14. For the *khuba* tradition and Buddhist revivalism in northern Thailand, see Keyes (1982), Tambiah (1984), Kwanchewan (1988), Tanabe (2004; 2012), and Cohen (2000).

15. The Living-Standards Development Project for Poor and Orphaned Children provides accommodation and education at the nursery, primary, vocational and university levels. The total number of pupils and students enrolled amounts to about seven hundred (late 2013).

REFERENCES

Buddhaghosa, Bhadantacariya. (1956) 1991. *The Path of Purification* (*Visuddhimagga*). Translated by Bhikkhu Nanamoli. Fifth Edition. Kandy: Buddhist Publication Society.

Carrithers, Michael. 1983. *The Forest Monks of Sri Lanka: An Anthropological and Historical Study*. Delhi: Oxford University Press.

Cohen, Paul. 1984. "The Sovereignty of the Dhamma and Economic Development: Buddhist Social Ethics in Northern Thailand." *Journal of the Siam Society* 72: 197–211.

———. 2000. "A Buddha Kingdom in the Golden Triangle: Buddhist Revivalism and the Charismatic Monk Khruba Bunchum." *The Australian Journal of Anthropology* 11(2): 141–54.

———. 2001. "Buddhism Unshackled: The Yuan "Holy Man" Tradition and the Nation-State in the Tai World." *Journal of Southeast Asian Studies* 32(2): 227–47.

Crosby, Kate. 2000. "Tantric Theravada: A Bibliographic Essay on the Writings of François Bizot and Others on the *Yogāvacara* Tradition." *Contemporary Buddhism* 1(2): 141–98.

———. 2013. *Traditional Theravada Meditation and Its Modern-Era Suppression*. Hong Kong: Buddha Dharma Centre of Hong Kong.

DeLanda, Manuel. 2006a. "Deleuzian Social Ontology and Assemblage Theory." In *Deleuze and the Social*, edited by Martin Fuglsang and Bent Meier Sorensen. Edinburgh: Edinburgh University Press.

———. 2006b. *A New Philosophy of Society: Assemblage Theory and Social Complexity*. London: Continuum.

Deleuze, Gilles. 1995. *Negotiations, 1972–1990*. Translated by Martin Joughin. New York: Columbia University Press.

Deleuze, Gilles, and Félix Guattari. (1980) 1987. *A Thousand Plateaus: Capitalism and Schizophrenia*. Translated by Brian Massumi. London: Athlone Press.

Deleuze, Gilles, and Claire Parnet. (1977) 1987. *Dialogues*. Translated by Hugh Tomlinson and Barbara Habberjam. New York: Columbia University Press.

Escobar, Arturo, and Michal Osterweil. 2010. "Social Movements and the Politics of the Virtual: Deleuzian Strategies." In *Deleuzian Intersections: Science, Technology, Anthropology*, edited by Casper B. Jensen and Kjetil Rödje. New York: Berghahn Books.

Foucault, Michel. 1982. "The Subject and Power." In *Michel Foucault: Beyond Structuralism and Hermeneutics*, edited by Hubert L. Dreyfus and Paul Rabinow. Chicago: University of Chicago Press.

———. (1967) 1986. "Of Other Spaces." *Diacritics* 16(1): 22–27.

Harvey, David. 2000. *Spaces of Hope*. Edinburgh: Edinburgh University Press.

Hetherington, Kevin. 1998. *Expression of Identity*. London: Sage.

Keyes, Charles F. 1982. "Death of Two Buddhist Saints in Thailand." *Journal of the American Academy of Religion, Thematic Studies* 48(3/4): 149–80.

Kwanchewan Srisawat. 1988. "The Karen and the Khruba Khao Pi Movement: A Historical Study of the Response to the Transformation in Northern Thailand." MA Thesis, Ateneo de Manila University.

Scott, James. 2009. *The Art of Not Being Governed: An Anarchist History of Upland Southeast Asia*. New Haven: Yale University Press.

Tambiah, Stanley. 1984. *The Buddhist Saints of the Forest and the Cult of Amulets*. Cambridge: Cambridge University Press.

Tanabe, Shigeharu. (1986) 2004. *Nung lueang nung dam: Tamnan khong phu nam chao na haeng Lannathai* [Wearing yellow robes, wearing black garb: The story of a peasant leader in northern Thailand]. Bangkok: Chulalongkorn University Press.

———. (1992) 2012. "Kho khit hen rueang ton bun latthi phra sri an lae latthi fuen fu satsana nai Lanna [Notes on *ton bun*, millennialism and revivalism in Lanna]." In *Phithikam lae patibatkan nai sangkhom chao na phak nuea khong prathet Thai* [Ritual and practice of the peasant society in northern Thailand], edited by Kwanchewan Buadaeng and Apinya Feungfusakul. Chiang Mai: Center for Ethnic Studies and Development, Chiang Mai University.

———. 2013a. *Seirei no jinruigaku: Kita tai niokeru kyoudousei no politikusu* [Anthropology of spirits: Politics of communality in northern Thailand]. Tokyo: Iwanami Shoten.

———. 2013b. "Spirit Mediumship and Affective Contact in Northern Thailand." In *Duai Rak: Essays on Thailand's Economy and Society for Professor Chatthip Nartsupha at 72*, edited by Pasuk Phongpaichit and Chris Baker. Bangkok: Sangsan.

Turner, Victor. 1967. *The Ritual Process: Structure and Anti-Structure*. Chicago: Aldine Publishing Company.

Wong, Deborah. 2001. *Sounding the Center: History and Aesthetics in Thai Buddhist Performance*. Chicago: University of Chicago Press.

# "THE MOUNTAIN OWNER HAS COME"
## Religious Assemblage across the Thailand-Myanmar Border

KWANCHEWAN BUADAENG

## Introduction

In January 2012, the Karen charismatic monk U Tuzana (also known as Myaing Gyi Ngu Hsayadaw in Burmese, or Phue Khaw Taw in Karen), who is based in the Myaing Gyi Ngu or Khaw Taw Pu area of Karen State in Myanmar, initiated the construction of a pagoda and other religious monuments on top and around the base of Tamo Mountain, in Doi Tao District of Chiang Mai Province. The coming of Phue Khaw Taw created much excitement among the Karen people living in the hill villages in the area. Many of them had been followers of the late Khuba Khao Pi (1889–1977) and Khuba Wong (1913–2000), the charismatic northern Thai monks whose monasteries—which became the centers of their activities—were in Li District of Lamphun Province. Khuba Khao Pi had stayed for twenty years at Wat Phra Bat Tamo (the monastery at the Temple of the Buddha's Footprint at Tamo), at the foot of Tamo Mountain, before he moved to Wat Phra Bat Pha Nam in Li District. The pagoda was successfully built in a month, during which thousands of Karen people came daily to labor, carrying sand, cement, and stone from the foot to the top of the steep, high mountain. The excitement was due not only to the coming of Phue Khaw Taw, but because his coming was in accordance with the prophecy given by the late *khuba*s. The late *khuba*s' words, "The mountain has an owner and one day he will come to build a pagoda on its top," are often referred to by Karen lay leaders.

"But how can you be sure," I asked some followers, "that it was Phue Khaw Taw that the *khuba*s were speaking of?"

A lay leader replied, "There is a sign, I am told. Only in the last few years has Tamo Mountain's cliff been standing upright; the cliff always leaned to one side until the coming of Phue Khaw Taw."

I used the term "*khuba* movement" in my study (Kwanchewan 1988) that focused on Khuba Khao Pi and his Karen followers who resided around Wat Phra Bat Pha Nam in Li District. The term "movement" is used because Khuba Khao Pi had resisted the order of the mainstream sangha, the centralized state organization of monks. The name Khuba Khao Pi, literally "Revered White Teacher Pi," came from the fact that he was disrobed by the state and sangha authorities but continued his monkhood by wearing a white robe instead of a yellow one. He had his own religious community in the distinctive *khuba* tradition: regular meditation, extensive religious monument construction, and vegetarianism. In addition, Karen followers saw Khuba Khao Pi as Ariya Metteya, the fifth Buddha, who would lead them to utopia provided that they practiced vegetarianism, upheld moral precepts, and supported religious monument construction. After the death of Khuba Khao Pi the nature of the movement changed. Although Khuba Wong followed Khuba Khao Pi's religious tradition, his position and operation, unlike Khuba Khao Pi, were fully controlled by the centralized sangha. After the death of Khuba Wong some Karen followers actively started to search for another messiah. The arrival of Phue Khaw Taw to construct the pagoda on top of Tamo Mountain was interpreted by some Karen elders, followers of Khuba Khao Pi, as the coming of the messiah.

The assemblage of the Karen followers of the late *khuba* and the new messiah, however, cannot be viewed simply as the continuation of the *khuba* movement. Many different agencies were involved in the construction of the pagoda at Tamo Mountain, and they did not all share the same identity, direction, and goals. They connected with each other and converged in the construction activity but did not necessarily form a unified whole. Thus the concept of "assemblage" is more fitting in this case than the term "movement," as it stresses the multiplicity of the nature of the convergence, following DeLanda (2006, 253), who notes that "assemblages are not Hegelian totalities in which the parts are mutually constituted and fused into a seamless whole. In an assemblage components have a certain autonomy from the whole they compose, that is, they may be detached from it and plugged into another assemblage." This chapter also follows Escobar and Osterweil (2010, 191) in that assemblages are viewed as "wholes characterized by relations of exteriority; the whole cannot be explained by the properties of components but by the actual exercise of the components' capacities." In this case, the different components of the assemblage—the Karen followers, Phue Khaw Taw, the abbot of Tamo monastery, and the financiers—do not fuse into a seamless whole, but their interaction, nevertheless, increases one another's capacity. The description in these pages of each component stresses its different identity and operation, and its independence from the others. Connections are made via particular persons, while the sacred mountain provides the space for convergence. The conclusion of this chapter analyzes the realization of Karen capacity as a result of their joining in this assemblage.

## Karen Followers of the Late Khubas

The Karen people who have followed and settled around Khuba Khao Pi's Pha Nam monastery are from the hill areas of Mae Sariang District in Mae Hong Son Province and from Hot and Omkoi Districts of Chiang Mai. Those who have followed and settled around Khuba Wong's Huai Tom monastery are from Mae Ramat and Tha Song Yang Districts of Tak Province, around the Thailand-Myanmar border. These are areas where both *khuba*s traveled extensively to renovate or construct religious monuments. They also lived with and taught the Karen, who were the majority in the area, to adopt their Buddhist tradition. The *khuba*s had a close relationship with local Karen leaders who transmitted the *khuba* tradition to their people and mobilized them for the projects of religious monument construction.

Another reason Karen followers from different areas attached to different *khuba*s was their different perceptions of *kacha* (lord). *Khuba* in Karen understanding is *kacha*. So Khuba Khao Pi they called *kacha wa*, a Skaw Karen term meaning "white lord" (because of his white robe), and Khuba Wong they called *kacha pho*, or "little lord," when he was a novice, and later, when he was a well-known monk, they called him *kacha pha* *do* (great lord). In daily usage, *kacha* is also used to mean "owner" (e.g., *ya kacha* means "it's mine"). Accordingly, in traditional Karen beliefs, "lord," a sacred being, is an owner of particular objects and places. For example, *thee kacha* is the "lord of the water;" *kaw kacha* is the "lord of the land." The great lords are propitiated annually by villagers for their well-being. Therefore, the two *khuba*s were also believed to be the owners of the areas in which they settled and built their sacred pagodas. Because of their greater power they suppressed the local spirits, the former owners of the water and the land, and became the new lords and owners.

When Karen learned that the *khuba* had come to build a pagoda and to stay in the hill areas around the Thailand-Myanmar border, not far from their villages, they willingly participated and contributed their labor to the building. Some had knowledge of Buddhism and merit-making from seeing the ruins of Buddhist monasteries in the area. For others, it was because their parents had joined Khuba Sriwichai in constructing the road to Doi Suthep in Chiang Mai city in the 1930s. After repeatedly joining the *khuba*s' construction activities they understood more and more about their Buddhist teachings. Nevertheless, while they worshiped the *khuba*s, they still also worshiped the spirits which resided in the area. After the *khuba*s returned to their monasteries in Li District, some Karen people went to visit them so often that they thought they should relocate to be close to the *khuba*s' monasteries. Those who decided to relocate also decided to give up spirit worship. The relocation of Karen people to Khuba Khao Pi's and Khuba Wong's monasteries took place in the 1970s.

In the case of Khuba Wong's followers, they said he suggested that they go to a monastery around Pa-an city, in Karen State in Myanmar, to get a sacred stone which they could use to protect themselves from evil spirits. They could soak the stone in water and drink the sacred water before they relocated to the *khuba*'s location. Even when they were staying with the *khuba* they could drink the sacred water any time they felt threatened by evil spirits. Getting a sacred stone from Pa-an, which is on the Burmese side of the Salween, was described by one Karen religious leader as going back to their mother's side of the Salween (*mo thee*) to cut off their umbilical cord—the Karen people believe that the west side of the Salween River, which is in Myanmar, is their mother's side, while the east side, which is in Thailand, is their father's side (*pa thee*). Another important piece of advice which Khuba Wong gave to the Karen who wanted to relocate around him was to be only vegetarian. This was to avoid evil spirits following and attacking. Spirits were accustomed to being fed with chicken and pork, so they would not trouble those who were vegetarian. Thus at least in the first few years, every Karen who settled at Huai Tom village around Khuba Wong's monastery was vegetarian. Similarly in Pha Nam, when Khuba Khao Pi was still alive, Karen followers living around his monastery were strictly vegetarian, devoted themselves to the *khuba*'s construction projects, and regularly attended the *khuba*'s ceremonies. After Khuba Khao Pi passed away in 1977, Karen followers in Pha Nam followed Khuba Wong and devoted themselves to Khuba Wong's religious activities. In the time since Khuba Wong passed away in 2000, however, Karen ascetic practices—especially vegetarianism—have declined, and this is increasingly noticeable.

Modernization and commercialization have now changed Karen people's way of life. In the beginning, the most common source of employment for people who had relocated to live near the *khuba* was construction work on the *khuba*'s projects, without payment. But now people are busy with cash cropping, or making silver or weaving textiles for sale. The younger generations complete their formal education and find employment elsewhere, outside the villages. The typical reason given as to why they cannot continue to be vegetarian is that being vegetarian is inconvenient when working outside the village or visiting a hospital in town.

Some Karen people, however, belonging to the earlier generation that relocated to the *khubas*' sites and now in their seventies and eighties are strict in their religious practices and their vegetarianism (along with some of their descendants). More than that, they have actively searched for the new *kacha*, the next "lord" who will oversee the Karen people. In 2005, 2007, and 2009, around twelve male and female elders and religious leaders from both Pha Nam and Huai Tom[1] organized a trip to important monasteries in Myanmar, in the Karen State, including Alangthaya[2] in the town of Thaton, Swe Kabin in Pa-an, and Khaw Taw monastery, near the Salween River. Lung Ni,[3] the lay leader from Pha Nam who initiated the trip to Myanmar, told me that on the first trip they briefly met Phue Khaw Taw, who hinted that he would come to build religious monuments on the Thai side of the border. According to Lung Ni, Phue Khaw Taw said that

Thai people had donated money for the construction of many religious monuments on the Burmese side, so it should be all right if he used Thai money for construction on the Thai side. In fact, he said, the two sides should be combined as one. Phue Khaw Taw also mentioned that he could visit to hoist the umbrella to the top of the great Sri Wiang Chai pagoda—almost finished—which was being constructed at Huai Tom.[4] Before they left, Phue Khaw Taw gave Lung Ni and the team some medicine and instructed them to continue being vegetarian. On the second visit, Phue Khaw Taw was not around to meet them. On the last visit, Lung Ni said that Phue Khaw Taw was seriously ill but managed to ask them where they were from and how many of them had come.

I asked Lung Ni and other elders why they had faith in Phue Khaw Taw, and Lung Ni told me about his dream. Just one day after Khuba Khao Pi passed away, the *khuba* had come to him and told him that he would stay in Omkoi (Lung Ni's hometown) for seven days. After that he would go to Alangthaya, on the Burmese side of the Salween. When I asked if Phue Khaw Taw was the reincarnation of Khuba Khao Pi, Lung Ni said that it was not necessary for Khuba Khao Pi to be reborn as Phue Khaw Taw, but that the spirit of Khuba Khao Pi had been merged in Phue Khaw Taw. He referred to Phue Khaw Taw's own words that "Khuba Sriwichai, Khuba Khao Pi, and Khuba Wong are now in me. . . . Any of the previous *khuba*s' unfinished construction projects will be continued by me." Lung Ni believed that the three *khuba*s mentioned, and also Khuba Chaoraj,[5] belonged to the same lineage: "They know the same things, and believe in the same things."

The prophecy of Khuba Khao Pi and Khuba Wong about the coming of the owner of Tamo Mountain is also often mentioned by Karen people who are now following Phue Khaw Taw. When asked who invited Phue Khaw Taw to come to Tamo, Lung Ni said, "Nobody. He comes on his own. He sees for himself that it is time for the mountain owner to come. It is not necessary to ask anyone." Another lay leader from Huai Tom also confirmed Khuba Khao Pi's words that when the Tamo cliff stands upright, its owner will come. He said that Khuba Wong, too, had confirmed Khuba Khao Pi's prophecy, adding that the mountain owner would come from the west. According to him, Khuba Wong explained that three charismatic monks who were in the same lineage were the late Alangthaya, Thammaya, and Phue Khaw Taw. They belonged to the mother's side of the Salween, while Khuba Chai Langka (Khuba Sriwichai's teacher), Khuba Sriwichai, Khuba Khao Pi, and Khuba Wong belonged to the father's side.

## Phue Khaw Taw and His Connections

Charismatic monks in Karen State in Myanmar are often popularly named after the places they have founded.[6] Phue Khaw Taw (1949–) is called after his monastery at Khaw Taw area or Myaing Gyi Ngu, literally "Big Forest River Bend" in Burmese. This reflects the concept of *kacha* as the lord who "owns" the particular place. Phue Khaw Taw is widely recognized as the spiritual leader of the Democratic Karen Buddhist Army (DKBA), set up in 1994, in the mutiny against the Karen National Liberation Army (KNLA), the military wing of the Karen National Union (KNU), which has long fought the Burmese government. His biography has been written in Burmese and translated into English (Myaing Nan Swe 1999) to offset his controversial image and actions by emphasizing his meritorious actions and his aim, which is not political power but the prosperity of the Buddhist lands of antiquity. The DKBA central committee writes,

> The Ministry of Myaing-Gye Ngu Sayadaw is not only for the betterment of the Kayin people but also for the improvement of the life of every individual. As he was prohibited to carry out his ministerial work, the Buddhist people who served in the KNU organization could not bear the injustice done to Sayadaw. As a result, they separated themselves from the KNU and formed the DKBA organization as a means of protection for the Buddhist people, the temple, pagodas, monasteries and other religious buildings. (Myaing Nan Swe 1999, 225)

The book describes Phue Khaw Taw's personal experiences, stressing his desire to devote himself to religion from a young age. He was ordained as a novice and received Buddhist education, but when family members fell ill he had to leave to help in the rice fields. He was later conscripted by the KNLA and then found the new goal of his life while traveling in the mountains and forests as a soldier. As the book describes, he found many zedis, stupas, shrines and pagodas in the forests and mountains which were ravaged by time immemorial. On seeing these ruined zedis, stupas, shrines and pagodas Maung Than Sein [Phue Kaw Taw's civil name] was moved with piety and he determined to rebuild these religious edifices when the opportunities arose.

After completing his military service, Phue Khaw Taw was ordained as a monk when he was twenty years old. He then devoted himself to disciplined meditation in the mountains, from which he gained his charisma and his reputation for magical powers (Rozenberg 2010). Later he began building and renovating many stupas and religious monuments in the hills on the Thailand-Myanmar border, following his vow to rebuild the peace and prosperity of the Buddhist lands of antiquity. In the two decades from the beginning of the 1980s he had built or renovated more than seventy pagodas and forty ordination halls in Karen State (Rozenberg 2010, 135).[7] His moral leadership was not new, as it had also existed in previous Karen charismatic leaders or prophets who had founded millenarian-like movements.[8] As summarized by Gravers (2010), "U Thuzana is the answer to the Karen quest for a moral leader who places peace, well-being and future prosperity above politics. His support is based on Karen traditional leadership, nationalism and modern development, as well as traditional Buddhist moral leadership."

In recent years Phue Khaw Taw has gone for medical treatment to a well-known hospital in Bangkok (Gravers 2010). I was told that many migrant Karen workers who had been following him since they were in Myanmar visited him at the hospital. Then the millionaire owner of a big agrobusiness company that employs migrant Karen workers learned about Phue Khaw Taw through his workers and invited Phue Khaw Taw to live in his grand religious park in Chonburi Province. Phue Khaw Taw has performed Buddhist and traditional Karen religious ceremonies for thousands of Burmese Karen laborers employed by the company.[9] His projects, such as the construction of the pagoda on top of Tamo Mountain, have also been sponsored by the owner of this company, which has branches in many regions of Thailand.

The reason Phue Khaw Taw chose to build the pagoda on top of Tamo Mountain is explained by a close disciple of his, a monk who came from

Khaw Taw monastery in Myanmar. This disciple says that Phue Khaw Taw had thought of building a pagoda in this place twenty years before, but it had not eventuated. This is understandable, I think, because that was a difficult time when the DKBA, led by Phue Khaw Taw, had just split from the KNU and there was fighting between them and with the Burmese army. I believe that Phue Khaw Taw learned about Khuba Khao Pi and Tamo Mountain from Karen people who were frequently crossing the border and from monks who had been ordained at Huai Tom Temple. As mentioned earlier, the *khuba*'s followers had conducted a pilgrimage to important religious sites in Myanmar and had met Phue Khaw Taw for the first time in 2005. Another monk told me another reason: "Phue Khaw Taw has magic eyes. From the Khaw Taw area he had seen that Thailand would be flooded. So he had asked the deities to lessen the amount of water and vowed to construct the pagoda in return."

Construction of the pagoda on top of Tamo Mountain was carried out by thousands of Karen people from many villages, including followers of Khuba Khao Pi and Khuba Wong living around the area. Around five hundred Karen people came each day to help, carrying heavy stone, sand, and cement up the narrow, winding trail to the top of the high mountain. I was also told that some Karen people who came to make merit with Phue Khaw Taw revealed that they had seen him in a vision before coming to see him in reality. With the contribution of Karen labor and the donation of materials and food from many sources, the construction of the pagoda was finished within a month.

During the construction of the pagoda, Phue Khaw Taw stayed overnight at many places: the construction site, Phra Bat Tamo monastery, and the area of Phra Bat Huai Tom Pagoda. He left the area for Bangkok, for other places in Thailand, and for the border area from time to time. In October 2012, I met many Karen monks and novices from Myaing Gyi Ngu monastery in Karen State, Myanmar, who had continued living in the area.[10] Although the pagoda was finished, there was still a lot to be done, including building a permanent road from the main road to the foothills of Tamo Mountain and then up to the pagoda. A monk who acted as Phue Khaw Taw's secretary told me that Phue Khaw Taw had just been there two days ago, but that it was always uncertain when he would be coming. Sometimes he phoned to let his people know that he would come, but sometimes he just arrived and stayed for twenty minutes before leaving again. He mentioned that Phue Khaw Taw had said, "It is as if the car is my monastery."

Construction of the pagoda on Tamo Mountain was possible because of the participation of different agencies—in this case, at least four. These agencies neither knew each other well nor shared the same reasons for contributing to the construction of the pagoda. First were the former Karen followers of Khuba Khao Pi and Khuba Wong, as described above. They perceived Phue Khaw Taw to be the mountain owner who would lead the Karen to a prosperous utopian future, in accordance with the prophecy of the two late *khuba*s. The second agency was Phue Khaw Taw himself and his monks and novices from Karen State, Myanmar. Around sixty to one hundred of these monks and novices worked permanently at the construction site, while local Karen came only on and off to help. A few of Phue Khaw Taw's monks had originally migrated from Karen State or had crossed the border with their parents when they were young. Of three monks who were known to be Phue Khaw Taw's secretaries, one had been ordained at a monastery in Mae Sariang District of Mae Hong Son Province and another in Tha Song Yang District of Tak Province; the third was ordained at Wat Phra Bat Huai Tom. Some of them had Thai citizenship and could communicate in Thai. They thus worked as coordinators with local people and sometimes with the officials who came to investigate the legality of the construction. A few monks had experience in building and could thus act as supervisors of novices working on the construction site.

Construction of the pagoda on Tamo Mountain aroused the suspicion of local officials because it was taking place without official permission and was led by Burmese monks and novices who had entered Thailand without legal documents. National security officials and those from other related agencies, such as the police, district officers, and forestry authorities, came to investigate. The person who helped most in defending the construction work was the third agency in the assemblage, Phra M, the abbot of Wat Phra Bat Tamo. His ethnic and educational background, as well as his religious practices, all differed from those of the *khuba*s, but he had faith in Khuba Wong and had actually been assigned as an abbot of the monastery founded by Khuba Khao Pi many decades earlier.

Phra M was born in 1955 in a middle-class family in Bangkok. He was influenced by his own brother, who was ordained as a Buddhist monk and was disciplined in his meditation practice. From the age of seventeen Phra M meditated, following in the footsteps of famous monks such as Luang Pho Ruesi Ling Dam (1916–92) and Luang Pho Cha (1918–92) and so on. He later met Khuba Wong when he went to central Thailand and joined a group organizing a *kathin* (robe offering) ceremony at Wat Phra Bat Huai Tom in 1979. In his biography on the temple's website (www.wattamor. com), he recounts how "the first time I met Luang Pho Khuba Wong, I felt very affectionate and respectful to him; we were like a father and son who had been parted from each other for a long, long time. . . . I believed that I had met a teacher who understood me." He also told me in an interview that he had been Khuba Wong's son for two past lives.

Although he was granted the position of squadron leader in the Royal Thai Air Force after he finished school in 1980, he always desired to become a monk. He was ordained in 1981 in Bangkok and later traveled to live with Khuba Wong. In 1982 he moved to become the abbot of Wat Phra Bat Tamo, which had been abandoned since Khuba Khao Pi had left in 1957. He explained that his desire to become a Buddhist monk had begun in his past lives. He could have been ordained then, but not until he was in his sixties. It was only in this life that he was able to be ordained as early as he had desired.

Phra M was actually the host for the construction of the pagoda because the mountain was in the vicinity of Phra Bat Tamo monastery. (As one Karen leader said, he was introduced to Phue Khaw Taw via an army general from Bangkok.) According to Phra M himself, the coming of Phue Khaw Taw was in accordance with Khuba Wong's prophecy that the owner, or lord, of Tamo Mountain would come to build a pagoda. He also praised Phue Khaw Taw for his ascetic practices of not receiving money and being vegetarian. He believed in Phue Khaw Taw's words that if the pagoda was not built, Bangkok would be flooded for eleven days continuously. So he acted as an intermediary between Phue Khaw Taw, Thai state officials, and also official sangha monks. He wrote a confidential letter to the officials concerned, informing them of why he had allowed Phue Khaw Taw to build the pagoda. He said that Thai officials should not offend Phue Khaw Taw because the monk also supported dam construction, which would help in Thailand's development. Phra M continued, saying that should he be treated badly, the monk could recall 25,000 Karen laborers back to Myanmar, which would greatly affect Thai business.

The fourth agency enabling the construction of the pagoda was the financial support of business people. One Karen leader told me that the cost of constructing Tamo pagoda and the surrounding buildings was around 80 million baht. The estimate might not have been from real calculations, but it was not far from reality. Although most of the labor was free, the cost of materials (the iron structure, cement, bricks, etc.) was high. Besides that, the monks' and novices' daily living expenses were also high. Phue Khaw Taw would come regularly to pay for construction materials, food, and other expenses. And this was not his only project, but just one of many going on at the same time. Others were the construction of the pagoda's ordination hall, a ceremonial hall, and other buildings in Chiang Mai and in central Thailand. Besides these, construction projects were also being conducted on the Burmese side of the border, including road and bridge construction. His followers at the border referred to Phue Khaw Taw saying that because the money that had been used to build many projects in Myanmar was from Thailand, he had to also build religious monuments in Thailand, beginning with the Tamo pagoda.

One of the chief financial supporters was the owner of the agroindustry company that was one of the biggest exporters of frozen chicken from Thailand. The company had branches in many provinces of Thailand and also operated in the border area in Karen State, reportedly hiring thousands of Karen workers from Myanmar. Besides this, it had contracted around one hundred thousand farmers in many regions to produce crops and animals.[11] The owner of this company was known as a religious man. He invited Phue Khaw Taw to live on his estate, built in a grand religious park with unique buildings and religious statues from many traditions. The park is one important node in the movement of Phue Khaw Taw, who sometimes stays there in between his travels around the country. Phue Khaw Taw travels frequently, He has to come regularly to a hospital in Bangkok, and he is often invited to preach at factories employing Karen migrant laborers in provinces neighboring Bangkok. Besides these trips, Phue Khaw Taw travels extensively to oversee construction projects around northern Thailand, on both sides of the Thailand-Myanmar border, and elsewhere; he also spends time at his monastery in Myaing Gyi Ngu. He had a few new cars donated by business people. His drivers, interpreters, and other assistants were Karen with Thai identification cards, who were faithful to him and ready to drive and accompany him elsewhere in Thailand.

## Linkages between Different Agencies in the Unstable Assemblage

As described above, each of the four different agencies—the Karen lay people, Phue Khaw Taw and his associates, Phra M, and the financial backers—had their own distinctive identity, experiences, and religious goals and practices. They converged not to form a synchronized organization but to exercise their individual capacities in the construction of the grand religious project, under the leadership of the revered monk. Relations among them were slight, for people in each agency did not necessarily know in detail about the backgrounds, desires, and objectives of the others. Their connections were more interpersonal: Phue Khaw Taw had linked up with the late *khuba*'s Karen followers who had gone to see him a few times in Myanmar; the Thai millionaire had linked up with Phue Khaw Taw via his Karen migrant laborers; Phra M had linked up with Khuba Wong and his officials, who had introduced him to Phue Khaw Taw.

Besides these interpersonal connections, the sacred Tamo Mountain also played an important role as a central link with the different agencies. Like other mountains with unusual features (e.g., very high, very large, perfectly cone- or square-shaped, or difficult to access), Tamo Mountain was believed to be the abode of sacred beings. According to Swearer, Sommai, and Phaithoon (2004, 22),

the mountain as a topographic feature of a landscape inspires awe, respect, fear, curiosity, and reverence. Its height serves as a point of special orientation and the axial center of a cosmological worldview associated with kingship. Imagined as the abode of autochthonous, Brahmanical, and Buddhist deities, spirits, and sacred beings, the mountain's wilderness environment serves as a magnet for spiritual virtuosi—shamans, ascetic monks, and hermits (*ruesi*)—as well as pilgrims who journey to the temples and monasteries located there.

Tamo Mountain is high, with a large rocky top clearly visible from the surrounding plain of Li and Doi Tao Districts. According to a myth told by Phue Khaw Taw's secretary and memorized by many other Karen followers, the mountain was long ago the abode of three hundred *yaksa*, demon-like beings. Like other tales of Buddha visiting sacred places,[12] when the Buddha arrived at the Tamo Mountain area, he challenged the three hundred demons to completely cover up his body. The demons could not, as the Buddha's body was too big to cover. So the demons believed in him and followed his instructions and became vegetarian, as otherwise they would have turned to stone. According to Khuba Wong (Phra Maha Nophadol 2009), the Tamo area was visited by four Buddhas who left their footprints, later visible in the area. The coming of Phue Khaw Taw to construct the pagoda to accommodate a Buddha relic helped to give credence to the myth of the Buddha's visit. The sacredness of Phue Khaw Taw, in turn, was also reinforced.

It is clear that the assemblage does have the effect of increasing the participants' capacities. In the case of the Karen followers of the late *khuba*s, who are now in their seventies and eighties, hope is rekindled for a future utopia. Before the coming of Phue Khaw Taw they were frail and rarely wandered far from home. When Phue Khaw Taw, the mountain owner, came according to the prophecy, they regained their strength. They excitedly told me of their happiness on meeting the charismatic monk and of their great desire to gain merit, which gave them energy to climb the mountain while carrying heavy sand or stone, and to walk up and down once or more often each day, until the pagoda was finished. They would not have normally been able to expend that much energy.

Charismatic leaders who are able to build grand religious monuments on top of sacred mountains are also recognized as being highly meritorious people. They certainly possess greater power than the sacred beings who formerly inhabited the place. This is also reflected in the ritual that Phue Khaw Taw usually conducts when he begins building a pagoda. The ritual is conducted on the spot to propitiate the guardian spirits. Trays are prepared holding coconut and other offerings. The top of the pagoda is of utmost importance, and the ritual of hoisting its umbrella is usually performed by a meritorious or revered person to add more sacredness to the pagoda and its surrounds.

By adding to this assemblage the support of wealthy Thai financiers, it is clear that Phue Khaw Taw has expanded his influence from beyond the Thailand-Myanmar border to the interior of Thailand, with more monasteries built in his name and with new networks of Karen followers.

However, this assemblage is not stable but always shifting. As summarized by Collier and Ong (2005, 12) in their study of global assemblage, "An assemblage is the product of multiple determinations that are not reducible to a single logic. The temporality of an assemblage is emergent. It does not always involve new forms, but forms that are shifting, in formation, or at stake." As found in this assemblage, in the age of globalization many different agencies have been able to connect and converge to act together. Facilitated by high-tech communication and transportation, they are easily mobilized.

As has been explained, not all Karen followers of Khuba Wong and Khuba Khao Pi are convinced that Phue Khaw Taw is the real mountain owner and the proper person to build the sacred pagoda. These nonbelievers pay no attention to the late *khubas'* prophecy on the coming of the mountain owner. More than that, they question the background of Phue Khaw Taw as the spiritual leader of DKBA and also his hidden agenda in building the pagoda at Tamo Mountain. Nonbelievers from Huai Tom village say that Phue Khaw Taw might be fleeing from Myanmar, that his actions are suspicious in that he always travels to the Li District area very late at night, that he obtains a lot of money from there, and that monks and novices who build religious monuments might be soldiers in disguise.

The lay leader of the village cautioned that years ago many Karen were defrauded by a monk who claimed to be an incarnation of Khuba Chaoraj. The monk asked for a lot of money from Karen villagers, promising that they would receive ten times the amount of money donated in return; the villagers never got their money back. The village leader worries that Phue Kaw Taw might be like that monk. This leader tries to persuade Karen villagers to be loyal only to Khuba Wong or Khuba Khao Pi, whose bodies are still kept in Wat Phra Bat Huai Tom and Wat Pha Nam, respectively. He says, "Our own construction activity is not yet complete, but many Karen people have gone to help Phue Khaw Taw's construction. This is not the right way to do things."

Those who believe in Phue Khaw Taw, on the other hand, are convinced that Phue Khaw Taw is the proper person because he is a strict vegetarian and devotes himself to the construction of religious monuments in the same tradition as Khuba Khao Pi and Khuba Wong. That Phue Khaw Taw is from Myanmar does not matter to this group. Some think that Phue Khaw Taw is creating an opportunity for them to make merit and they do not hesitate to take this opportunity. As one person explains,

> He is actually Karen, the same as us. . . . I am interested in helping. . . . Making merit is for myself. . . . I am the owner of that merit. . . . I am satisfied with this. . . . I join the activity like my forefathers who helped Khuba Sriwichai build the road to Doi Suthep. . . . Villagers who do not believe in Phue Khaw Taw told me not to go, that he [Phue Khaw Taw] is a Burmese. . . . I said I don't care. . . . I am interested only in merit-making.

## Conclusion

This chapter applies the concept of assemblage to understand the convergence of many different agencies in the construction of the pagoda on top of Tamo Mountain. The multiplicity of the assemblage is evident in the different goals and the different ethnic, educational, and occupational backgrounds of the agencies. Even within one agency, in fact, such as the Karen followers, there are differences in ideas and practices. Nevertheless, these disparate agencies are linked in interpersonal networks that converge on the Tamo Mountain, a sacred space with a sacred meaning and the memory of the visit of the Buddha, and the prophecy of Khuba Khao Pi and Khuba Wong regarding the mountain owner.

Furthermore, the interaction in the assemblage has increased the capacity of each agency. The amount of money required is high; seeing the Karen people donate their labor to construct the grand and elaborate projects inspires wealthy donors to give more. The Karen people's hopes for utopia are revived; at the same time, the resources and energy that they invest in the construction work increases. The accomplishment of a grand project legitimizes the great, meritorious leader. The construction has actualized the power of the sacred mountain and turned the marginalized area into a grand utopian community.

This assemblage also reflects the change in the regional socioeconomic and political context, especially on the Thailand-Myanmar border. The increasing porosity of the border due to industrialization and commercialization has facilitated the movement of people, objects, and ideas. High-tech communication, media, and transportation have brought people from different areas together. Phue Khaw Taw, Karen migrant workers from the Karen State, and sponsoring businessmen from Bangkok all join the assemblage operating in the area of Doi Tao, a remote district of Chiang Mai. However, the assemblage is unstable and rife with various kinds of tension, most notably between Karen people who have different ideas and over legal issues surrounding the construction. So the assemblage is always in the process of becoming, and new assemblages may arise, following new connections and conditions.

## NOTES

1. More or less the same people joined each trip.

2. Alangthaya monastery is also famous for the construction of many stupas in the area of Thaton, which is in Bago Region and not far from the Karen State capital, Pa-an. The charismatic monk who led the construction was from Pa-O background. Like the *khuba*s, he was a vegetarian and practiced meditation regularly. He passed away many years ago and was succeeded by another monk.

3. A Pwo Karen in his sixties from Omkoi, interviewed on October 15, 2013.

4. The grand pagoda was built following the model of the great Shwedagon pagoda in Yangon. It took eleven years to finish, from 1995 to 2006.

5. Khuba Chaoraj was a charismatic Pwo monk from Pa-an, in Karen State, who had set up his monastery in a rural district of Lamphun Province in the 1960s and 1970s. He was recognized as being close to Khuba Khao Pi. He also drew large numbers of Karen followers from the surrounding hills to resettle around his monastery (see also Gravers 2012).

6. For instance, revered monks Thammaya Hsayadaw and Taungale Hsayadaw were named after the monasteries they constructed at the places called Thammaya and Taungale, respectively.

7. Rozenberg (2010) also includes Phue Khaw Taw in his study as one of eight contemporary revered monks widely worshiped in Myanmar.

8. Gravers (2004) writes about charismatic Karen leaders claiming to be vegan

ascetics or *minlaung*, righteous rulers fighting with the British army from the eighteenth century until Burma (Myanmar) gained its independence. These leaders were present in the Yunzalin and Salween River areas, and led in the construction of pagodas to prepare the way for the coming of the future Buddha, Ariya Metteya.

9. Some religious ceremonies performed in the grand hall of the religious park, presided over by the company owner and attended by thousands of Karen migrant workers, are recorded in video form and distributed widely. In one video Phue Khaw Taw asked Karen workers to work harder and to be honest with the company.

10. Phue Khaw Taw's secretary told me that there were around seventy monks and novices constructing the road. Phue Khaw Taw had planned to bring more monks and novices to the construction site, but only this number had arrived. The monks and novices did not wish to come because the place was too hot compared with Myaing Gyi Ngu.

11. The company web page writes that it dominates the markets in Japan, England, Germany, China, the Netherlands and Belgium (see www.sahafarms. com/main.php).

12. The Buddha's journey throughout Lanna, the name of a former kingdom covering upper northern Thailand, is recorded in many chronicles and legendary histories. While visiting many great mountains he encountered autochthonous people and demon-like beings which inhabited those places. He showed his sacred power and taught the *dhamma* (Buddhist moral principles) to those demon beings and local peoples who were moved by his teachings and decided to convert to Buddhism. The legend of the Buddha's visit usually relates to the history of a stupa, built by a king or nobleman to accommodate a relic of the Buddha that was either given by the Buddha himself or came to the place by itself after the Buddha passed away.

## REFERENCES

Collier, Stephen J., and Ong, Aihwa. 2005. "Global Assemblages, Anthropological Problems." In *Global Assemblages: Technology, Politics, and Ethics as Anthropological Problems*, edited by Aihwa Ong and Stephen J. Collier, 3–21. Oxford: Blackwell Publishing.

DeLanda, Manuel. 2006. *A New Philosophy of Society: Assemblage Theory and Social Complexity*. London: Continuum.

Escobar, Arturo, and Osterweil, Michal. 2010. "Social Movements and the Politics of the Virtual: Deleuzian Strategies." In *Deleuzian Intersections: Science, Technology, Anthropology*, edited by Casper Bruun Jensen and Kjetil Rödje, 187–217. New York: Berghahn Books.

Gravers, Mikael. (1993) 2004. *Nationalism as Political Paranoia in Burma: An Essay on the Historical Practice of Power*. Routledge Curzon.

———. 2010. "The Monk in Command." *The Irrawaddy* 18:5.

———. 2012. "Waiting for a Righteous Ruler: The Karen Royal Imaginary in Thailand and Burma," *Journal of Southeast Asian Studies* 43(2): 340–63.

Kwanchewan Buadaeng. 2002. "Khuba Movements and the Karen in Northern Thailand: Negotiating Sacred Space and Identity." In *Cultural Diversity and Conservation in the Making of Mainland Southeast Asia and Southwestern China: Regional Dynamics in the Past and Present*, edited by Yukio Hayashi and Thongsa Sayavongkhamdy, 262–93. Bangkok: Amarin Printing and Publishing.

Kwanchewan Srisawat. 1988. "The Karen and the Khruba Khao Pi Movement: A Historical Study of the Response to the Transformation in Northern Thailand." MA Thesis, Ateneo de Manila University.

Myaing Nan Swe. 1999. *Myaing Gye: Ngu Sayadaw; A Jahan Who Shines the Light of Dhamma*. Translated by Shin Khay Meinda. Myaing Gyi Ngu Special Region, Karen State (DKBA): Mann Ba Nyunt Pe.

Phra Maha Nopadol Siriwitho. 2009. *Prawat wat phra putthabat Tamo* [History of Tamo Buddha footprint monastery]. Chiang Mai: Nathaphol Kan Pim.

Rozenberg, Guillaume. 2010. *Renunciation and Power: The Quest for Sainthood in Contemporary Burma*. Translated by Jessica Hackett. Yale University Southeast Asia Studies, monograph 59.

Swearer, Donald K., Sommai Premchit, and Phaithoon Dokbuakaew. 2004. *Sacred Mountains of Northern Thailand and Their Legends*. Chiang Mai: Silkworm Books.

Tanabe, Shigeharu. 2011. "Theories on Community, Network, and Assemblage." Lecture for postgraduate students of the Faculty of Social Sciences, Chiang Mai University, July 18.

# THE FOLK MEDICINE REVIVAL MOVEMENT IN NORTHERN THAILAND
## The Exercise of Healers' Capacities and Legitimization of Healing Practices

NOBUKO KOYA

## Introduction

Interest in Thailand in integrating both traditional medicine and folk medicine into the body of institutionalized medical treatment options has increased over the past few decades. Thai traditional medicine (*kan phaet phaen Thai*) has developed and been institutionalized mainly by the Institute of Thai Traditional Medicine at the Ministry of Public Health, established in 1993.[1] Folk medicine (*kan phaet phuen ban*) is the indigenous healing method perpetuated by and transmitted among folk healers in rural areas. Though it has a number of practices in common with Thai traditional medicine, knowledge and skills vary among healers and across regions. Thai traditional medicine services are now provided at various places, such as public health stations and hospitals. Northern Thai folk healers, on whom this research focuses, also have experienced increased opportunities to more actively engage in society as the folk medicine revival movement has progressed.

Because folk healers' position in the Thai medical establishment has changed, understanding their contributions to healing cannot be furthered by assuming that their place remains in the framework of past medical resources. Of particular interest are the changes to their relationship with the central authority. For example, some healers recently have been invited to treat patients at public medical institutions. Moreover, some folk healers are government-certified to practice folk medicine. In the context of "health care systems" as defined by Kleinman (1980), some folk healers tend to move into the professional sector from the folk sector.[2] Weisberg (1982) divided northern Thailand's early 1980s medical resources into two distinct spheres—the "officially sanctioned" and the "locally sanctioned"— and he located folk healers in the locally sanctioned sphere. However, in Thailand today, healers can be officially sanctioned, albeit only in part. This study is about the "locally sanctioned" folk healers who are looking to enter the officially sanctioned sphere or the professional sector.

This study has two objectives. First, it aims to describe—through direct observation of folk healers—the legitimization of the folk medicine revival movement in northern Thailand that began around 1990. As a group, folk healers have been developing their knowledge and skills and changing their practices while cooperating and negotiating with various people and organizations. This chapter elucidates how folk healers have evaluated their practices within multiple legitimacies that relate to social authority, national laws and regulations, or traditional customs.

However, healers differ in their means of evaluating their practices. The concept of assemblages, as proposed by Deleuze and Guattari (1987) and developed by DeLanda (2006), is useful for understanding this process. As explained in the introduction to this book, assemblage theory presents a theoretical alternative to the notion of organic totalities, because assemblages are wholes (units) consisting of components that are defined by their relations to elements of exteriority. These relations imply that component parts of an assemblage may be detached and plugged into a different assemblage. The actual exercise of the components' capacities by interacting with other components determines the properties of the assemblage. The concept may be understood as an ecosystem consisting of different plants and animals in which each component (plant or animal) is self-sufficient, yet the relationships among them are in symbiotic coevolution. These relations among the components or parts of assemblages are contingently obligatory. In other words, the interdependence of components depends on circumstances and context and is not ideal—and neither are the logically necessary relations that are present in organic totalities (DeLanda 2006; Escobar and Osterweil 2010).

The second objective of the study is to examine the connections among the components and the ways in which these components exercise their capacities in the folk medicine revival movement. In particular, this study demonstrates the unique capacities of each healer and how these distinct capacities are exercised in relation to other components. The folk medicine revival movement in northern Thailand has, at this point, evolved into an assemblage with relations among various components, such as folk healers, medical institutions, nongovernmental organizations, central government and its local-level agencies, Buddhist monks, HIV/AIDS and other patients, and media (e.g., radio, television, books and magazines, and the Internet). In addition to such social actors, material things such as herbal medicines or tools used for rituals, and institutional norms such as national laws and regulations, are also components of an assemblage and affect healers' exercise of their capacities. While healers strive for and maintain individuality, they also experience the coevolution that is emblematic of assemblage theory.

The data used in this study for the ethnographic descriptions were drawn from observations of and interviews with folk healers who were participating in healers' networks in Chiang Mai and neighboring districts of Chiang Mai Province. Fieldwork on *mo mueang* was conducted between 2005 and 2013.

## Legitimacy Based on Traditional Customs and Laws regulating Thai Traditional Medicine

The folk healer (*mo phuen ban*), who is central to this research, is the principal actor in folk medicine. Folk healers in northern Thailand, referred to locally as *mo mueang*, are the subjects of this study. There are two dimensions of folk healers' knowledge and skills. The first is physical and relates to the healing work performed on a patient's body. Massage, herbal medicine, and dietary advice are features of this dimension of the folk healers' work. The second dimension is religious or spiritual in nature and is directed toward a patient's mind. Some examples of the spiritual aspect are divination, the application of charms, and rituals. These two aspects combine in actual practice, resulting in a holistic way of healing that is acknowledged by researchers and folk healers. However, this holistic approach to healing is only partly accepted by public health care, which only accepts the physical aspect—that is, the knowledge and skills related to work performed on the body (such as massage).

Although most folk healers' practices are not legally legitimate, they are traditionally legitimized by the knowledge and skills that are passed down from *khu* or "teachers."[3] The *khu* is a collective concept of teachers, including everyone, past and present, who has transmitted the knowledge and taught healing skills to others (direct teachers, teachers' teachers, and even divinities). Healers conduct sessions at the request of patients. They form *pho liang* and *luk liang* (foster father and foster children) relationships.[4] In the healing practice, healers place puffed rice, flowers, incense, candles, and token money as offerings onto a small tray with a pedestal called a *khan khu* and then pray to *khu* for a successful healing. There is typically an altar for *khu* inside a healer's house.

Folk healers do not have a history of charging patients for their services and are, instead, rewarded with gifts—including money—when the patients have recovered or during the Thai New Year festival (Songkran). Some patients offer their labor instead of gifts. This is part of the practice called *dam hua,* which is the northern Thai custom of visiting elders with gifts to show respect. Some patients perform *dam hua* for healers every year. Neither healers nor patients discuss these gifts. Healer-patient relationships are traditionally based upon general reciprocity. Traditional customs—having *khu* and conducting healing as giving—have been the main motivations for people to recognize folk healers (fig. 1).[5]

The healing practices of folk healers, as well as those of Thai traditional medicine practitioners, are regulated under the Practice of the Art of Healing Act (*Phraratchabanyat kanprakop roksinlapa*) of B.E. 2542 (1999), the Drug Act (*Phraratchabanyat ya*) of B.E. 2510 (1967), and the Sanitorium Act (*Phraratchabanyat sathan phayaban*) of B.E. 2541 (1998). To gain legal legitimacy for their healing practices, folk healers must obtain a license of medical practice in Thai traditional medicine, regulated by the Practice of the Art of Healing Act of B.E. 2542. There are four kinds of license: Thai medicine, Thai pharmacy, Thai midwifery, and Thai massage. Practitioners of Thai traditional medicine must attend courses offered by certified teachers and pass examinations on theory and practice. However, it is difficult for folk healers to obtain a license this way because most of them are aged and less educated. Moreover, the standard names of herbs appear in the textbooks and are required in the examinations, but such names are often different from the local names that healers know. Alternatively, folk healers who obtain guarantees from a person working in a field related to folk medicine and who meet the conditions defined by the Committee of Thai Traditional Medicine also can obtain a license. In this scenario, a person working for a hospital, university, NGO, or other public institution creates the required candidate healer documents and submits them to the Committee of Thai Traditional Medicine for consideration on behalf of the candidate. Since around 2010, folk healers who have obtained licenses this way have appeared in Chiang Mai Province, though only gradually. This opportunity is offered to a limited number of people—usually those who cooperate with or have connections to public institutions.

Even if a folk healer holds a license, there are legal issues regarding the production and sale of herbal medicines, and the healer must obtain permission from the Food and Drug Administration of Thailand (FDA) to produce and sell these medicines. Obtaining FDA approval is difficult because meeting the demands of a suitable facility for production of the medicines, with sufficient space and a sterile environment, is costly. As a

FIGURE 1. Legitimacy of *mo mueang* based on traditional customs

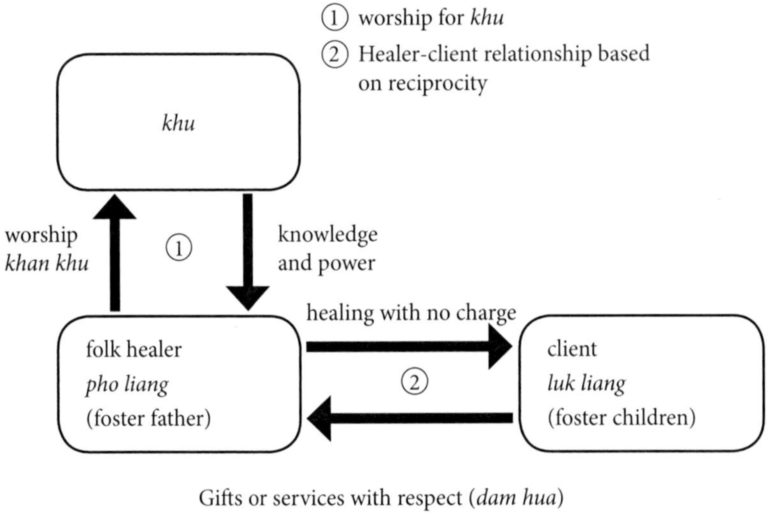

67

result, folk healers rarely sell herbal medicines with FDA approval. Yet FDA approval is not important to village patients because they are accustomed to being treated by folk healers and are familiar with the folk healing tradition. However, today, folk healers accept various patients who may feel differently from the villagers, so some healers have become more careful about selling medicines (as will be discussed later).

## *Mo Mueang* Grouping and Networking

The main actors of the folk medicine revival movement are individual folk healers and their organized groups. Individual healers undertook a process of grouping and networking, and this process resulted in the Lanna Mo Mueang Network (*Khrueakhai mo mueang Lanna*). Healers' groups and networks developed over three phases.

### Contact among healers in their communities and the creation of groups: Early 1990s

The HIV/AIDS crisis that occurred in the early 1990s when the prevalence of HIV-infected people and AIDS patients rapidly increased created an opportunity for folk healers to increase their presence in and engagement with various institutions of the larger society. For instance, in 1994, an NGO called the NorthNet Foundation launched the Community Healthcare Project (*Khrongkan sukhaphap phuea chumchon*) as a way to attract patients into the network of institutions (hospitals, administration offices, schools), and folk healers were invited to join the network.[6]

In 1995, NorthNet invited folk healers in Mae On District of Chiang Mai Province to form a group called the Panchasila Herbal Club (*Chomrom samunphrai panchasila*). Some original members of the group had been providing care to HIV/AIDS patients in their homes or in hospitals. This group worked in cooperation with the community hospital and nearby health stations. The Panchasila Herbal Club facilitated cooperation and the mutual exchange of knowledge and skills among its club members. The club members, supported by Mae On Hospital, exchanged knowledge, learned and refined medicinal processing skills, and went on field trips to the forest. The Panchasila Herbal Club also offered courses in Thai traditional medicine, particularly on the subject of Thai pharmacy. Fifteen of about forty members attended the classes, five finished the one-year course, and three healers passed the exam and earned licenses of Thai pharmacy in Thai traditional medicine.

In 1997, NorthNet received a European Commission grant through the ASEAN Institute for Health Development at Mahidol University to improve the comprehensiveness of the program. Under this grant, NorthNet created a new (and ongoing) project called the Holistic Healthcare Project (HHP). The HHP established holistic health centers at district, subdistrict (*tambon*), and community levels and brought together medical staff, local villagers, HIV/AIDS patients, and folk healers. The healers associated with each of these centers were organized into three groups. The names of the healers' groups and the places where the centers were established are as follows: Fang Mo Mueang Club (*Chomrom mo mueang Fang*) at Fang Hospital in Fang District, Ratanasila Club (*Chomrom ratanasila*) at Mae Hoi Ngan Health Station in Doi Saket District, and Chaturasila Club (*Chomrom chaturasila*) at an abandoned temple (Wat Denchai) in Hang Dong District. They held meetings in which they exchanged their opinions and folk healing knowledge and provided healing services.

## Links among groups: Building the Chiang Mai Mo Mueang Network in 1997

During the late 1990s, the number of folk healers' groups increased, and they began to interact with each other. In 1997, in cooperation with the Northern Coordination Center for Thai Traditional Medicine (the northern branch of the Institute of Thai Traditional Medicine of the Ministry of Public Health), the HHP formed the Chiang Mai Mo Mueang Network (*Khrueakhai mo mueang Chiang Mai*) of eight groups of folk healers, including the Panchasila Herbal Club and the three groups mentioned above.[7] Thirty-eight groups were included in the network in 2001 according to the list of member groups (Samnakngan khrueakhai mo mueang Chiang Mai 2002).

The Chiang Mai Mo Mueang Network held meetings attended by a few representatives from every folk healers' group, and it organized an acting committee of forty members with a president, vice president, and secretary, and in which the staff of the HHP and the Northern Coordination Center for Thai Traditional Medicine were advisors. According to a staff member of the Northern Coordination Center for Thai Traditional Medicine, though folk healers had not been familiar with such systematic ways of organizing their community, they gradually learned the skills needed to operate the network and better negotiate with governmental officials, referring to it as "political training." The folk healers persevered even though they were unfamiliar with the methods and sometimes found it to be quite challenging.

### Decline of activities, return to individual practice, and building the Lanna Mo Mueang Network

Sometime around 1999, because of internal interpersonal conflicts, some folk healers left the network. Similar conflicts among members also occurred in the healers' groups that constituted the network. When some group members were asked why their group stopped their activities, two reasons often given were financial shortages and differences of opinion among members.

Because the costs to this large network's operations were burdensome, the HHP decided to focus on a smaller target—the Lanna Mo Mueang Network, a gathering of folk healers in what they called "natural networks." During fieldwork for this research in 2006, ten folk healers who also belonged to the Chiang Mai Mo Mueang Network normally participated in this network's activities, as described below.

## Lanna Mo Mueang Network Activities: Public Events

Members of the Lanna Mo Mueang Network exchanged knowledge about folk healing and brought this knowledge to the general public. For example, healers met to exchange knowledge about types of tumors and how to treat them, or how to care for paralyzed patients. During these meetings, healers' experiences were freely shared among all for the purpose of improving each healer's practice. When introducing knowledge to the public, a healer presented individual as well as group knowledge and skills to improve public understanding of folk medicine. For example, folk healers spoke about folk healing or health-care practices at workshops or on radio programs, and they organized and participated in public events to provide healing services to visitors. Public events were organized on two levels, both of which legitimized folk healers' work through their engagement in such events. These events also provided each healer with opportunities to exercise his or her capacity.

## Public events at the local level

One example of a public event at the local level was held at a local temple in Hang Dong District of the Chiang Mai Province.[8] Two local healers in the district organized the event in cooperation with the HHP staff and other healers. They managed the budget, prepared lunch for the participants and visitors, and set up the site. They contacted the temple, local governmental agencies, and people in the community to ask for their cooperation. After some negotiation, the local municipal office decided to pay for the lunch-related expenses.

A healer (the head of the network) spoke during the opening ceremony. He explained the purpose of the event, stressed the dangers of eating chemically contaminated foods, and spoke on the importance of maintaining and transmitting folk wisdom. He also explained that the fees for services at this event were much lower than the usual fees at shops, and he encouraged the visitors to freely try the healing services being offered. Following his talk, the municipal mayor spoke about his interest and experience in folk healing and his expectation that many people would come to the event to learn about folk healing and to try the healing services. Then, the participant healers introduced themselves and briefly explained their individual healing techniques.

Inside the temple hall, healers provided various services, including massage, *tok sen, yam khang, chet haek, thian bucha*, and palm reading.[9] At the front of the hall, near a table where handmade herbal products were displayed and sometimes sold, they distributed a free powdered herbal medicine called *ya hom* and a decoction. Before the event opened, they worshiped *khu* together, and each folk healer put *khan khu,* or a tray with a pedestal, for *khu,* nearby. Visitors who were treated placed money on the tray in recognition of the services they had received. The amount was not fixed and depended on the visitor.

At these public events, healers can effectively introduce their healing knowledge and techniques by simultaneously showing various kinds of herbal medicines and different ways of healing. To provide a wide variety of techniques and knowledge, healers must work together to specify and divide their roles; for instance, if one healer presents *yam khang*, other healers must choose a different technique. Each healer's presentation is based on his or her specialty and personal learning experiences that are developed before joining the group activity. Healers also benefit from these meetings, workshops, public events, and personal interactions with other healers by observing and learning new techniques. This improves the breadth of their knowledge while they become more aware of their own specialty and distinctive experience by sharing with others. Healers' self-awareness also may be heightened by the HHP staff or outside actors. When some groups contact the HHP to ask for help coordinating a project, the HHP staff chooses and accompanies an appropriate healer to join the project.

**Public events at the national level**

An example of a public event at the national level in which healers participated as exhibitors was the National Herb Expo. This has been held annually in a suburb of Bangkok since 2004. Department for the Development of Thai Traditional and Alternative Medicine[10] of the Ministry of Public Health organizes the event. I observed and participated with the folk healers during the third National Herb Expo, in 2006.[11] Invited by the organizer, these folk healers exhibited their knowledge and skills at the booth for the northern region, which was among booths that helped introduce the culture of the four regions of Thailand.

The healers created an altar for *khu* at the center of the booth and worshiped *khu* together each morning for the five days of the event. After worship, a *khan khu* was put aside for each healer, and he or she then provided healing services to visitors until evening. The healers organized the techniques and knowledge among themselves according to the organization of roles that the HHP and the healers had decided upon in a prior meeting. The organization, structure, and methods were similar to those used at the local public events.

In a meeting room outside the exhibition hall, a participating healer I will refer to as B twice facilitated a workshop on *ao man*, a type of folk massage used in rural villages to relieve pain and fatigue from agricultural work. Urban people, including practitioners of Thai traditional medicine who are familiar with Thai massage, took interest in it because of its rarity in their communities. With assistance from the HHP staff and a few experts of Thai traditional medicine, B demonstrated massage techniques and taught massage to the workshop participants. After each workshop, B presented each participant with a certificate of attendance issued in the name of the director of the Department for the Development of Thai Traditional and Alternative Medicine. In the workshop, participants referred to B as "teacher" and showed their respect to him by greeting him politely. As a result of this experience, B appeared more confident in his knowledge and practice than before the workshops. This example demonstrates how these events are opportunities for folk healers to exercise and expand their capacity. B's capacity as a massage practitioner was actively exercised relative to the HHP, Thai traditional medicine, and the urban people who participated in the workshops.

These two public events demonstrate that folk healers are creating a social space in which they are legitimizing their role as healers by relying on both accepted formal authority and accepted traditional authority. One of the local administrative offices or the Ministry of Public Health validates their healing practices and encourages people to accept and believe in these practices. The worship of *khu* and the acceptance of money through *khan khu* is evidence of healers being traditionally recognized. The optional utilization by participants of *khan khu* is a clear acknowledgement of legitimacy because it refers to the exchange of gifts instead of the sale and purchase of healing services. Legitimacy based on traditional customs was more important as a representation of northern Thai folk healers' identity to the central Thai people at the National Herb Expo than at the local public event because at the National Herb Expo it differentiated them from the companies exhibiting and selling herbal products at other booths.

## Individual Experiences: Three *Mo Mueang*

While the preceding sections about group activities, group identity, and group outcomes focused on the ways that folk healers' group behavior brings legitimacy to them and to their practices, individual experiences also provide useful insights into the changes experienced in the folk medicine revival movement. The three case studies below describe the experiences of individual folk healers.

## The healer who became a "doctor" at a health station

"P" is a male folk healer in his sixties who is currently employed at a health station as a massage practitioner. He lives in San Kamphaeng District of Chiang Mai Province, and his father was also a healer. P started learning about folk healing in his teens when he was in the temple as a novice monk. Sometime around 1994, when he was in his forties, his practice became active when the local hospital requested his help in caring for HIV/AIDS patients. Shortly thereafter, in 1995, he joined the Panchasila Herbal Club as one of the original members, and then, together with nearby healers, he opened a folk health center at his house. The center became a place for both treatment and the social gathering of patients.

Every Tuesday and Friday from 2007 to January 2009, P and another healer sold four kinds of medicine each containing a single herb (*marueng*, *khamin*, *fathalaichon*, or *matum*) and administered massage to patients at the hospital in San Kamphaeng.[12] In February 2009, he was advised to move his practice to the health station located in the business area of San Kamphaeng so that he could receive more patients. The staff at the health station prepared the required candidate healer documents that demonstrated P's career as a folk healer, his healing techniques, and his participation in workshops and meetings organized by public institutions. They submitted the documents to the Committee of Thai Traditional Medicine. P said, "We folk healers have always worked together with the hospital staff; I have also wanted to work with the health station and hospital staff; then patients will come to seek folk healers." This case is an example of folk healers gaining legitimacy by working with medical personnel in the professional sector—the officially sanctioned sphere.

## The village healer

"B" is a male healer in his fifties living in Hang Dong District of Chiang Mai Province who successfully ran workshops at the National Herb Expo described above. He learned about folk healing, particularly about herbal medicine and massage, from his grandfather and his father, who were also folk healers. He actively began to practice folk healing in the early 1990s when a fellow villager died of AIDS. He visited villagers and asked for their help in solving HIV/AIDS-related problems. According to B, some villagers said that he had gone mad, because they feared and discriminated against HIV/AIDS patients. However, B continued working to persuade the villagers to help these patients. Gradually, he gained their understanding and cooperation. He opened a care center at an abandoned temple near his house to treat HIV/AIDS patients and people suffering from other diseases; this became one of the three holistic health centers of the HHP. At the care center, he established and was the head of a folk-healer group called the Chaturasila Club.

In 2006, B constructed a new building in the compound where his house is and named it the Center for Learning Folk Medicine. Today, he uses this building to treat patients and teach people about folk healing and customs. Word of his success and expertise has spread beyond his home village, and now his patients are not limited to those from Chiang Mai Province. People also know about B through articles introducing his healing activities in caring for HIV/AIDS patients. When a patient living far away telephones to ask B for help, to discuss symptoms, or to receive a diagnosis, B sends the patient the appropriate medicine. The cost of the medicine and the postage are paid to B's bank account after the patient receives the medicine.

As in the case of B, today many folk healers have patients around the country who belong to various social classes. Some healers even have foreign patients who visit them at their houses. Healers appear at public events and on the radio and television or in books and magazines. Moreover, broad Internet access has increased the interest in folk healers. I asked B, "Since you began to practice as a folk healer, have you had any difficulties with the related laws?" He said,

Yes, of course. I have helped people infected with HIV before. At that time, some people said that I did social medicine with AIDS patients. Even if we didn't treat them, AIDS patients would come to us. Even if our behavior was not in conformity with the law, they would come. Actually, what we practice is not Thai traditional medicine. We really practice as folk healers. The folk healer is a villager. We don't have the license, but we are folk healers. That is enough for me. It is OK that we treat patients in the way of villagers, not aiming to gain profit. If they come, we help them. If they don't come, we do nothing.

The third case, "S," is a male healer in his forties living in Mae On District of Chiang Mai Province. His mother's father was a folk healer, and he has been familiar with folk medicines since childhood. For a long time, there were no female traditional birth attendants (midwives) in his village, and his grandfather assisted with all of the childbirths until 1969. Around that time, pregnant women were able to travel to hospitals to deliver by using a villager's car. After it became common for villagers to go to see doctors at hospitals when they were sick or pregnant, the interest in folk healing declined. Moreover, S's grandfather found it to be difficult to treat patients without holding a license to practice medicine. Thus, he retired from practicing folk healing because he was afraid of being accused of illegal practices.

S started to learn about folk healing while he was living in a temple in his teens, and he started his practice in earnest at age twenty-eight (in 1993) when he cared for his HIV-infected neighbor. He joined the Panchasila Herbal Club in 1995 and quit his job in motorcycle repair so he could treat patients full time. He learned about Thai traditional medicine and attended the course offered by the Panchasila Herbal Club. In 1997, he passed the Thai pharmacy exam and earned his license in that subject.

As with B's patients, S's today are also spread far and wide, and he often deals with patients living far away. He welcomes more patients, but he feels somewhat anxious; he says he thinks that increased media attention to folk healers is a double-edged sword. Some people have challenged S on the telephone with statements and questions such as "Your medicine is not clean" or "Does this really work?" or "Do you have permission from the FDA?"

When I asked him how he answers these challenges, he said, "I'll tell them this. I am doing things in the way of a villager. I don't have enough money to construct a clean factory. If you say that, provide financial help to me please." He is very careful about selling medicines to people who do not believe in their healing effects or to patients who are seriously ill, because he worries about being accused by the patient's family if the patient worsens or dies.

## Legitimization of *Mo Mueang*

There are three paths in the legitimization process for northern Thai folk healers in the folk medicine revival movement of the last two decades.

First, healers are legitimized by their networks and by the group outreach activities in which they participate. Most folk healers practice without legal legitimacy (i.e., formal certification). Before they joined a healers' group, these healers did not actively or openly practice healing because they were afraid of being arrested by the police. Folk healers' groups and networks, run in cooperation with medical institutions, administrative agencies, and NGOs, provide an umbrella of legitimacy that protects them and helps to validate their activities and status. Under the umbrella of group legitimacy, these folk healers are openly practicing folk healing.

Being part of a legitimate network of healers also provides folk healers with public trust gained gradually through their healer networks. For example, some healers attend meetings or workshops at the Ministry of Public Health under the wing of an NGO that serves as a liaison. Some folk healers work on research projects at colleges, and some exhibit their healing knowledge and skills at large, national events such as the National Herb Expo. Within these institutions and at these events, healers accumulate experience that serves to validate their authenticity as *mo mueang*. The general public trusts that the knowledge and skills of these folk healers are valid because researchers and medical personnel (i.e., legitimate experts) are trusting them and paying attention to them. The attention paid to folk healers by these professionals is a comforting factor that appeals to the general public, particularly to educated, middle-class people and university graduates who live in cities.

Organizing folk healers into groups and networks has been a way for people and institutions working in the field of folk medicine to expand their reach and increase their public exposure because they can make the target population clear when planning their projects. Folk healers' networks function as places that connect healers not only to each other, but also to a wide variety of people and institutions, enhancing healers' legitimacy. In other words, when influential individuals, groups, and government agencies cooperate with healers' groups, folk healing gains informal legitimacy in the eyes of the public and the outside entities involved with the healers. Moreover, legitimacy is increased in the minds of the healers themselves. The influence of these external parties may be even more far-reaching and important to the legitimacy of folk healing and folk healers than the efforts and exposure brought about by the activities of healers' groups.

The second path of legitimacy is through formal, legal means. Nonhealers involved in the activities of folk healers' groups and networks or their projects related to folk medicine have helped healers to acquire licenses to practice Thai traditional medicine in two ways. First, they support healers' efforts to learn about Thai traditional medicine and take the necessary exams—for example, the course offered by the Panchasila Herbal Club. They also prepare the required documents on behalf of the candidate healer and submit them to the Committee of Thai Traditional Medicine as was described, for example, in the case of P. Folk healers are now inclined to be legally legitimized, compared to their attitudes in the past, although most folk healers are not certified in Thai traditional medicine. While this path to legitimacy may have become more popular of late, even with a license, there are legal problems blocking the practice of folk healing, particularly regarding the preparation and dispensation of herbal medicines. Thus, legitimacy based on traditional customs may play a more important role in qualifying folk healers in the eyes of society.

The third way that folk healing and healers are becoming legitimate is by emphasizing the symbols of traditional spaces. During public events that introduce folk healing knowledge and skills, the members of folk healers' networks represent that they are traditionally legitimized through their worship of *khu* and their enactment of reciprocal relationships with patients by using *khan khu* as a medium for value exchange. These symbolic gestures form the basis of folk healers' practice, status, and identity. The examples of B and S, described above, illustrate that legitimacy based on traditional customs may be emphasized by folk healers to distinguish themselves from practitioners of Thai traditional medicine or medical professions and to separate their herbal medicines from the consumer-oriented, profit-based nature of medicines produced at factories with FDA approval. Folk healers present themselves not as professionals but as villagers practicing their healing based upon their customs. In this way, they may avoid being labeled as illegal practitioners or medicine sellers in terms of national laws and regulations.

## Contact between *Mo Mueang* and Other Actors: Capacities Exercised in Assemblage

In the early 1990s, during the beginning of the folk medicine revival movement, some folk healers had direct contact with HIV-infected people and AIDS patients in their villages. Other villagers were fearful of and strongly prejudiced against AIDS patients, yet healers like P, B, and S helped and cared for these patients with compassion and a sense of mission. These folk healers' altruistic capacities were exercised because of their interaction with the pain and suffering of the patients. At the same time, hospitals began to treat these patients, and NGOs (e.g., NorthNet) and academic researchers implemented studies aimed at solving HIV/AIDS-related problems. Inevitably, folk healers came into contact with people and organizations working toward the same end of easing the suffering related to HIV/AIDS. The HIV/AIDS patients themselves and their self-help groups were also included in that interactive space.

In addition to the connections formed as a result of the HIV/AIDS crisis, folk healers connected with people and institutions working with Thai traditional medicine, especially the Northern Coordination Center for Thai Traditional Medicine, to share folk healing knowledge and improve the understanding of healers' actual practices. People's concerns about folk healing also increased at that time. Healers' groups and networks emerged to facilitate cooperation among healers and revitalize healers' practices. These groups also began gathering folk healing knowledge, seeking alternative health-care solutions, and promoting folk wisdom to the public, particularly when grant money was available. As a result, folk healers expected to reap benefits by joining groups and network activities: development of their existing knowledge and skills, improved social recognition (legitimacy), and financial support for their healing practices.

The visibility of healers—on the radio or television, in books and magazines, and via the Internet or public events—also made it possible for the public to get to know them and learn where they practice, which facilitated each healer's further contact with people and institutions interested in folk medicine. Through these avenues of direct contact, healers' capacities to commodify herbal medicines and some skills (such as massage) were exercised. For example, greater visibility exposes folk healers to people who live outside their home villages, and through word of mouth, patients outside a healer's village seek help from that healer. They telephone to ask for herbal medicines, and they forward payment for the medicine and postage to the healer's bank account. The traditional process of value exchange of folk healing services for gratuity (*khan khu*) is not feasible over long distances. In this way, herbal medicines are commodified because the healer must indicate their costs, and payments must be monetary. However, it is important to note that the capacity to keep folk-healing gifts is also exercised both in individual healers' practices and in group activities, such as public events.

Yet all folk healers are not alike. They differ in age, sex, specialty, and orientation as well as in their knowledge, experience, and skills. Therefore, their capacities also differ. Particularly, healers with a great deal of experience and knowledge who prescribe medicines, as is true for B and S, attract patients with persistent diseases such as HIV/AIDS, cancer, diabetes, and gout. Due to their relatively wide public visibility and their patients' conditions (which are difficult to cure), these healers tend to incur more legal problems related to certification and FDA approval than healers who specialize in massage. Because of this, emphasizing that their practices are based on their village's customary methods of healing, and differentiating themselves from practitioners of Thai traditional medicine or medicine sellers seeking profit (as did B and S) can be effective ways to protect folk healers from legal problems.

# Conclusion

Focusing on the folk medicine revival movement in northern Thailand since the 1990s, this study has examined the grouping and networking process of *mo mueang* and their group activities and individual folk healers' experiences. The study found that folk healers have tended to be legitimized by a central authority through their cooperation with medical personnel and institutions or by gaining a license in Thai traditional medicine. But by entering an official medical system centered on modern medicine, they passively come under the control of those in institutional power.

However, the study also found that folk healers' practices related to traditional customs have not declined but instead increased. Even after folk healers engage in larger society beyond local communities and develop their knowledge and skills, they continue to rely on custom and village traditions as a source of legitimacy. As a result of contact with other actors, they reflectively emphasize traditional customs to differentiate themselves from the practitioners of Thai traditional medicine and to avoid their healing and herbal medicines being regarded as simple commodities. The folk medicine revival movement has great potential due to folk healers' awareness of their conscious choice to become *mo mueang*.

## NOTES

1. A coherent medical system and a body of knowledge that might be called a theory of medicines, which continues to be a part of Thai traditional medicine, has been among Thai people at least since the reign of King Narai the Great, who reigned 1656–88 (Somchintana 1989, 27, 58).

2. In the inner structure of health-care systems, health care is described as a local cultural system comprising three overlapping parts: the popular, professional, and folk sectors. The popular sector is the lay, nonprofessional, nonspecialist, popular culture arena (e.g., family) in which illness is first defined and health-care activities initiated. The professional sector comprises the organized healing professions of modern medicine and—in certain societies— professionalized indigenous medical systems (e.g., Chinese medicine, Ayurveda). The folk sector comprises nonprofessional, nonbureaucratic specialists, and it shades into the other two sectors of the local health-care system. In Taiwan, where Kleinman (1980) conducted field research, herbalists and bonesetters work on the boundary between the professional sector and the folk sector.

3. *Khu* is a term in the northern dialect. The corresponding word in standard Thai is *khru*.

4. *Pho liang* in northern Thailand is an honorific title addressed not only to folk healers but also to rich peasants. When villagers address anyone as *pho liang*, they indicate their respect for the person in the utterance (Wijeyewardene 1971).

5. The act of giving creates a twofold relationship—one of solidarity and one of superiority—between giver and receiver (Godelier 1999). Both of these relationships are found between healers and patients. In addition to giving, the difference between the sacred *khu* and the secular patients also contributes to forming a relationship of superiority.

6. For more examples of coping with AIDS-related problems in northern Thailand, see Seri (1996). For folk healers' experiences caring for HIV/AIDS patients, see Rangsan (2001).

7. The four other groups are the Sarawatchakkasila Club (*Chomrom sarawatchakkasila*) in Saraphi District, the Saichon Nuea Mo Mueang Club (*Chomrom mo mueang saichon nuea*) in San Sai District, the Mae Tha Mo Mueang Club (*Chomrom mo mueang Mae Tha*) in Mae On District, and the Chai Prakan Mo Mueang Club (*Chomrom mo mueang Chai Prakan*) in Chai Prakan District (Yingyong 2001, 34–35).

8. This event was the Fourth Mo Mueang Network's Street Fair (*Khrueakhai mo mueang sanchon khrang thi 4*) held at Wat Nong Bua in Hang Dong District on November 14, 2005.

9. *Tok sen* involves tapping energy lines using a small wooden hammer and cylindrical wedge. *Yam khang* is "treading plowshare." A Healer puts his foot with herbal medicine on a heated iron plowshare to warm it and then massages his client's body. *Chet haek* entails wiping or shaving poison off with special tools such as leaves, parts of wild animals, and a healer's magical knives. A *thian bucha* is a prayer candle.

10. The Institute of Thai Traditional Medicine was established under the Department of Medical Services in 1993 and was transferred to be under the Department for the Development of Thai Traditional and Alternative Medicine, which was established in 2002 (Pennapa and Anchalee 2005, 103).

11. This event was the Third National Herb Expo (*Mahakham samunphrai haeng chat khrang thi 3*) held at IMPACT Muang Thong Thani in Pathum Thani Province from August 29 to September 3, 2006.

12. The scientific names of *marueng, khamin, fathalaichon*, and *matum* are *Moringa oleifera, Curcuma longa, Andrographis paniculata*, and *Aegle marmelos*, respectively.

REFERENCES

Deleuze, Gilles, and Félix Guattari. 1987. *A Thousand Plateaus: Capitalism and Schizophrenia*. Translated by Brian Massumi. Minneapolis: University of Minnesota Press.

DeLanda, Manuel. 2006. *A New Philosophy of Society: Assemblage Theory and Social Complexity*. London: Continuum.

Escobar, Arturo, and Michal Osterweil. 2010. "Social Movements and the Politics of the Virtual: Deleuzian Strategies." In *Deleuzian Intersections: Science,*

*Technology, Anthropology*, edited by Casper Bruun Jensen and Kjetil Rödje, 187–217. New York: Berghahn Books.

Godelier, Maurice. 1999. *The Enigma of the Gift*. Translated by Nora Scott. Chicago: University of Chicago Press.

Kleinman, Arthur. 1980. *Patients and Healers in the Context of Culture: An Exploration of the Borderland between Anthropology, Medicine, and Psychiatry*. Berkeley: University of California Press.

Pennapa Subcharoen and Anchalee Chuthaputti. 2005. "Kingdom of Thailand." In *WHO Global Atlas of Traditional, Complementary and Alternative Medicine*, edited by G. Bodeker, C. K. Ong, C. Grundy, G. Burford, and K. Shein, 103–6. Kobe: WHO Centre for Health Development.

Rangsan Chanta. 2001. *Phumpanya phuen ban: Miti thang watthanatham nai kan dulae raksa phu tit chuea lae phu puai et nai phak nuea khong prathet Thai* [Folk wisdom: Cultural dimensions of the treatment of HIV-infected people and AIDS patients in northern Thailand]. Chiang Mai: Khlet Thai.

Samnakngan khrueakhai mo mueang Chiang Mai. 2002. "Khrueakhai mo mueang Chiang Mai" [Chiang Mai Mo Mueang Network].

Seri Phongphit. 1996. *23 prasopkan kan tham ngan kiao kap rok et phak nuea* [23 experiences of working with AIDS in northern Thailand]. Nonthaburi: AIDS Division, Department of Communicable Disease Control, Ministry of Public Health.

Somchintana Thongthew Ratarasarn. 1989. *The Principles and Concepts of Thai Classical Medicine*. Bangkok: Thai Khadi Research Institute, Thammasat University.

Weisberg, Daniel H. 1982. "Northern Thai Health Care Alternatives: Patient Control and the Structure of Medical Pluralism." *Social Science and Medicine* 16:1507–17.

Wijeyewardene, Gehan. 1971. "A Note on Patrons and Pau Liang." *The Journal of the Siam Society* 59(2): 229–33.

Yingyong Taoprasert, ed. 2001. *Lanna Traditional Medicine as a Dimensional Response to AIDS: A Case Study in Northern Thailand*. UNAIDS.

# EBB AND FLOW OF ASSEMBLAGE IN CAMBODIAN NGO MOVEMENTS
## Diaspora Returnees' Human Rights Initiatives on the Khmer Rouge Tribunals

TOSHIHIRO ABE

## Diaspora Returnees as Marginal Man

A social phenomenon typical of the post-conflict country is the return of the diaspora and refugees. Many of these returnees have lived in a foreign country for many years. Furthermore, some assimilate deeply into the foreign society during this period, thus forming their own identity. Some diaspora never return to the country of origin, while others do. The term "diaspora returnee" describes the latter category and aptly depicts the quintessential character of this group, which can be thought of under the sociological concept of "marginal man." After returning to their country, they recognize and must face gaps between themselves and those nationals who stayed during and after the conflict, between their image of the homeland and the reality of the society, and finally between the foreign society where they have lived and toward which they feel an implicit sympathy on the one hand and the society of their origin where their identity should have been developed on the other. In responding to these gaps, some leave their mother country once again, returning to the place where their identity was actually formed. Others remain in the mother country while making use of these gaps. For these returnees, assimilation into and accommodation of the mother country may be a natural strategy—for example, by using their competencies in a foreign language or their business skills acquired in the foreign country. In cases where the systems and rules are not just and fair toward the returnee, resisting the authorities of their mother country may be another option.

This dichotomy of assimilation and resistance is a tool for analysis and not a term used to classify the situation. The reservation that the actual actors should be somewhere between these dichotomies needs to be considered. In summary, diaspora returnees begin their activities by being expelled against their will, then live in a foreign country as outsiders, and then return to their country, where, although they might be a just and legitimate part of the society, they are treated by the remaining nationals as outsiders once again, thus becoming "marginal man."

This paper covers two Cambodian nongovernmental organizations (NGOs) led by Cambodian diaspora returnees and explores how these movements have related to society, generated a unique communality, and changed the nature of their activities in the course of the judicial process of the Khmer Rouge Tribunals. In terms of assemblage, the thematic concept of this collection, their activities can be better understood from the viewpoint of the concept of "embryonic assemblage."

## Context of the NGO Movement

### A brief outline of the Khmer Rouge Tribunals

The Khmer Rouge Tribunals, officially named the Extraordinary Chambers in the Court of Cambodia (ECCC), were set up to try the Pol Pot clique for the mass atrocities that occurred in Cambodia in the second half of the 1970s. The scale of the massacre, with between 1.7 and 2.2 million victims (Etcheson 2005; Heder and Tittemore 2004), the length of time since the incidents happened (more than thirty years ago), and the extremely ideological political system which mobilized and drove people are tall barriers obscuring the formation of a picture of responsibility clear enough to persuade everyone.

However, abandoning judicial attempts to face these barriers is seen by those inside and outside Cambodia as accepting the extreme atrocities and their illegality, leading to approval of a culture of immunity. Mainly based on such international demands for justice, the Cambodian special tribunal was established in 2006.

The ECCC is mandated to judge the culpability of the persons most responsible for the violation of international law and crimes against humanity that occurred from April 1975 to January 1979, when the Democratic Kampuchea (DK), the Khmer Rouge government, ruled Cambodia. Severe political control by the DK during that time resulted in widespread death of Cambodian nationals. It was impossible to establish any legitimate accountability mechanisms earlier because of the long-lasting civil war in the 1980s and the political instability that followed in the 1990s, even after the Paris Peace Accords were signed in 1991.

The idea of establishing a Khmer Rouge tribunal was aired in 1997, when the former co–prime ministers of Cambodia, Norodom Ranariddh and Hun Sen, requested the UN's assistance in setting up such a court.[1] However, the plans of the Cambodian government for the tribunal diverged greatly from those of the UN task force established for this endeavor, and difficulties emerged in balancing the domestic and international legal applicability of the tribunal with the mandate of the ECCC judiciary.[2] The ECCC was finally established in 2006 and comprised both international and domestic legal staffers and laws. It reflected the principle of local ownership at the institutional level, similar to the tribunals for Sierra Leone and Peru.

Since its establishment, the ECCC has ruled on two cases. The first, Case 001, investigated the legal culpability of Kaing Guek Eav, alias Duch, the former director of the S-21 torture center in Phnom Penh. The second, Case 002, concerns war crimes and crimes against humanity allegedly committed by Nuon Chea and Khieu Samphan,[3] two former Khmer Rouge cadres who occupied top positions in the DK regime. The trial chamber passed a verdict on Case 001 in July 2010 and the supreme chamber announced its decision in February 2011; for Case 002, the guilty verdicts against Nuon Chea and Khieu Samphan were delivered in August 2014, reflecting only on crimes against humanity perpetrated during the evacuation of Phnom Penh in 1975. Two additional lawsuits, Cases 003 and 004, have been repeatedly opposed by the Cambodian government (*Phnom Penh Post*, 27 October 2010) and were still at the pretrial stage as of December 2015.

Some observers consider that the court compensates for its relatively slow proceedings by indirectly instilling judicial norms in a fragile transitional society, but others criticize it for failing to match the expectations of victims of the DK era by not reflecting their sense of justice in the legal process.

## The ECCC, victim participation, and the NGO

The ECCC is unique when compared to other similar entities in the international judiciary because of its mechanism for victim participation under the name of a civil party. Rule 23 of the Internal Rules, adopted in June 2007, states that the purpose of setting a civil party status is to participate in criminal proceedings by supporting the prosecution, and to acknowledge the right of the victims to appeal for collective and moral reparations. Any person who has experienced physical, psychological, or material harm in the regime is eligible to apply as a civil party. However, the actual condition of victim empowerment in the first stage betrays the court's internal rules. Even though the clause for victim participation was written, the Victims Unit was not immediately established by the court. The Victims Unit started its outreach operation in 2008 without a budget, and the job attrition rate at the office was high (Elander 2013, 107–8).

In such circumstances, local Cambodian NGOs have assumed the role of disseminating information on the court and mobilizing locals to participate in the various outreach programs of the court. Chhang Youk, the director of the Documentation Center of Cambodia (DC-Cam), manages the organization's work in a way that is similar in his mind to a truth commission. A truth commission is a policy in transitional justice that involves gathering as many testimonies as possible throughout the country rather than adopting judicial procedures such as those in court. Theary Seng, the former director of the Center for Social Development (CSD), emphasizes the significance of the ideal of reconciliation at the center's public forums, even though morning sessions in the forums are held in order to foster communication between ECCC officials and local participants. This means that Seng implicitly brought the center's message to forum participants that justice is not enough. In so doing, the NGO tried to address the deficiency of the court's outreach programs and the court's pursuit of justice.

In summary, owing to the lack of an adequate budget in the court for victim empowerment, NGOs have for many years (since the inception of these court activities) taken on the role of informing locals and mobilizing them to participate in the process. DC-Cam and CSD are the most prominent actors led by diaspora returnees in the context of an NGO's engagement in the ECCC process.

# Ebb and Flow of Assemblage in the Initiative of Chhang Youk

## 1. Fixing the basement: Starting as a unique repository of historical materials on the Khmer Rouge era

DC-Cam developed in parallel with Youk's footprints in post-conflict Cambodia, starting in 1995 as the local branch of Yale University's Cambodian Genocide Program, tasked with researching and documenting material relating to the Khmer Rouge regime. Youk was the first local leader of the project and continued to run the center after its inception as an independent Cambodian NGO in 1997. DC-Cam's main activities first involved identifying the secret mass graves around the country and developing a database of written materials related to the DK regime. He recalled an episode in 2001 during an encounter with a former Khmer Rouge soldier who wanted to sell the photos of Pol Pot and other Khmer Rouge leaders as well as a "confidential" videocassette of a meeting of Khmer Rouge leaders. While the materials may have been valuable, his policy that money could not be paid for justice precluded this suggestion (*Searching for the Truth*,[4] May 17, 2001, 1). Even though the center was allocated only twenty-five dollars per month in 1995 for the work, he remained motivated in engaging in this solitary task. His sense of justice is evident in the following lines:

> DC-Cam maintains a strong stance that it will distribute all documents it has to every institution for the sake of truth and justice. DC-Cam is ready to provide our documents to the tribunal, various organizations or the media. (*SFT*, December 2003, 3)

At that time, holding historical material was akin to intellectual armament for Youk. However, this statement also shows the center's relative lack of influence at that time.

## 2. Arrangement of the gathering space: Still showing himself as one of the victims

In April 2003, DC-Cam started publishing the English version of the magazine *Searching for the Truth*. Prior to this, they had, since 2001, only published the monthly magazine in Khmer. Almost one year later, they translated the contents of the previous issues into English. Publishing the magazine as an English quarterly meant accepting the input of foreign scholars and donors as well. DC-Cam could then translate the articles written by foreign writers on the DK regime or issues faced by the Khmer Rouge. DC-Cam thus created a bilateral space for readers both inside and outside the country.

Bilateral communication has been key to the various work at DC-Cam since 2003. In this regard, they changed their direction from gathering and keeping materials and evidence to preparing a space for new relationships. They approached the Cham community, a Muslim ethnic group in Cambodia, in 2003 to record their experiences as a religious minority. This community had not been addressed as a special minority who had possibly been dealt with differently from other victims during the DK era. An essay competition in 2003 on peoples' past experiences in the DK regime, organized with the Cambodian Writers Association, was another attempt to delve into locals' memories. The methodology allowed relative autonomy to the writers compared to other authentic research methods such as an interview or the questionnaire survey. DC-Cam's interviewing project in 2004 extended the line of minorities to include Buddhist nuns, other Muslims, torture victims, and students, clearly showing their intention to connect with people accorded minority status in Cambodia. Put another way, the vague phrase "victim of the Khmer Rouge era" was elaborated upon. In March 2004, DC-Cam again proceeded to create a public space for gathering information when they announced the opening of a public information room, like a private library with a lot of historical materials which they had sourced and stored for nine years. In the following year, Rutgers University in the US announced their cooperation with DC-Cam to house the Khmer Rouge archive on campus. Youk's stated desire to search for possible connections or form networks with international societies, foreign NGOs, and victims who had shared similar experiences (*SFT*, December 2005) was a remarkable idea from this diaspora returnee. Ordinary Cambodians either had never pursued the idea publicly, or they had no practical skills with which to pursue networks with foreign actors. In February 2006 (informally in October 2005), a big project called "Legal Response Team," with backing from American experts, followed.

During this time, while DC-Cam had extended its outreach not only to domestic minority groups but also to foreign human-rights experts, they still maintained their position that they were victims as well. While they were certainly leading the project, they at the same time implied that the movement was conducted by the Cambodian victims of their own accord. In particular, Youk repeatedly mentioned his experiences during and after the DK era.

> I was a teenager during those years and suffered like almost all of my compatriots. When I picked water grass for my sister, who was pregnant and starving, I was considered to be a criminal, hit with an axe, pushed to the ground, and tied up with ropes. I was put in jail for weeks. . . . Another of my sisters died because she did not have enough to eat. When Khmer Rouge soldiers accused her of stealing a small amount of food, she denied their charges. To test her veracity, they cut open her stomach. They found no food there, and she died soon after from her wounds. (*SFT*, March 2004, 2)

> Thirty years later, our family is divided over whether putting the Khmer Rouge on trial would bring them justice for my sister's death. . . . I take a different view [from his family]: that the tribunal is important and that we need prosecution before we can ever reach the point of true forgiveness. (*SFT*, September 2007, 4–6)

He also let his young subordinates write their stories as family members of victims (*SFT*, June 2006, 52).

While extending their programs from 2003 to 2008, Youk directly demonstrated his perceptions of justice in the following expression regarding the history textbook edited by DC-Cam:

> We have recently completed a history text on Democratic Kampuchea for high school students. . . . It is the first such text written for this age group by a Cambodian. . . . We hope that the text will be published soon; if the government doesn't agree to publish it, DC-Cam will print and distribute it free throughout the country. (*SFT*, September 2006, 5)

He also takes a critical stance toward the ECCC when the suspicion of corruption among Cambodian court officials was reported, knowing that all the officials belonged to the ruling party, the Cambodian People's Party (*SFT*, March 2008, 5).

DC-Cam and Youk then maintained the relative uniqueness and independence of their work from official bodies such as the ministry and government. This view is confirmed by Youk's statement that they have critical information (archives and a history textbook), which can be used independently against the state's power only based on their own will. Through these activities, they created a space for communication among various victims. It was also a space where minority groups could represent themselves as unique entities with different historical experiences from other victim groups. DC-Cam thus allowed the various victims—including the minorities who were also victims but were neglected by the official proceedings of the ECCC—to speak out for themselves, while fostering public discourse and creating a sense of victimhood among them that had formerly not been elaborated on in a public space. These twofold aspects of DC-Cam's activities fit well into the concept of embryonic assemblage. However, this figure would change in the following years.

## 3. Institutionalization and authorization: Representing the People of Cambodia (2009–present)

The first change in their character was DC-Cam's inclination to be a pseudogovernmental organization, cooperating closely with the ministries. This started with the official approval of DC-Cam's history textbook and the distribution of the textbook in 2007. In September 2006, Youk once referred to the possibility of distributing the textbook on their own, contrary to the government's decision. However, after publication, DC-Cam started to emphasize collaboration with the Ministry of Education, Youth, and Sport, as well as the Royal Government of Cambodia.[5]

The close relationship with ministries and the government did not result only in publishing and distribution. An instruction manual for teachers using the textbook was then required, and thus, the "collaboration with the Ministry of Education" continued and deepened (*SFT*, June 2009, p.1). This was followed by an official teachers' training.[6]

Training of an authentic historical understanding of the Khmer Rouge era was further extended to civil servants. In July and November 2011, DC-Cam conducted sessions to educate police officers and university teachers.[7] Army officers entered into DC-Cam's educational campaign in July 2012.

Undoubtedly, DC-Cam has now become a state-backed organization in charge of historical education. DC-Cam became not a body that encouraged the gathering of various views but rather a body that provided *legitimate* knowledge. This direction has almost completed the process of obtaining government approval for establishing a permanent genocide education center. In December 2008, DC-Cam explained their future plan to establish such a center, which is to be "the leading Asian institution focused on genocide studies, one that will be connected to leading scholars and other institutions throughout Asia and the wider world" (*SFT*, December 2008, 1). Finally, the year 2012 saw the Ministry of Education transfer a parcel of land (4,785.61 square meters) to DC-Cam to build its permanent center, called the Sleuk Rith Institute.

Through such a process of institutionalization and authorization, Youk has become increasingly aligned with the political establishment. In 2010, after his return from a lecturing trip to American universities in April, he wrote about the responsibility of ASEAN member states for accepting at least implicitly the Khmer Rouge hold on power (*SFT*, December 2010, 1). When a US delegation visited Cambodia in November 2011, Youk, rather than Cambodian government officials, was put in charge of guiding the delegation through the historical sites of the DK era.

The above impression was also confirmed in October and November 2011 when DC-Cam organized a conference with minority groups in Cambodia to understand and share their experiences during the DK era. The conference comprised a film screening, lecture, and discussion as would be typical for a forum of this kind. However, a noticeable item was included in the schedule: Memorializing the Minority Groups. According to the conference summary, in this session

DC-Cam Director Youk Chhang and Andrew Cayley [an acting international prosecutor of the ECCC] presented memorials to representatives of the five minority groups in attendance [Cham

Muslims, hill tribes, monks, Chinese, and Vietnamese]. It was a solemn and meaningful affair. (http://www.d.dccam.org/Projects/Public_Info/pdf/Understanding_Genocide_Report_November_24_2010.pdf)

Memorial plaques were inscribed for the groups. The one for the Cham Muslims read:

This commemorates the suffering and death of the Cham people of Cambodia from 1975 to 1979. It also expresses the solemn hope and resolve that justice will be done and that these events will never happen again—anywhere. To the young who read this in future years, whoever you are, never forget what happened to the Cham people. Do your utmost every single day of your lives to respect and love one another. *Genocide, Truth, Memory and Justice. Phnom Penh, 25 October 2010. Andrew T. Cayley, ECCC International Co-Prosecutor.*

For hill tribes:

This plate recalls with love and compassion those members of the Highland people of Cambodia who suffered torment and death between 1975 and 1979. And remember that whatever the differences are between us humanity's most basic common link is that we all inhabit this small planet. We all cherish our children's future. And we are all mortal. *Genocide, Truth, Memory and Justice. Phnom Penh, 25 October 2010. Andrew T. Cayley, ECCC International Co-Prosecutor.*

Even though the person named on the plate, who holds the authority of this symbolic instrument, is an acting foreign prosecutor, there is no doubt that Youk Chhang is someone who can admit to the victimhood of the Khmer Rouge regime. The point where this plate was ceremonially presented is far from the previous point of the DC-Cam's stance to the people toward whom the center reached.

In the previous section, the center's activities showed the shift from gathering to sharing, publishing, and networking. Here a new element was added: giving as a patron. Youk's and DC-Cam's expression of policy amounted to such behaviors. Clear nationalistic statements increased, as in this statement on the opening hearing of Duch's trial:

> Today is a turning point for Cambodia. . . . This journey [for genocide justice] is essential for us to come together as a nation. The Khmer Rouge trials are not only about justice; they are also about the Memory of Our Nation. (*SFT*, March 2009, 1)

The apex of his nationalistic inclination is shown in the project launching the *Preah Vihear Times*:

> It will be the third English-language newspaper in Cambodia and the first run by Cambodians. . . . The conflict worries ASEAN member countries and became a major agenda item for the organization. Thus, as well as being a symbol of Cambodian heritage, Preah Vihear is an example of the types of regional conflicts on which the paper intends to focus. (http://www.d.dccam.org/Projects/Preah_Vihear_Times/pdf/ The_Preah_Vihear_Times.pdf)

Though they received a publication license from the Ministry of Information in August 2010 and secured a well-known American journalist as the international editor,[8] the *Preah Vihear Times* has still not yet been published. Regardless of the success or failure of publishing the *Preah Vihear Times*, DC-Cam under Youk's guidance created a space that nurtured assemblage among Cambodian minorities, became more fixed in its direction as an authentic institution, and naturally departed from its previous line.

## Assemblage and the Radical Activities of Theary Seng

### Changing the image and scene of human rights activity with Theary Seng's American style (2006–9)

Another example is of the rise and fall of the movement led by a Cambodian woman named Theary Seng, who had returned from New York as a young, smart lawyer. Born in 1969, she was thirty-seven years old when she took up the position of executive director of the Center for Social Development (CSD) in April 2006. The CSD was founded in 1995, and until Seng joined, the center had organized several programs, such as the Parliamentary Watch Project and the Court Watch Project, both of which fall under the category of monitoring. These are standard activities for a human rights organization, and despite having little direct impact on the society, they are safe for donors because they tend to be relatively free of political pressure. Monitoring itself does not mean directly challenging the ongoing political status quo. However, the atmosphere inside the CSD must have, to Seng, seemed insufficient for meeting the ideals of a human rights organization. In the first year of her leadership, she set out to reform behavioral rules inside the center, saying,

> I knew that CSD must be run like a business enterprise. . . . We wanted to marry business efficiency, professionalism and accountability with humanitarian goals. (Center for Social Development 2006)

Upholding the values of good business may have impacted the younger generation, who may otherwise not have had an accurate image of the workings of a human rights NGO. Her career and sophisticated manner soon attracted foreign donors. They received US$534,000 in the first year, which was double the center's budget of the previous year. It was a surprise for staff in a country where the average salary of a school teacher was about US$80–120 per month.

The young, high-performing leader soon started a radio program to promote dialogue on human rights issues, broadcasting seven days a week and covering nineteen provinces and municipalities. This might be normal in a democratic society, but it was new in Cambodia, "allowing everyone to be on the 'same page,' and the foundation for other outreach efforts or reinforcements" (Seng 2010).

In January 2007, Seng signed a contract with the German governmental aid agency Deutscher Entwicklungsdienst for a three-year, US$300,000 fund to organize public forums around the country. The record of this forum is a good indication of the lively atmosphere of the center of that time. Twenty-one public forums entitled "Justice and National

Reconciliation" were conducted around the country by the CSD from 2006 to 2009. At that time, the ECCC was preparing to open public hearings on Case 001. The forums mainly comprised disseminating basic information about the ECCC, calling for civilian participation in court proceedings, collecting testimonies on past experiences, and facilitating dialogue on various topics, such as reconciliation, justice, and healing. CSD forum participants were encouraged to express their "questions and doubt" or "hope[s], expectations, and benefits from the tribunal" and their opinions on "whether Khmer Rouge history should be taught to the next generations."[9] This shows the forum was organized as a space to supplement and utilize the ECCC process to deepen the local people's own perception of their experiences. The forums then comprised between one hundred fifty and two hundred participants, with an age and gender balance. Although these participants are by no means representative of the Cambodian population as a whole, their responses nevertheless provide critical illustrations of local perceptions of the ECCC. In addition to CSD staff, court officials and representatives from other NGOs were present at each event. At the forum in Pailin on October 24, 2008, for instance, people attended a question-and-answer session featuring the ECCC judge, co-prosecutor, public affairs officer, defense section officer, and witness protection unit officer.

The unique nature of the forum was to allow questioning, which was fundamental but tended to detract from other official communication between locals and the authorities. Even questions doubting the legitimacy of the court were often provided to the official staff from the ECCC:

> I don't have any questions to ask, but I wonder: Many questions [have been] asked, but the answer is still that the law doesn't allow [foreign actors or other stakeholders] to be sentenced and the agreement [between the UN and the Cambodian government] doesn't allow [them] to be sentenced. In this regard, can the tribunal [bring] justice to the victims? … Whether only answering that the law and agreement don't allow [them] to be sentenced will give justice and please the Khmer people or not, [I'm not sure].[10]

An NGO staffer at this same forum inquired, "Was the law to try the Khmer Rouge leaders established with the consultation of the people? Do the government and foreign countries use this method?" These comments challenge the officials' desire for forum participants to understand and accept the principles and mechanisms of the ECCC. Additionally, official claims that foreign involvement guaranteed international judicial standards met with queries regarding the legitimacy of international organizations such as the UN.

Such a straightforward expression in a public space is rare in the Cambodian context, particularly when the topic is related to politics. It is unclear whether those who showed their ideas in such a manner did so after being motivated by Seng's activities; however, it can be said that the diverse expressions, such as the one above that is critical of the ECCC, are not in the open-access records of other NGOs. In this sense, Seng's engagement in outreach on the ECCC was unique among local movements.

Theary Seng's ability to attract the progressive, younger generation was amplified through the publicity gained through a television program, *Youth Leadership Challenge*, sponsored by the US Agency for International Development (USAID). "Loosely modeled after American TV shows like 'The Apprentice' and 'American Idol,'" the program was designed to promote civic activism among Cambodian youth (US Department of State 2009).

A former CSD staff member remembers Seng's popularity and influence among young students at that time, stating that the government must have been watching her actions closely because her political positions were closely aligned to those of the opposition party.

On May 23, 2008, the first evidence of this appeared when the CSD canceled its annual meeting because two police officers visited the CSD office to hand over a letter from the Ministry of Interior demanding they fire Seng. However, the center's staff did not accept it because this was not following legally correct procedure. This was a precursor to the next incident.

## Collapse of the CSD and attempts to create a new space

The board members of the CSD seemed to successfully rebuff the action to remove Seng from the position. However, in July 2009, representatives of the Phnom Penh Municipal Court visited the CSD office with an injunction to suspend Theary Seng's position as executive director and replace her with Vi Houi, who claimed Seng violated an internal rule (*Phnom Penh Post*, July 22, 2009).

Not to be stopped in such a manner, Seng immediately moved to establish another NGO, the Center for Justice and Reconciliation (CJR), in August 2009 with (somehow) government permission from the Ministry of Interior. As early as October 2009, the CJR gave tutorials to the ECCC staff on victim support. In December 2009, at Pannasastra University, a well-known private university, the CJR held a public forum with ECCC officials, continuing with the same program deployed at the former CSD. At that time, the general impression was that the former NGO was taken over by people close to the ruling party; however, in reality, Seng was able to resume the same activities in a new and freer space. By March 2010, CJR staff were looking forward to expanding the center's outreach with a more community-oriented approach. When the Duch verdict was handed down in July 2010, Seng organized another conference at Pannasastra University. This was attended by several active court officials from the ECCC as well as famous foreign scholars; this collaboration showed that the CJR was maintaining its public status and reputation and developing its outreach efforts smoothly. Yet a new source of internal discord emerged during 2010, and some core Cambodian staff members left the CJR.

Perhaps partly owing to this internal incident, Seng established yet another NGO, the Center for Cambodian Civic Education (CIVICUS). The play *Speak Truth to Power: Voices from Beyond the Dark*, which was performed in Cambodia in February 2011, was organized by CIVICUS, not the CJR. The play, written by Ariel Dorfman and based on a book by Kerry Kennedy and Eddie Adams (2000), was "adapted from the book and has been performed all over the world by world-famous actors." This event introduced a "world-famous play" that featured people facing similar hardships to those faced by Cambodian victims and searching for a possibility to connect with one another (CIVICUS, "Speak Truth"). However, the notion that the foreign good could enlighten Cambodia was clearly in the forefront. This idea was incorporated into the program to educate monks and teachers on human rights issues between October 2011 and May 2012. The program textbook, *Khmer Courage Curriculum*, was introduced as follows:

This is your book! . . . The drafting of the Khmer curriculum . . . is based on extensive discussions between CIVICUS Cambodia in Phnom Penh and RFK Center in Washington, D.C., with comments and ideas from Kerry Kennedy after her visit to Cambodia in February 2011. (http://www.civicus-cam.org/programs/civiceducation/speaktruthtopower/82)

Seng had organized places for dialogue to provoke alternative views on justice in regard to the Khmer Rouge issue. Her background as a returnee from the US, and her outstanding character, worked to exhibit the various ideas. However, this project differed from the previous one in that it delivered something directly from abroad to locals, only allowing locals to translate the text.

The play related to this project was performed in September 2011 for three nights at Meta House Phnom Penh (German-Cambodian Cultural Center). The center is open to locals; however, given the nature of the venue, the expected audiences were undoubtedly foreigners in Phnom Penh.

In 2011, Seng organized a victims association for victim empowerment in the ECCC process; yet this may have lost any clear connection with the people mentioned in the following explanation:

The Association of Khmer Rouge Victims in Cambodia . . . is a network of survivors of the 1975–79 killing fields. . . . The members of the Victims Association are from overseas and spread across the provinces and capital of Cambodia, coming together as a result of the public forums . . . since 2007. They include widows and orphans; former child soldiers and former prisoners; hard-working farmers and middle-class city-dwellers; well-known actresses, playwrights, authors and journalists; as well as teachers, translators, security guards, taxi drivers, *inter alia*. (Association, c. 2013)[11]

## The return to a single activist: Vanishing of the embryonic assemblage

On November 15, 2011, Theary Seng abruptly published a press release announcing her resignation from the position as a civil party lawyer at the ECCC:

Ms. Seng no longer wishes to have any legal association with this ECCC which is mocking the dead, her and other victims and embedding impunity. . . . She denounces this ECCC as a political farce, an irreversible sham of extraordinary perversion in denying justice to victims, exploiting their suffering, soiling the memories of their loved ones and embedding cynicism in an already fragile population living in paranoia, mistrust and distrust.

She denied the legitimacy and significance of the judiciary, and introduced an alternative way forward with the slogan "Poetic Justice." Media, particularly foreign media, favored her action, and she consequently set up press conferences. Her strategy was to attract the foreign media specifically and appeal to the critical understanding of Cambodian authority, including the ECCC, through this channel.

In the week following her resignation, she went to a riverside space in front of the FCC cafe in Phnom Penh, where foreign tourists gather, and played a public game of darts on a dartboard superimposed over Nuon Chea's face.

She planned to play this dart game again in 2012 when US president Barack Obama visited Cambodia, but the result was a mess sparked by a raid by twenty police officers.[12]

Her experience clearly demonstrated the political atmosphere in Cambodia at the time, and the video footage of the incident provoked cautious reactions from some ordinary Cambodian locals. Her attitude was politically radical, which did not allow the locals, who were still afraid to express themselves, to behave in the same way, namely in a Western display of human rights. Foreign media favor her, but one former CSD staff member said even foreign donors were becoming unwilling to risk not being able to capitalize on their investment because of a political clash with authority.

Seng once succeeded in constructing various activist movements around her actions based on her uniqueness as a returnee. She started her work among Cambodian locals as a fellow citizen returning from the US. Usage of local media as channels of human rights work, such as TV programs for youth or radio shows with a Cambodian DJ, must have been surprising for local students. Emphasis on business sense and frank introduction of UN personnel into CSD events attempted to build potential motivation for diverse expression from the locals. CSD was unique in adopting new approaches for communication among former victims. Through these flexible channels, CSD's initiatives once brought the status of embryonic assemblage to the context of the Cambodian human rights movement.

However, in deepening the conflict with the government and in diverging from local staff members' mentality and behavioral tendency, she isolated herself. Specifically, since resigning from her position at the ECCC in 2011, her activities have been performed mostly for foreign media and human rights organizations. Her role as a human-rights activist can be seen as similar to that of an artist, which does not eliminate the possibility of creating an assemblage. Political or social circumstances may influence the future responses of other people to her appeal.

## The Rise and Fall of Embryonic Assemblage within the Two Initiatives

Chhang Youk's movement changed along an arc of institutionalization and authorization, and the nature of the assemblage was dissolved during that progression. Theary Seng's movement has also changed its direction, but in a different way from Youk's—that is, in the dispersing of its solidarity.

Both NGOs expanded the space for communication and networking with local minorities who in the past were not dealt with as public actors in the justice arena. The viewpoint of returnee took on a significant role in developing such opportunities. Yet in the authoritarian social context, DC-Cam underwent institutionalization and authorization while the CSD collapsed. The movements, which promoted American-style democracy, inevitably changed their courses, being affected by different social circumstances. The surrounding circumstances also included the people who served as the movements' supporters. For instance, the people engaging in this new NGO movement had some level of foreign language competence for communication with foreign donors and thus were largely limited to the young generation who had no experience in the Khmer Rouge era. Furthermore, young participants who could afford to go to university and master English were more likely to have rich parents whose sympathies lie with the ruling party. In other words, it was difficult for the NGO staff to direct harsh criticisms at the current government due to some staff members' backgrounds. Partly, in terms of this point, the CSD would not have been able to keep the support of its young staff. In sum, in the social circumstances where various political ideas are not allowed to be disseminated, assemblages that encourage people to speak out about victimization and appeal for their rights as victims may be forced to change course, whether that entails institutionalization or sporadic action.

These two returnees' movements faced the reactions of local stakeholders. The gap between the returnee who began the movement and the local people who joined the movement was clear in many areas, such as linguistic competence, computer skills, and financial knowledge. At the beginning, the gap itself worked as a positive difference that gave the locals new motivation for social change. However, the nature of their relationship changed, from one with horizontal partnerships to a vertical one, showing the gap had not been resolved. Finally, it became a relationship in which the locals were put in the position to just follow the superior returnee leader. On the other hand, the returnee, namely the marginal person in the Cambodian social context, faced the difficulty that they lost the supportive reaction of the locals when the locals started identifying the returnee as an outsider.

NOTES

1. Though the direct trigger to establish the present ECCC was the letter to the UN by the Royal Government of Cambodia (RGC) in 1997, Hun Sen and his colleagues had repeatedly appealed to the UN to establish a tribunal to try Khmer Rouge cadres since 1990 (Heder 2011, 4–15).

2. For details on the negotiation process between the UN and the Cambodian government, see Heder and Tittemore (2004); Heder (2011); Youk (2007, 157–72); and Dacil (2010, 4–6).

3. The case started with two more cadres. Ieng Thirith left the process in September 2012 because of her Alzheimer's disease, and Ieng Sary passed away in February 2013.

4. Hereafter cited as *SFT*.

5. See, for example, page three of a DC-Cam report from 2010 at http://www.d.dccam.org/Projects/Genocide/pdf/DC-Cam_Genocide_Education_Report_to%20Belgium--2010.pdf.

6. See a DC-Cam document for 2013 at http://www.d.dccam.org/Projects/

Genocide/pdf/MOU_Between_DC-Cam_and_MOEYS_2011-2013_Eng.pdf.
7. Detailed in a DC-Cam document available at http://www.d.dccam.org/
Projects/Genocide/pdf/GENOCIDE_EDUCATION--Police_Academy_of_
Cambodia.pdf.
8. Joel Brinkley, the former editor at the *New York Times* and Pulitzer Prize winner, is designated as a foreign editor for the planned newspaper.
9. Facilitator, CSD Forum, Kampot, June 14, 2006.
10. Unidentified local participant, CSD Forum, Siem Reap, March 2, 2007.
11. The website this quote is taken from is no longer functioning, which suggests internal dissent in the organization.
12. For an account, see http://latitude.blogs.nytimes.com/2012/11/20/protests-greet-obamas-visit-to-cambodia/.

REFERENCES

Association of Khmer Rouge Victims in Cambodia. n.d. Home page. http://www.akrvictims.org (site discontinued).
Center for Social Development. 2007. *CSD Annual Report 2006*. Phnom Penh: Center for Social Development.
CIVICUS Cambodia. "Speak Truth to Power (Courage without Borders)." http://www.civicus-cambodia.org/speak-truth-to-power-courage-without-borders/.
Elander, Maria. 2013. "The Victim's Address: Expressivism and the Victim at the Extraordinary Chambers in the Courts of Cambodia." *International Journal of Transitional Justice* 7(1): 95–115.
Heder, Steve. 2011. "A Review of the Negotiations Leading to the Establishment of the Personal Jurisdiction of the Extraordinary Chambers in the Courts of Cambodia." http://www.cambodiatribunal.org/sites/default/files/A%20Review%20of%20the%20Negotiations%20Leading%20to%20the%20Establishment%20of%20the%20Personal%20Jurisdiction%20of%20the%20ECCC.pdf.
Heder, Stephen, and Brian D. Tittemore. 2004. *Seven Candidates for Prosecution: Accountability for the Crimes of the Khmer Rouge*. 2nd edition. Phnom Penh: Documentation Center of Cambodia.
Kennedy, Kerry, and Eddie Adams. 2000. *Speak Truth to Power: Human Rights Defenders Who are Changing Our World*. New York: Umbrage Editions.
Keo, Dacil Q. 2010. "The UN, Cambodia, and the Khmer Rouge: Politics before Victims?" *Searching for the Truth*, 4th quarter: 4–6.
Seng, Theary C. 2010. "Public Forums on Justice & Reconciliation (March 2006–July 2009)." http://thearyseng.com/peace-builder/42/54.
US Department of State. 2009. "High School Student Wins Youth Leadership Challenge." http://cambodia.usembassy.gov/youth_leadership_2009.html.
Youk Chhang. 2007. "The Thief of History: Cambodia and Special Court." *International Journal of Transitional Justice* 1:157–72.

# PART II
# *COMMUNITAS* AND REFLEXIVITY

# THE MUSLIM COMMUNITY IN MAE SOT
## The Transformation of the Da'wa Movement

RYOKO NISHII

## Introduction

Situated on the Thai-Myanmar border, Mae Sot has a distinctive
demographic mix. Comprising some 4.8 percent of the town's population
(63,439), there were 3,036 Thai Muslims living there in 2013, according to
the Mae Sot Municipal Administration Office. There is no official data on
the Burmese Muslim population, but some NGO research shows 8,461
Burmese Muslims living in Islam District, where the population is mostly
Muslim (Mae Sot Zakat Organization for Occupation and Education, 2013).
There are also many Burmese Muslims living in other areas of Mae Sot;
there are reputed to be a total of 20,000 to 30,000 Burmese Muslims living
there illegally. Residents of the town also estimate that there are ten times
more Burmese Muslims than Thai Muslims. Most Thai Muslims trace their
origins to Bangladesh, Pakistan, and India. So it seems natural that the Da'wa
movement, which started in India, would enter Thailand through Mae Sot.

The purpose of this chapter is to sketch the dynamism of the Muslim
community in Mae Sot through analyzing the transformation of Mae Sot's
Da'wa movement. I will reconsider the classical concept of "community as
a totality" by applying assemblage theory, inspired by Deleuze's concepts.

Assemblage theory hints at a method for going beyond polar concepts
of "person as a part" as opposed to "community as a whole" to better
approximate the actuality of the living world. As Shigeharu Tanabe
described in the introduction, an assemblage consists of a contingent
configuration of heterogeneous forces, institutions, individuals, groups,

things, and nature, where certain autonomy among its constituent elements and "the virtual" or potential of individuals and parts, instead of the unified totality, have significant roles. In a similar theoretical direction, Escobar and Osterweil also pointed out that assemblage theory differentiates itself from theories that rely on concepts of totality and essences and that assume the existence of seamless webs or wholes. They explain, "Assemblages are wholes characterized by relations of exteriority; the whole cannot be explained by the properties of components but by the actual exercise of the components' capacities." (Escobar and Osterweil 2010, 191). I intend to describe the Muslim community in Mae Sot as an assemblage in which persons as parts maintain diversity, nationality, and other local conditions, giving the community irreducible complexity. Instead of assuming community to be an entity, casting community as an assemblage sheds light on the ongoing process of transformation of community in which people pursue their own lives in differentiated conditions, making the potential and the virtual emerge into the present contingent configuration of community.

## Outline of the Da'wa Movement

### Historical background

Numerous Da'wa organizations are currently active, including the Afmadiyya Mission in India, Darul Arqam in Malaysia, Hizbud Da'watil Islamiyya in Iraq, and Jama'at Islami in India and Pakistan (Masud 2000, xxvi). In Thailand, the most popular Da'wa movement is Tablighi Jama'at; this chapter describes the activities of Tablighi Jama'at[1] at the local level. However, instead of this name I will typically use "Da'wa," the word the villagers use when referring to their own activities.

In Arabic, *da'wa* literally means "to call" and can connote an invitation to a meal, a prayer, an invocation, a vow, an appeal, a claim, or a lawsuit. The verb *da'wa* usually means to "call on," or "pray" if the call is addressed to God. Tablighi, in the organization name, is the adjective form of *tabligh*, which is only used in Urdu in India, adopted from Arabic. This word also has a number of meanings: to reach one's destination, to arrive, to achieve one's objective, to come to hear, or to come of age. The verb form *ballagha*, from which the noun *tabligh* is derived, means to cause something to reach a destination, to communicate, or to report. In the Qur'an the word *balagh* (communication of revelation) is used instead of *tabligh*, but the two words are considered synonymous. In modern usage *tabligh* and *da'wa* are often used interchangeably. In modern Urdu usage *tabligh* by itself has acquired the meaning of "mission" or "to proselytize." However, probably to avoid this particular sense of *tabligh* and *da'wa*, the Tablighi Jama'at has defined *tabligh* without reference to conversion (Masud 2000, xx–xxi). Rather than literally "calling others toward one's religion," the avowed purpose of the Tablighi Jama'at is to bring about spiritual revival among Muslims themselves. Tablighi Jama'at calls Muslims back to Islam through the regular practice of Islam modeled upon the life of Prophet Mohammed (Preeda 2001, 110).[2]

Masud characterizes Da'wa movements as typically focused on one of three main aims: modernization, revivalism, or renewal of faith. Modernists want to reform traditional Islam to meet the challenges of modernity. Revivalists reject modernity and tradition; they call for the revival of the original Islam, and oppose modernity as secularist and materialist. Those motivated to bring about a renewal of faith also reject modernity as a manifestation of materialism and secularism. Renewal of faith is the goal of Tablighi Jama'at, which also speaks of revival and reform. The need for this renewal is explained by asserting that the true faith has been corrupted and needs to be renewed. The movements asking for faith renewal are often rooted deeply in their local contexts (Masud 2000, xxix).

While there is some controversy about when Tablighi Jama'at actually began its work, most researchers agree that the founder Mawlana[3] Llyas began his activities in the mid-1920s. Some report that Mawlana Llyas began Tablighi in Mewat to the south of Delhi in central India, sometime after his return from haj in 1926 (Masud 2000, 9). Throughout its history, the South Asian Muslim community has remained conscious of its minority status. Living on the periphery of the Muslim world, fear of absorption into the local Hindu majority has made the community sensitive about its separate religious identity. This sensitivity was heightened with the advent of modernity and the arrival of Christian missions under British rule. When Muslims began converting to Hinduism and Christianity, it was feared that modernity was corrupting the faith. It is quite common to describe Mewatis as Muslim in name only. Often, Mewatis are described as nominally Muslim or even under influence of local Hindu tradition, or "regionally Islamic." But Mewatis who consider themselves Muslim insist that they remain ethnically distinct from the Hindus around them (Masud 2000, xxxvii).

The historical headquarters of the Tablighi Jama'at is at Nizamud Din in Delhi, India. The movement currently operates in more than eighty countries (Masud 2000, vii). The movement's annual gatherings in many countries are generally well-attended. The largest congregation occurs in Raiwind, just outside Lahore, Pakistan. It may accommodate over a million people under makeshift arrangements at any one time (Azmi 2000, 239). In effect, "The Raiwind International Conference of the Tablighi Jama'at has become the second-largest congregation of the Muslim world after the Hajj" (Ahmad 1991, 510).

## The loose organization of Tablighi Jama'at

Tablighi Jama'at emphasizes participation, group work, and changing one's personal environment by travel beyond one's place of work and residence. It is held that each person should spend three days each month for Tabligh activities that immerse participants in thinking about religion and studying Islam. Each year, with the intention of spiritual improvement, a Tablighi Jama'at adherent should spend at least one *chilla* (forty days) out with Tablighi Jama'at, and three *chilla*s in his or her lifetime (Masud 2000b, 26). These requirements are vague, and people give conflicting accounts on this matter. According to interviewees in Thailand, three days each month should be spent on Tablighi Jama'at travel, and forty days or four months' travel in a lifetime.

In Thailand, Tablighi Jama'at is a loosely structured organization or network. Because the structure is so tantalizingly undefined, it is hard to actually describe it unequivocally as an organization. Masud has pointed out that of the sixteen Da'wa movements that he discovered, only Tablighi Jama'at does not maintain regular membership. Anyone can join in or abandon the Tablighi Jama'at activities at any time and there is no membership fee (Masud 2000a, xxvi). He also mentioned that in countries such as Morocco, Belgium, and France, where religious groups can operate only as registered societies, national Jama'at groups have established structured organizations. In Thailand, no membership register is maintained. It is only at the local level where any count can be made of people who are involved in Jama'at activities. The network is based on personal relationships. As Masud said, while a hierarchical structure is present and is relatively continuous through the territorial levels from village level to national level, it is mostly loose and temporary.

Each level has leaders called *shuro*. The most basic level is the *mahalla*, centered on the village mosque. Above this level is *harko*, which encompasses several *mahalla*. At least one of the local leaders is known at the level above *harko* because a representative attends a weekly meeting at the *markaz* (center) for provincial (*changwat*)[4] liaison. This is known as *markaz changwat*.[5] These meetings are held every Friday night, and leaders from each *harko* are expected to attend. There are from ten to twelve *shuro changwat*. The national *markaz prathet* is the highest level of the Thai hierarchy. There are two *markaz prathet*: one at Bangkok and one at Yala. Meetings are held once every two months, alternately at Bangkok and Yala. All *shuro* in the *markaz changwat* should also attend *markaz prathet* meetings. Fifteen *shuro* attend the *markaz prathet*, and four of them—one each from Mae Sot, Min Buri, Narathiwat, and Songkhla—are leaders of the *shuro prathet*. Any Jama'at activities of more than forty days have to be registered at one of the *markaz prathet*.

The loose organizational structure is viable owing to the principle of self-finance. Activists and leaders receive no salaries. A Tablighi is supposed to meet all of its own activities' expenses. Moreover, Tablighi adherents pay no contributions or fees to the organization (Masud 2000b, 30).

## The Da'wa movement in Thailand

The Da'wa movement is reputed to have been spreading throughout the country since the 1980s. The most popular Da'wa organization in Thailand is Tablighi Jama'at (Preeda 2001, 110). The introduction of Tablighi Jama'at around forty years ago is usually attributed to Haji Yusuf Kan, a resident of Mae Sot who died in 2000. He is said to have been of Indian Muslim origin. In August and September 2007, during research in Muslim communities in Chiang Mai, I discovered that Tablighi Jama'at had spread into northern Thailand earlier than other areas, including southern Thailand, where the majority of Thai Muslims live. Many Muslims in Chiang Mai had known Haji Yusuf Kan personally and informed me that twenty to thirty years ago most Muslims in the communities were already attending Tablighi activities. As mentioned previously, there are presently two main Tablighi Jama'at centers, in Bangkok (Min Buri) and Yala (started less than thirty years ago).

When I interviewed Bai[6] T in 2007, a man of Indian origin who was living in the Chang Khlan community in Chiang Mai, he told me that when he was twenty-two years old he first encountered members of Tablighi Jama'at who had come from South Africa and were of Indian origin. They kept to themselves at Chang Khlan mosque and did not try to teach or persuade others. After that, other groups came from Sri Lanka. In those days Haji Yusuf had influence (*ithiphon*) and he propagated Tablighi Jama'at all over northern Thailand. Bai T told me that Haji Yusuf's son had become addicted to drugs, but when he returned after four months traveling in a Da'wa group, he had become a good Muslim. This transformation so impressed Haji Yusuf that he mobilized many Muslims in northern Thailand to spread Tablighi Jama'at.

Initially, the movement spread among ethnic Pakistani, Bangladeshi, and Indian Muslims in the city.[7] It later spread into villages. Still today, the Tablighi movement uses peculiar words (of Urdu origin) in referring to their activities, organization, and institutions. Their distinctive style of dress, such as long robes, also follows South Asian Muslim style, and is different from that worn by local Muslims in Thailand. Villagers can recognize Tablighi adherents when they see them walking in these robes.

## Da'wa Movement in Mae Sot, Past and Present

### Introduction of Da'wa into Mae Sot

In August 2012, I visited Mae Sot to verify and expand on the information I had learned from Bai T. I was able to meet several informants who participated in the beginning period of the Da'wa movement in Thailand and many descendants of first-generation participants. Having occurred only forty years previously, the events were still in living memory. I discovered that Haji Yusuf had some Da'wa precursors. In Mae Sot, informants said that the first persons to introduce the Da'wa movement were Nana Suai and Tongsuk.

Nana Suai was born to an Indian Muslim father and a Thai mother who had converted from Buddhism to Islam in 1908. His father was a doctor in India during the colonial period.

Nana Suai spoke Urdu fluently but could not speak Thai very well. He started the Da'wa movement with Tongsuk who, born in 1934, was a much younger man. As with Nana Suai, Tongsuk's father was also an Indian Muslim and his Thai mother had also converted to Islam. His father however, was a businessman. Tongsuk could speak Burmese and Thai; he was interested in language, so he had learned Burmese at a Burmese temple near his house. Of these two men who went around northern Thailand preaching Islam, their descendants remarked that they were not so rich but they were very kind.

Tongsuk recorded in his diary that the first day he went on Da'wa was February 4, 1970. Tongsuk diligently noted important days in his dairy, which his daughter showed me. In the volume containing the entry for the beginning of Da'wa, he wrote on the cover, "Tongsuk's best one. There is no book better than this." In another volume, Tongsuk recorded the first overseas Da'wa, to Bangladesh. The year was 1979, almost ten years before Haji Yusuf began to explore Da'wa, according to an informant.

Nana Suai died on May 22, 1980, at the age of seventy-two. Fifty-one days before his death, in front of the mosque near Nana Suai's house, there was a traffic accident involving an old man, a pregnant woman, and a student who was Nana Suai's pupil. Nana Suai helped to deal with the accident. During that night, he could not sleep and ended up taking sleeping pills three times. The next morning, his daughter found her father paralyzed and unable to speak. He simply lay on his bed until he died. Tongsuk suffered an illness and died in 2002 at the age of sixty-eight.

## Support and opposition toward the Da'wa movement

In Mae Sot some people feel positively and others negatively about the Da'wa movement. While it is said that more than 90 percent of Muslims in Mae Sot have been on Da'wa, not everyone is an enthusiastic or even willing participant. One Mae Sot Muslim reckoned an even split between those who think Da'wa is a good thing and those who do not.

One enthusiast said, "Da'wa teaches us to practice good things and avoid bad things." Another said, "The purpose of Da'wa is personal practice. It is more about practice than about speaking".

One characteristic tenet of Tablighi Jama'at is that travel is the most effective means of personal reform. In previous research in Chiang Mai, one Muslim who used to go out on Da'wa told me, "When I was out on Da'wa, I felt that I touched the truth." When on Da'wa, adherents are cut off from their ordinary lives and are absorbed only in religious activities. They stay in a mosque and address the afterlife and religious matters. To them, Da'wa is a means of personal transformation.

This is what Mumtaz Afmad takes to be the secret of Jama'at's success:

> The core of its methodology is to isolate individuals from their familial, occupational, and geographical environment for a period of time, form them into a micro-community or group, and as a result of the group's inner dynamics and exclusive internal network processes, organize a system of religious learning and other devotional activities. (Afmad 1991, 515)

When adherents go out on Da'wa, they travel in a group of at least ten persons. They stay three days at one mosque and then move to another. Whether the duration of the retreat is three days, forty days, or four months, the pattern is basically the same. Da'wa enthusiasts say that seclusion from their daily lives reminds them of Islamic teaching and practice, and that these activities transform people.

This same seclusion can evoke anti-Da'wa sentiment. The grandson of Nana Suai, Chat[8] (fifty-eight years old), and his wife, Sut (fifty-seven years old), are now anti-Da'wa. Sut told me Nana Suai used to go out for Da'wa after planting and harvesting rice—that is, after securing food for his family—but today, Da'wa participants abandon spouses and children, leaving them hungry, claiming that Allah will help them. Nana Suai's daughter-in-law was likewise negative towards Da'wa as it is practiced today. Whereas Nana Suai went out for teaching only after ensuring that his family would not have difficulties, she said, recent Da'wa participants are largely from a younger generation and tend to neglect their families to follow their own pursuits.

Da'wa participants have an ethnic bias. The present majority are Burmese Muslims. In 2013, one Burmese Muslim teaching Islam to Burmese children told me that many Burmese Muslims came to Mae Sot for the Da'wa movement. He said 95 percent of Burmese Muslims attend Da'wa activities.

Here, I point out the connection between ethnicity and attitude to the Da'wa movement: pro-Da'wa is associated with Burmese, and anti-Da'wa with Thai. Very few interviewees openly refer to this association between Da'wa and ethnicity. Of course, this alone cannot delineate the boundaries of groups for and against Da'wa. Some Thai Muslims are involved in the Da'wa movement, and a few of them also practice Da'wa activities enthusiastically.

## Transformation of the Da'wa movement

In this section I will explore how the Da'wa movement has been transformed by analyzing criticisms by Da'wa detractors, such as Chat's and Sut's assertions that the Da'wa activities of Nana Suai's and Tongsuk's time are different from those in the present. Suk, the imam of Nurun Islam Mosque, the oldest and biggest mosque in Mae Sot, is Nana Suai's son. Imam Suk studied in Libya for seven years and told me that he was the first child in Thailand to go for Da'wa when he went with his father at age eleven or twelve (interviewed December 26, 2013).

He said,

The way of Da'wa of my father was different from the present. Da'wa does not mean to stay at mosques. Islam is the law of the way of life. My father went to look around to see whether Islam was taught or not. He wrote books for teaching Islam in Burmese, in Urdu, and in Thai. He printed them and gave them to Muslim communities. If there was no teacher, he looked for teachers. Da'wa activities at present just involve preaching at mosques. But the way of my father was different. If there was no book, he gave. If they were too poor to buy books, he helped them. He took poor children from Nakhon Sawan, Chiang Mai, Tak, to his house and gave them education. My mother cooked with a big pot without complaining. Now they have grown up and gotten good jobs or become Islamic leaders.

He noted that his father Nana Suai was not a rich businessman like Haji Yusuf Kan. He farmed a rice field, bred goats and chickens, cultivated fish, and planted trees in the garden.

Nana Suai set up an Islamic school in Mae Sot, now with more than six hundred students from elementary school to junior high school—70 percent Burmese, 30 percent Thai. At school, he taught both Thai language and Islam. Nana Suai's curriculum is now the model for the Thai Ministry of Education in other areas of northern, central, and southern Thailand.

Imam Suk told me that to him Da'wa means activities to promote knowledge of Islam's way of life. He said that Chat (Nana Suai's grandson, who was staying with us when I interviewed Imam Suk) is thus properly practicing Da'wa by broadcasting a radio program preaching Islam at a local studio at his house. The purpose of Da'wa activities in the days of Nana Suai was to contribute to the Islamic community through spreading Islamic knowledge.

Comparatively, the aim of Da'wa in the present is to obtain personal salvation. As a Da'wa participant told me, Da'wa is a means of personal transformation. Most modern Da'wa participants seem uninterested in the present political situation in Thailand. When I did research in December 2013, many Muslims in Mae Sot were watching TV broadcasts of democracy demonstrations in Bangkok all day long. But when I asked Da'wa enthusiasts what they thought of the political demonstrations, everyone answered uniformly that they were not interested and did not concern themselves with the present political disturbance. Their focus is personal salvation and their personal afterlife. For a rewarding afterlife, they try to adhere to Islamic ways as emphasized by Da'wa teaching in this lifetime, including following Prophet Mohammed's example and adhering to prescribed ways of eating and drinking.

The character of the Da'wa movement in Mae Sot has transformed from social activities to disseminate Islam to personal salvation. Da'wa activities have also become more strictly formalized. For example, ten years ago girls used to be able to attend Da'wa accompanied by an aunt-uncle pair, but at present each girl must go with a male relative whom she cannot marry, in a strict male-female pair.

# Mae Sot as an Interface between Thailand and Myanmar

Muslims enjoy comparatively greater religious freedom in Thailand than in Myanmar. One Da'wa leader who is originally from Myanmar told me the story of his son's hardship in Yangon. Burmese Buddhists set fire to the Islamic school where his son studied, and he barely escaped with his life. His brother, who recently came from Myanmar to Mae Sot, said that Islam is relatively tolerated in Thailand. In Myanmar, Da'wa activities are watched vigilantly by soldiers. He said, "Here in Thailand, police do not arrest Da'wa participants. In Myanmar, they arrest and examine every word. We can't enjoy religious activities. But in Thailand, they regard those who engage in religious matters as good people. So I don't want to stay there [in Myanmar]. Going for journey [Da'wa] is not enjoyable there." He teaches Islam at a Burmese school with about one hundred thirty students.

Differences in boundaries for Thai Muslims and Burmese Muslims arise from their nationalities. I met one Thai woman at the Burmese Talim (women's study group). Amina (fifty-nine years old) is married to a Burmese Muslim aged forty-six. She was born Buddhist and married a Thai Muslim man, but her first husband drank alcohol and indulged in gambling. She eventually divorced him and met her present husband at the market in Bangkok where he was selling meat. They moved to Mae Sot—her present husband's hometown—and have begun to go for Da'wa. Now they have found jobs selling roses to traders from Myanmar. She had previously gone on three-day journeys for Da'wa. As mentioned before, women must go with their husbands, or men they cannot marry, like their sons or brothers. These journeys by male-and-female pairs are called *masturo*. *Masturo* participants must be in a strict man-and-woman pair. In Mae Sot, most Burmese women have no authorization to go beyond the Mae Sot area. Amina herself can go everywhere because she has Thai nationality, but her predominantly Burmese Muslim friends do not. She needs to form *masturo*s with her Burmese friends to go on Da'wa. This limits her to Da'wa activities within the Mae Sot area, despite the relative freedom afforded by her own nationality.

On the other hand, there are ambiguous aspects to the boundaries between Thai and Burmese Muslims in Mae Sot daily life.

The first man I interviewed for research in December 2013 was Sam, aged fifty-three. I met him the day following my arrival in Mae Sot, when I visited the newly built mosque, which had not been finished at the time I conducted the previous year's research. He introduced himself and said that as his father was Bangladeshi and his mother was a Burmese Muslim. He was born in Thailand and graduated from the elementary school near the border. He subsequently began to work in Thailand, but liked to study so he had returned to finish high school seven or eight years previously. His son had escaped the school fire set by Burmese Buddhists. As he spoke with a perfect Thai accent I initially took him to be a Thai Da'wa participant and was surprised when his Burmese origins were later revealed.

On my last day of research in December 2013, I attended Burmese Talim. One Burmese participant who could not speak Thai invited me to meet her husband, who was an Islamic teacher and who could speak Thai, so I visited her house after Talim. I interviewed her husband, Lam (fifty-three years old). He could speak Thai, but had a slight foreign accent and occasional difficulty explaining in Thai. When he was a child, he said, he used to study at a Thai school near the border, but he had lived in Myanmar for such a long time and had moved to Mae Sot just six years before, so I took him to be a Burmese Muslim. When the interview was almost finished, I stopped the tape recorder. He served me *mohinga* which he described to me as a Burmese version of *kanom chin* (a kind of Thai noodle with coconut milk sauce). I told him that I was interviewing Thai Da'wa participants and asked him, "Do you know Wahid?" He said, "Yes, I used to go Da'wa with him." I then asked if he knew Wahid's close associate and fellow Da'wa leader, Sam. Lam replied, "He is my brother!" I was very surprised. I had assumed that the man I met on my first day was a Thai Muslim. This man was a Burmese Muslim. I wondered how they could be brothers.

In fact, though all of his children have Thai nationality, Sam's application for Thai citizenship is still pending. Had I not met Lam, Sam's brother, I would not have known that Sam was not Thai. In Mae Sot, distinguishing features between Thai and Burmese are fluid. There are no uniform characteristics for either Thai or Burmese Muslims. Individuals develop unique characteristics given the environments where they grow up, study, work, and go through other life milestones. Even apparent nationalities can be changed with little difficulty if the situation warrants it. This is characteristic to residents of Mae Sot.

## Muslim Communities as Assemblages

### The Mae Sot Muslim community as an assemblage

Mae Nani (eighty-five years old) was born a Thai Buddhist and converted to Islam when she married a man from Pakistan. She has nine children and now acts as a sort of intermediary between Thai and Burmese. Mae Nani's house is often visited by Burmese. The wife of one of Mae Nani's sons was a Burmese Buddhist and then converted to Islam.

When Mae Nani converted to Islam, she tried sincerely to follow the instructions of older Muslim women around her, including on how to cook and how to bathe. She could thus be accepted as a member of the Muslim community. She said that if she had not been accepted, no one would visit her house. In those days, the Muslim community mostly comprised Thai Muslims and was smaller than at present. Muslim women met each other every week for lectures on Islam at a house near the mosque. A Thai Muslim woman in her sixties told me that it was fun eating sweets together after the lecture. She has since stopped attending as study group membership has shifted from those in the older Thai Muslim community to the Burmese Da'wa group.

Mae Nani began holding Talim, a Da'wa women's study group, ten years ago. Four years ago the group began to take turns holding Talim every two months in rotation among four houses. Meetings are held every Friday in Burmese and every Sunday in Thai.

I attended Talim in Burmese for the first time in August 2012. Among twenty-three participants only three could speak Thai. Most of them wear a black chador daily in public, which covers the whole body including the face. Sitting in a small crowded room, they removed their veils and showed their faces. After reading a chapter of the Qur'an, Maorana (a male intellectual) delivered a lecture through a curtain. During the talk, the light in the women's space was turned off. In this dark congested space full of women I felt hot and sleepy. After the lecture, the light was turned on again. Finally, tea and Burmese snacks were served. The gathering began at two o'clock and finished at 3:50 p.m. The all-female chador-wearing participants covered their faces again before going outside, as if they were hiding themselves from the secular world and maintaining a sacred space inside their chador.

In December 2013 I had the chance to attend Talim in Thai. Among the twelve participants, four were Burmese. I also attended another Talim in Burmese in 2013. There were twenty-six participants, with only one Thai and the others Burmese. I felt that the Burmese Talim was more active than Talim in Thai.

When we consider the changing composition of the Muslim community in Mae Sot, we can also say that the assemblage of the Muslim community is transformed. As the population of Burmese Muslims has grown, the Muslim community has hosted a newly emerging community within it. Mae Sot's Muslim community has become more heterogeneous, containing both Burmese Muslims and Thai Muslims. The Da'wa movement develops in this composite environment.

## Burmese and Thai Da'wa assemblages

The boundaries between Burmese and Thai Muslims are not clearly defined, but we can see how the communities are articulated by focusing on people involved in the Da'wa movement. As I mentioned earlier, an important factor here is an inflow of migrant Burmese into Mae Sot's Burmese minority.

I observed two women who have joined the Da'wa movement: Saida, who is Thai, and Fatima, who is Burmese. Saida (thirty-eight years old) attends Da'wa enthusiastically with her husband. We met at her Thai Da'wa Talim study group. She wears a black veil in public that covers the face except the eyes. But at Talim, in rooms without men present, she takes off her veil and shows her face. She and her husband were working in Bangkok when they began participating in Da'wa. Her husband resigned from his air-force job and Saida also resigned from her job at an IT company. They returned home to Mae Sot in 2003 when Saida was twenty-eight years old. When Saida returned to her parents' home with a covered face, her mother did not permit her to enter the house. Her father did not acknowledge Saida, he said, because he could not recognize his daughter. They said their daughter was too religious.

Saida is a typical example of a present-day Da'wa life transformation. Saida changed her life with her husband, and discarded her high-paying job to return to her hometown, where it is easier for them to devote themselves to Da'wa activities. Her friends and former colleagues are now earning 40,000 to 50,000 baht per month, but she does not regret her decision. Even in religious life there are minor everyday dissatisfactions and disorder, but she leads a life peacefully believing Allah will help them. She previously valued professions with high social status, such as medicine or law, but after changing her life she wants her children to follow Da'wa teaching and lead a religious way of life.

Fatima (twenty-eight years old) is a Burmese Muslim. She moved to Mae Sot with her parents and seven brothers fifteen years ago. As she speaks Thai fluently, she translated Burmese to Thai for me at the Burmese Talim in 2012. I met her at Mae Nani's house. She helped to prepare the morning service of drink and sweets for children. On my second visit to Mae Sot, in 2013, I discovered she was living with her ten-year-old son. She had married twice. When she was fifteen years old her parents made her marry a twenty-year-old Burmese Muslim man. She disliked him and ran away to Bangkok to stay with her relatives. Her parents eventually persuaded her that he was a good man, and that she should stay with him. They lived in Bangkok with her father's younger brother. She soon became pregnant after living together, but when she was seven months pregnant, her husband died in a traffic accident.

She came back to Mae Sot and married again when her son was one-and-a-half years old. The second husband was forty-five years old, much older than her twenty-two years. He already had a wife but no children. He said that her child was pitiful without a father, and that he would like to be the boy's father. He himself was Muslim but his first wife was Buddhist. He came to ask Fatima and her parents three times to request permission to marry her. They turned down his proposal twice, but on his third attempt she decided to marry him because she wanted to give her son a father. The second husband sold *roti* at Ko Samui in southern Thailand with his first wife. He often came back to Mae Sot, where his parents lived, to generously give her a hundred baht per day. But after marriage, she found that her new husband had a quick temper and hit her and her son. Sometimes he throttled her to the point where she could not eat. He also whipped her son with electrical cords. She told me that she could endure her own mistreatment, but not his violence toward her son. Her son hated his stepfather and once said, "I will avenge mommy. I will stab him with a knife." Fatima eventually divorced, after seven miserable years of married life in which she was hit every day while they stayed in Mae Sot.

She went on her first Da'wa while still in her second marriage. Her son warned, "Mommy, you had better not to go to the mosque, or father will hit you again." On Da'wa, she was surprised at how helpful and affectionate everybody was. She said, "They share food by eating from the same plate with their hands. Though we are not brothers and sisters, we helped each other, washing dishes and sleeping next to each other. Allah is great and Mohammed is great. After three days journey, we cried when we separated even though we are living in the same community [Mae Sot]." When she went on Da'wa with Pakistanis later, she was asked why she did not cover her face. The Pakistanis said to her, "Every man has his taste; some prefer fair skin, some like dark skin. [If women show their faces] men will desire the women, and this will create problems. The prophet does not like women to show their faces." Fatima is beautiful though she thinks her skin is rather dark. She started veiling her face on that Da'wa and decided to continue even after returning from Da'wa.

Fatima wondered at first if she could persevere with covering her face but soon found that covering her face felt beneficial. When she began wearing the veil, she had not yet divorced. Her husband did not like this and tried to make her give it up. She said, "He doesn't fear hell. He doesn't want heaven." Though covering her face may not have led to divorce, it is of note that Fatima's newfound Da'wa women's network—who similarly practice face covering—assisted her with food and other basic necessities. Fatima goes to every Da'wa meeting riding a motorcycle borrowed from a friend. Now when her ex-husband returns to Mae Sot, she can avoid him in the street without greeting him. She said, "As I cover my face, I can ignore him".

The economic conditions of Thai Muslims are much better than those of Burmese Muslims. Mae Sot slum quarters house mostly Burmese, while Thai Muslims tend to live in upscale residential areas. Saida, the Thai Muslim woman, lives modestly and with the help of her parents has little difficulty finding enough money for food and her children's education.

Saida's family live in a townhouse which her parents own, and she runs a clothes shop in front of it.

Contrast her with Fatima, the Burmese divorcée who lives with her son. Fatima's parents also live in Mae Sot but have difficulty assisting Fatima and her son. Her father, fifty-seven years old, pedals a trishaw. Her mother, fifty-four years old, is not in good health, but loans out an old trishaw for thirty baht per day. I was impressed by Fatima's grasp of inequality between households when she said, "In some families only one member working can earn enough money, but in some families ten members work but cannot earn enough money." For Burmese Muslims, the Da'wa movement is useful as a network to integrate them into the Mae Sot community and help them survive there.

The Muslim assemblage in Mae Sot is articulated by, and spans, the Thai and Burmese Muslim subgroups. The Da'wa movement is practiced most actively by Burmese, with the Thai Da'wa-practicing minority holding both joint and separate activities. Mae Sot's Da'wa assemblage also links to Da'wa networks nationally and globally.

## Intermediaries between Thai and Burmese

Mae Nani holds a unique position among Mae Sot Muslims. As mentioned before, she was born Thai Buddhist, and later converted to Islam. Now, she plays an intermediary role.

Every Friday, she opens her house to Muslim children who come to study Islam, and treats them to tea and snacks. She began doing this fourteen years ago. In those days, many poor Burmese Muslim children came around to her house to beg. She did not want them to get too used to begging, so she gave them notebooks, socks, and other things they needed. Then she began hiring Islamic teachers every Friday to give the children a chance to study Islam. As a result, the Burmese children stopped begging.

Several Burmese Muslim women come to help Mae Nani prepare the tea parties on Friday mornings. One of them, Fatima, whom I described in the previous section, told me, "Mae Nani does not make distinctions. She treats Burmese indiscriminately. She does not care that they are poor. She loves equally. If they want to marry but have no money, she helps them to marry [by offering her house, preparing food, etc.]. She is not selfish and calculating. So many people love Mae Nani." Mae Nani herself said,

"I have never said Burmese should not enter my house because they are dirty. During Ramadan, Burmese visit from Yangon and Myawaddy [the town on the opposite side of the border to Mae Sot in Myanmar] every year." Fatima said, "They know Mae Nani is kind and her daughters-in-law [one of whom is of Burmese origin] are good. They dare not visit another Thai Muslim house" (interviewed December 20, 2013).

Mae Nani and her children trade gems between Myanmar and Thailand. Her children have several shops in the market on the border. Though Muslim, Mae Nani and her female relatives do not veil their faces like other Da'wa participants. They explain that it is not convenient for business. Mae Nani takes a peculiar position at the interface of the Burmese Muslim–Thai Muslim assemblage in prioritizing her business and the convenience of herself and her associates.

## Concluding Remarks

Mae Nani's life parallels the transformation of the Muslim community of Mae Sot. When she converted to Islam, the Muslim community was small and everybody met one another regularly. Even in those days the Muslim community was heterogeneous, including Indians, Bangladeshis, and Pakistanis, because of Mae Sot's location as a crossroads serving South Asian and Southeast Asian populations.

How can we use the disparate parts, themselves actualized assemblages, to describe the greater assemblage of Mae Sot's Muslim community?

To recap, the Da'wa movement was introduced in the 1960s by Nana Suai and Thongsuk, then disseminated throughout northern Thailand by Haji Yusuf Kan, a man of Indian origin.[9] Many Muslims in Mae Sot at the time became involved in this movement. Most Mae Sot Muslims currently over forty years of age have experienced going on Da'wa.

As the number of Burmese Muslims in Mae Sot grew, the Muslim community found a new community emerging from within. The Da'wa movement as an assemblage shows multiple characteristics. In particular, the Burmese Muslims displaced the Thai Muslims as the majority within the movement. Though each participant has individual motivations, the assemblage of the Da'wa movement is important for Burmese Muslims as a whole, such as Fatima, the Burmese divorcée. On the other hand, for many Thai Muslims like Chat, the grandson of Nana Suai, the meaning of Da'wa has shifted disappointingly from social activities for disseminating Islam toward personal salvation. Many Thai Muslims have become anti-Da'wa, but a minority of them practice Da'wa activities enthusiastically, mingling with their Burmese counterparts. Here we can see the ongoing transformation of a community in which people pursue their own aspirations in diverse conditions, making the potential or virtual emerge from the community's present configuration.

Mae Sot is an attractive town because of the dynamic interaction between differing religions and ethnic groups. Persons as multiple and heterogeneous forces live there, creating a transformational assemblage on the border of two nation-states. The energy generated by the ever-changing interplay of various people and their circumstances creates a uniqueness in Mae Sot which transforms the Da'wa movement itself.

## NOTES

1. Several other observers have mentioned this movement: for example, it is referred to in Malaysia as Jemaah Tabligh (Nakazawa 1988) and Jema'ah Tabligh (Nagata 1980); in Thailand as Jema'ah Tabligh (Preeda 2001); and in South India as Tablighi Jama'at (Masud 2000; Oishi 2002; Afmad 1991). I follow the original referent in Urdu in this paper when I explain this movement. Because most villagers in Thailand call this movement "Da'wa," when they go on a Tablighi journey they say "*ok* Da'wa" (going out Da'wa). The Da'wa movement in Malaysia is called Dakwah (Shamusul 1997, Nakazawa 1988).

2. Gaborieau writes that "scholars also drew attention to the fact that the Jama'at no longer aimed only at helping Muslims to strengthen their faith: it also attempts, often with success, to convert non-Muslims to Islam" (Gaborieau 2000, 121). This new tendency has not yet become apparent in southern Thailand, although village rumor has it that missions to convert hill people in northern Thailand have succeeded in a few villages.

3. Mawlana is an honorific, meaning "our master" in Arabic.

4. A leader of the *harko* told me that eight *shuro* of this *harko* are appointed by the Yala center.

5. *Mrkz* in Urdu means "center." In Chiang Mai, they refer to the *markaz changwat* level as *harko*. It used to be called *markaz* at *changwat* level, but with the proliferation of *markaz*, they came to be called *harko*. Even now, people from southern Thailand still refer to this level as *markaz*. In northern Thailand divisions are not made according to *changwat*. Areas are divided into six

*changwat*. Chiang Mai itself comprises one area with Mae Hong Son. There are twelve *shuro* and the leaders of the *shuro* take turns every month in a yearly cycle including all twelve *shuro*.

6. *Bai* is a reference for a "brother" of Indian origin in Chiang Mai. The original Urdu word would be *bhai*, meaning brother, but with the Thai pronunciation of the aspiration, it becomes *bai* (comment by Prof. Maichida Kazuhiko, a linguist specializing in South Asian Languages, ILCAA, Tokyo University of Foreign Studies).

7. Muslims in Chiang Mai are often classified into two major groups: subcontinental Muslims and Yunnanese Muslims (Suthep 1977; Scupin 1980). Tablighi Jama'at spread to subcontinental Muslims first and then to other Muslims, including Yunnanese.

8. Names referred in this chapter are pseudonyms except for historical persons such as Nana Suai and Tongsuk.

9. Some Muslims in Chiang Mai told me that the Da'wa of Nana Suai and Haji Yusuf Kan were different; in his own version of Da'wa, Nana Suai just disseminated Islam in his own way, not in the Tablighi Jama'at way of Haji Yusuf Kan.

REFERENCES

Afmad, Mumtaz. 1991. "Islamic Fundamentalism in South Asia: The Jamaat-i-Islami and the Tablighi Jamaat of South Asia." In *Fundamentalisms Observed*, 457–530. The Fundamentalism Project, edited by Martin E. Marty and R. Scott Appleby. Chicago: The University of Chicago Press.

Azmi, Shaheen H. 2000. "A Movement or a *Jamāʿat*? Tablīghī Jamāʿat in Canada." In *Travellers in Faith: Studies of the Tablīghī Jamāʿat as a Transnational Movement for Faith Renewal*, edited by Muhammad Khalid Masud, 222–39. Leiden: Brill.

Escobar, Arturo, and Michal Osterweil. 2010. "Social Movements and the Politics of the Virtual: Deleuzian Strategies." In *Deleuzian Intersections: Science, Technology, Anthropology*, edited by Casper Bruun Jensen and Kjetil Rödje, 187–217. New York: Berghahn Books.

Gaborieau, Marc. 2000. "The Transformation of Tablīghī Jamāʿat into a Transnational Movement." In *Travellers in Faith: Studies of the Tablīghī Jamāʿat as a Transnational Movement for Faith Renewal*, edited by Muhammad Khalid Masud, 121–38. Leiden: Brill.

Masud, Muhammad Khalid. 2000a. "Introduction." In *Travellers in Faith: Studies of the Tablīghī Jamāʿat as a Transnational Movement for Faith Renewal*, edited by Muhammad Khalid Masud, xiii–lx. Leiden: Brill.

———. 2000b. "The Growth and Development of the Tablīghī Jamāʿat in India." In *Travellers in Faith: Studies of the Tablīghī Jamāʿat as a Transnational*

*Movement for Faith Renewal*, edited by Muhammad Khalid Masud, 3–43. Leiden: Brill.

Nakazawa, Masaki. 1988. "Jemaah Tabligh: Malay Islam genrishugi undo shiron" [Jemaah Tabligh: Essay on Malay Islam fundamentalism]. In *Malaysia shakai ronshu 1*, 73–106. A Comparative Study on the Modes of Inter-Action in Multi-Ethnic Societies, Institute for the Study of Language and Cultures of Asia and Africa (ILCAA), Tokyo University of Foreign Studies.

Oishi, Takashi. 2002. "Tabligi Jama'at." In *Iwanami Islam jiten*. Edited by Otuka et al, 613. Tokyo: Iwanami Shoten.

Preeda Prapertchob. 2001. "Islam and Civil Society in Thailand: The Role of NGOs." In *Islam and Civil Society in Southeast Asia*, edited by Mitsuo Nakamura, Sharon Siddique, and Omar Farouk Bajund, 104–16. Singapore: Institute of Southeast Asian Studies.

Scupin, Raymond. 1980. "The Politics of Islamic Reformism in Thailand." *Asian Survey* 20(12): 1223–35.

Shamsul A. B. 1996. "Identity Construction, Nation Formation, and Islamic Revivalism in Malaysia." In *Islam in an Era of Nation-States*, edited by Robert W. Hefner and Patricia Horvatich, 207–27. Honolulu: University of Hawai'i Press.

Suthep Soonthornpasuch. 1977. "Islamic Identity in Chiengmai City: A Historical and Structural Comparison of Two Communities." PhD diss., University of California, Berkeley.

# REVITALIZING THE POWER OF SPIRITS
## A Local Contestation of Small Peasants in an Urbanizing Context of Northern Thailand

ARIYA SVETAMRA

## Changing Context of Uncertain Lives and Local Contestation

In a small town not far from the city of Chiang Mai, there is an abundance of natural resources that make this area an ideal tourist destination. During the boom in land values starting around 1990–91, many people from Bangkok flocked to buy the land to build vacation homes, business resorts, golf courses, or longan gardens. Meanwhile, many of the local residents, suffering losses from poor yields, have fallen into debt and sold their lands. Today, most of the local people in this area earn their income from daily wages and are elderly or children, while the young people go to study or work in the city.

There has also been the emergence of the Vipassana Meditation Center, attracting two hundred urban middle-class practitioners (monks, nuns, and lay people). Non-Buddhists who are adherents of the local beliefs are excluded. The inundation of people who possess economic and social power, and bring with them an ideology based on capitalism and the nation-state, has caused feelings of anxiety and uncertainty in the local inhabitants.

This exclusion has its roots in the creation of the modern Thai state, when the Bangkok authorities assumed that a rationalized form of Buddhism would provide the most unity and harmony. They were convinced that "true religion" was a matter of rational doctrine and belief, and judged that traditional Buddhism was too superstitious. Consequently, the Thammayut sect became the model for modern state Buddhism. In 1902 a sangha bureaucracy was legally created. This modern ecclesiastical system brought the unorganized sangha in line with the civilian government hierarchy. It disdained all traditions in which folk stories and parables were used to teach the *dhamma* and where local culture was integrated with Buddhism (Kamala 1997, 3–7).

These traditional representations of locality are currently being disrupted or modified, symbolically or organizationally, along with the advancing reorganization of spatial and social divisions by the nation-state and increasing involvement in capitalist relations. All the spirit-cult practices (i.e., matrilineal ancestor cults, village-spirit cults, and *mueang* guardian spirit cults) are increasingly inconsequential and losing their efficacy and reality in the life circumstances of the people (Tanabe 2002, 52).

The revitalization of spirit possession rituals of the town spirit and various related traditions may be regarded as a consequence of the interaction with modernity by the group that did not embrace such modern views and chose not to migrate to the city. Included in this group are the traditional irrigation leaders who collaborate with the village headmen, and the elderly in the community. This revitalization can be viewed as the manifestation of a method to cope with the anxiety, insecurity, and uncertainty of living in this changing environment.

The group of traditional irrigation leaders takes responsibility for water management in local agriculture. In recent years, irrigation systems have been scaled down as the government's dam construction and water management have fallen into the hands of government officials.

In 1998, there were conflicts over watershed management between the Chom Thong lowlanders and highlanders. The lowland leader of these conflicts was the Chom Thong Watershed and Environment Conservation Club. Traditionally, lowland farmers managed their water resources through their water users' organization called *mueang fai* (meaning "weir"), which operated fifteen weirs and three reservoirs in Chom Thong. In 1989 they established the Chom Thong Watershed and Environment Conservation Club, which eventually included the operation of all the weirs in the district. In this conflict, the club became allied with the Dhammanat Foundation for Conservation and Rural Development, which was founded by a Buddhist monk, Phra Achan Pongsak Techadhammo.

The conflicts not only became a controversial issue among local lowland and highland residents but also involved many groups, such as government (at local and national levels), NGOs, universities, and so on. This wide participation intensified the debate about the relationship between lowland and upland communities. Communities in the lowland, supported by various interest groups, demanded that upland ethnic minority villagers be resettled in order to place their lands under state protection and conservation. On the other side of this debate, the upland people and their supporters maintain that rights of indigenous upland communities to practice sustainable forest management are being usurped and that the decrease in water is being caused by changing weather patterns and growing agricultural pressures in the lowland (Aquino and Lawrence 1999, 98–104).

During the water conflicts between the lowlanders and highlanders in 1998, the Watershed and Environment Conservation Club, together with the traditional irrigation leaders, organized roadblocks and Buddha-image confiscations, as well as aggressive demonstrations against intellectuals defending the indigenous rights of the lowlanders who were suffering from water shortages and economic hardship at a time of financial crisis. With the assistance of other environmental NGOs, the Conservation Club demanded that the government overturn a series of 1997 cabinet resolutions that strengthened the rights of local communities to manage their forests. In June 1998 a new resolution effectively canceled the previous resolutions supporting the rights of upland communities and returned authority to the Royal Forestry Department (Aquino and Lawrence 1999, 100).

The traditional irrigation leaders become the key actors in the negotiations with the Tambon Administration Organization (TAO) for the budget on water management. Eventually, they negotiated a TAO budget to preserve the traditional knowledge and culture, including repairing the traditional irrigation system and the spirit house. In addition, the traditional irrigation leaders performed the annual ritual ceremony making an offering to the spirit of the weir, and the prolonging of life ceremony of Inthanon Mountain. Their actions asserted the common belief and understanding that there are essential linkages between the status of water resources and the state of forest conservation on the one hand and their self-management and development of the natural environment on the other.

# Revitalizing the Power of Spirits

The revitalization of the town spirit, named Phya Angkharattha, emerged after the grandson of the traditional irrigation group's leader was chosen by the spirit to be the spirit medium.

Nat (pseudonym), a twenty-five-year-old spirit medium, was born into an agricultural family. His family lived in a house belonging to his grandfather, a traditional irrigation leader. Their family did not have much land for planting crops to make a living. Most families in the area have only about two or three rai of land. Nat's father made a living as a tailor and his mother worked as a maid in the local hospital. He also has one younger brother, who is currently studying for his bachelor's degree.

When he was still in elementary school, Nat enjoyed spending time with his elders. He liked to listen to them talk about making merit, and instead of playing with the other kids, he would accompany his grandparents whenever they went to the temple. He would also always beg his grandparents to see the spirit mediums during their annual ceremony. As he grew older he mostly kept to himself; he preferred to stay home and read rather than go out with his friends.

When he began to get nearer to the age when he would be chosen as a spirit medium, he began to exhibit some strange behaviors. When he was a senior in high school he attended a science camp. While there he fainted and was rushed to the hospital by his teacher. However, as soon as he got there he regained consciousness, and the doctor could not find anything wrong. At twenty-one years old he started to study medical science at Chiang Mai University. During this time he began to have more strange symptoms, such as heart tremors and incoherent speech. His grandfather then recited an incantation and blessing, and he began to feel better; he then told his parents that he wanted to go to the spirit house during the annual ceremony. When they went to the doctor, the doctor again said that there was nothing wrong with him. During his fourth year, his physical condition deteriorated further; there were times when he would stop breathing and needed to be rushed to the ICU. Upon reaching the ICU, however, the doctor would check and find him in perfect health. This repeated many times until the doctor finally said that he was suffering from *ton bun* (holy man) sickness. He decided to go and seek the help of the abbot at the temple. He found that while meditating with the abbot his condition improved but would again deteriorate after leaving.

One day it so happened that his meditation coincided with the annual ceremony for the town spirit. Nat wandered out from the temple sanctuary and over to the ceremony. He found his way to the stairs leading to the spirit house, where the annual spirit-dance and spirit-possession ceremony was taking place, and the dancers were entranced due to spirit-possession. One spirit medium came and invited him into the spirit house. Upon entering they gave him traditional clothes to wear and bowed to him. Once he was accepted as being a spirit medium he found that he was able to name the other spirit mediums who had been possessed by the town spirit before him. He also is reported to have exhibited supernatural qualities when possesssed. One year during the annual worship ritual in the spirit house, the spirit medium was sitting on the ground when he quickly climbed up to sit on the spirit shelf, next to the Buddha image. The onlookers were amazed, reporting that the medium just floated up to the spirit shelf. Another year a food offering was made on a *khan tok* (a pedestaled food tray). The spirit medium sat on the tray and when he got down nothing on the tray was broken, even though some items were very fragile, such as puffed rice. The people took this to be a miracle, and the story soon spread.

None of Nat's family wanted him to become a spirit medium because usually this was a role that was fulfilled by women. They were afraid that Nat would be teased in school and that Nat himself was still a student and needed to concentrate on his studies. When Nat was born, his grandfather had had a dream in which he was told that a deity would be born into his household. At that time he gave this no further thought but was beginning to think that his grandson may be some sort of spirit reincarnation. Nat's mother said that whenever Nat tried to wonder about the existence of spirits, he would fall ill. Eventually, his mother went to consult a well-known spirit medium in Chiang Mai for advice. He told that her son was indeed a spirit reincarnation. People recounted that after the last spirit medium, who was a woman, died at ninety years old, the town spirit, *Phya Angkharattha*, was looking for a new spirit medium but had not yet chosen anyone. Moreover, two other spirits had to confirm whether a candidate could become the spirit medium. The two elderly women who had been possessed by these spirits confirmed Nat's appointment.

After becoming a spirit medium, his health improved and he was able to study even better than before. After finishing his studies at the university, he got a job at a hospital. He then enlisted in the armed forces in January 2014 and received his sword in a ceremony. People said that others had to wait for a long time for this ceremony, but "he was just taking what was already his" since he was the medium of the town spirit, who protects the town. Outside of his time spent as a spirit medium, he lived his life quite normally. He went to work and had a girlfriend, who had studied at the same university and continued with her master's degree.

After fully accepting his role as a spirit medium, he had to follow many restrictions. He was not allowed to eat at funerals, perform spirit possession rituals on Buddhist holy days, or ask for money at religious ceremonies; any money that he does receive from such ceremonies is to be given to the temple or used for preparing the next ceremony. He is responsible for participating in the annual ceremony of the town spirit. On his free days he travels back home from the nearby province where he has been working to assist the sick and injured. Nat's mother says that many times he came home unexpectedly to find sick people waiting for him, as if he knew they were coming. When this happens he jokingly refers to them as "emergency patients" and always performs a ritual for them even on Buddhist holy days. Many people come to request blessings to pass their exams, to get a good job, or to solve a problem, but not for lottery numbers.

To begin the ceremony, clients must present an offering including a white flower, incense, and money (three baht) in order to invite the spirit to possess the medium, and then another twelve baht for calling on the teacher spirit. Present at the beginning of the ceremony are the *tang khao*, women who act as intermediaries between the clients and the spirit medium, to invite the spirit and put the offering onto the ceremonial shelf. At this point the spirit medium begins to feel engulfed by nausea, as if he wants to vomit. This feeling vanishes once the spirit enters his body. The spirit medium, who was wearing regular clothing, will then begin to change into the clothes of the town spirit. These normally include a northern Thai outfit and a headscarf in the traditional style. He will then begin to chew on the betel nut and, if it is the annual ceremony, drink local whiskey. The transformation of the spirit medium is total, causing the mannerisms of the young man to assume those characteristic of an older man of about eighty. Along with a curvature of the spine, the chewing of betel and drawn-out speech, the shy young man turns into a confident man who dares to talk with people.

The room for the ceremony is set up underneath a two-story wooden house. It has a large shelf with flowers and urns for incense offerings. Underneath that shelf is a small sitting area with antique pillows, a water jug, and a tray of betel nuts. To the left of the spirit shelf is an altar table with Buddha images and various offerings, a picture of Khuba Sriwichai (the northern Thai monk who was acclaimed a "saint"), and another of Luang Pu Thong (the abbot of Wat Phra That). Near this table are small statues of Prince Chumphon (son of King Rama V) and a drawing of the town spirit that the spirit medium made on his computer.

Peng, aged sixty, is one of the *tang khao*, or intermediaries for the town spirit. She was once quite ill, her body fatigued and sore. She had to eat standing up. She tried to visit the doctor at the hospital, but her condition did not improve. The doctor could not figure out the cause of her symptoms so he simply gave her pain relievers, which helped only a little. One day her husband took her to see the spirit medium. The town spirit asked if she would consent to being an intermediary for him. Because she was desperate for some relief she then agreed, and soon was back to full health. Whenever the town spirit wants to ask a client a question he will ask Peng. It is her duty to ask the client the question and repeat their answer to the town spirit. It is also her responsibility to prepare the clothing, betel, and water for him.

Peng says that before she was the only *tang khao*, but presently three more people, Kaew, Moon, and Mae Kaew, have come to assist her or replace her when she is not available. Kaew says that she was also sick, but after agreeing to help the town spirit her condition has improved. Mae Kaew's role is to prepare food when it is necessary for the ceremonies. She says that the town spirit makes her feel sick in order that she seek the spirit's cure and render her service to the spirit. Mae Kaew believes this was the town spirit's way of contacting her and selecting her for service. Moon's duty is to assist Mae Kaew in the kitchen. Moon says that a spirit from her rice field almost caused her death. After agreeing to assist the town spirit, the spirit from the rice field left her.

Aon, aged sixty-five, fell ill and the doctor said that she would have to do dialysis, but she refused. Instead she went to see the town spirit to be cured. He performed a ceremony and had her drink sacred water. When she went back to the doctor for a follow-up appointment, her doctor said that she would not have to do dialysis anymore.

Gon, aged sixty-three, came to the town spirit because he was suffering from back pain brought about by his job at the construction site. He said that whenever he lay down it was difficult to get up. After going to many hospitals and other spirit mediums without any improvement, someone recommended that he see the town spirit. The town spirit explained that his problem came from a spirit at his construction site and that he had to do a propitiation ceremony to appease the spirit. The town spirit then blessed a bottle of water. After performing the ceremony, Gon's health slowly returned to normal.

Sud, a sixty-five-year-old former headman, recounted an incident at his pig farm. He said that during this time a disease spread, causing pigs to die at many different farms. When the number of his pigs rapidly declined, he went to ask help from the town spirit. The town spirit told him to bring a monk to preach at his farm and surround it with a sacred thread and pictures of the town spirit. The remaining pigs at Sud's farm survived even though all the pigs in the surrounding farms perished.

Kham Noy, aged fifty-five, told about how she came to see the town spirit because she was feeling sore and in pain. The doctor had not been able to help her, so the town spirit told her to drink sacred water and take some home to drink at home as well. A few days passed and Kham Noy began to feel better. She returned to pay her respect to the town spirit and often assists in his ceremonies. She also says she wears a coin of the town spirit around her neck at all times to protect her from danger.

Lai, aged fifty-eight, says that most people come out with some kind of sickness due to various misfortunes. She says that whenever the town spirit gives advice or performs a ritual, the sick are cured and the misfortunes overcome. Usually the beneficiaries return to assist and participate in the ceremonies in accordance with the counsels of the town spirit. Lai came because her daughter had a dream that she lost a tooth. The town spirit said that misfortune will befall someone in her house and that she should go back and perform a ritual to ward off the bad luck, and then everyone would be better and free from danger.

## Spirit Possession Rituals as a Local Movement

The spirit possession rituals allow people to negotiate with the external other to find ways of controlling their decisions, achieving emotional stabilization, and acting out fantasy to gain a new status and change circumstances (Tanabe 2002, 61–62). In addition to the role of the spirit medium in magical healing, blessing, and warding off bad luck, all of which reduce people's anxiety and insecurity, there is the annual spirit-possession ritual. This ritual might be considered as helping strengthen the sense of community. In the past, the ritual was held at *dong luang* (great jungle, or spirits of the jungle) to the south of the temple. Now it is held at the spirit house, called *ho luang* (great spirit house), located one hundred meters from the temple's wall at the site the temple rents out for the people's market. Every year the households around the temple contributed to the cost of ritual sacrifices and helped prepare offerings.

In 2011, a wooden, Lanna-style new spirit house was constructed using donations, both cash and in-kind, such as construction materials like teak wood or labor. The total cost of materials and labor was about one million baht. Inside the spirit house, there is a statue of the town spirit in royal Lanna regalia, with his left hand raised to bless and his right hand holding a sword placed on his right knee. The statue sits on a *khan tok* (pedestaled food tray), which according to tradition signifies abundance. This statue was designed by the spirit medium using a computer graphics program and was communicated to him in a dream. There was a ceremony to celebrate the statue before enshrining it in the spirit house, and monks were invited for merit-making rituals that included a homily. In addition, the image of the spirit was paraded through the town with occasional stops for people to offer donations as they rendered homage to the sacred image. Coins of the town spirit were made for fundraising, and a miraculous story became associated with them when a police officer who was believed to have died in a fatal car accident purportedly survived because of the sacred coin.

The aforementioned activities were organized by the Disciples of Phya Angkharattha Club, which was established by the head of the traditional irrigation leaders, with a committee of office bearers including the president, vice-president, secretary, and treasurer. The president is a former headman, the vice-president is the head of the traditional irrigation leaders, and the secretary and the treasurer are former members of the municipal council. One of the club's committee members noted that the club was made up of residents in the community who believed and participated in activities related to the town spirit. The membership of the movement is not fixed but fluid, depending on their needs and interests. When I asked the reason why the statue was built, the same committee member said, "It will make the spirit as visible as the statue of the Buddha." Normally, there is no image of the spirit in spirit-cult practices. Therefore, the construction of the spirit image under the influence of the Buddhist tradition suggests a strategy of the group in their adjustment to the modern era of visual and virtual technologies and mass communication. Modern technologies, such as the computer, the design of the spirit's image and statue, the use of smartphones prior to the ceremony, and the notebook computer for playing local songs at the opening of the ceremony, are all tools of the young spirit medium. Yet all devotees unequivocally believe that the authentic communications are from the spirits. However, the spirit medium still engages in traditional practices such as dress, behavior, ceremony, and food. In addition, the club also revives those erstwhile traditional events of the community; examples include the town spirit possession ceremony in the ninth lunar month of the Lanna calendar, the *dam hua* ritual (pouring water to pay respect to elders) of the town spirit during traditional New Year festival (Songkran), and the *tan lua hing fai phra chao* (burning of the firewood as offerings of warmth to the statue of Buddha during winter) tradition.

The town spirit possession is a ritual held annually with about two hundred devotees. Most of them are middle-aged and elderly women. They said they attended the annual ceremony because it has been a tradition since the time of their ancestors. Besides, they participated out of gratitude for the spirit's protection against misfortune and to guard the town from disaster. The town spirit is considered to be the head of local spirits, and there are other spirits who are his soldiers.

At the ceremony, the place was crowded with hundreds of people who sat around the spirit house with an accompaniment of loud traditional songs provided by local musicians. In the middle, there was a tent with plastic sheets laid on the ground, with thirty spirit mediums getting seated in the tent. There were some middle-aged women who wore cotton blouses and traditional sarongs, with a small towel over their shoulders to wipe their faces. These spirit mediums were women dressed up mostly in men's traditional colored costumes. There were only a few who dressed in female costumes. It should be noted that most of the spirit mediums and participants were female, including some dressed as men (i.e., for male spirits). There was also one male spirit medium. The younger spirit mediums preferred to wear fashionable clothes. Everyone carried small bags or briefcases with costumes and cosmetics inside. After arriving, they began to dress up or put on makeup. Each person suffers from some discomfort symptomatic of spirit-possession. These devotees would raise the trays of offerings to pay respect to the town spirit.

There are some new emergent spirit mediums who respond to individual needs or anxieties. These have no connection to the town history or historical figures of the town as the traditional spirit mediums do. They are related to local or national heroes, heroines from other areas, the Chinese bodhisattva Kuan Yin, or the Hindu god Shiva. Some of these spirit mediums joined the ceremony and some did not.

The ceremony began with a Buddhist ritual inviting a monk to receive *sangkhathan* (making merit for the dead by giving offerings to the monk) and offer sacred chants. Once completed, the monk returned to the temple. Then the old man who was the lay leader of the temple invited the spirit using a local chant. He raised a tray of white flowers, candles, and joss sticks above his head as a sign of reverence. Then the head of the subdistrict (*kamnan*) offered sacrifices to the spirits. His offerings comprised local food, whiskey, sweets, fruits, betel, areca, flowers, and joss sticks. The first group to pay homage to the town spirit was the head of the subdistrict, the head of the municipal council, and members. After sacrificial offerings to the spirits, they distributed food to all the participants.

Around two or three hours into the ceremony, live bands played for a "trance dance" of all the possessed spirit mediums, except those associated with the town spirit and some of his soldiers, who sat together in the spirit house. These spirits were very friendly. People could come close to talk with them and touch them. The mediums of the town spirit sat in the spirit house (the same place as the monk sat). They offered blessings, tying of the wrists with white threads, and reciting incantations over water that provided magical healing.

With the ambience of the slow and continuous rhythm of northern traditional music and the scent of joss sticks, all the spirit mediums seemed to be in a state of trance while dancing. Some turned their faces upwards to the sky and cried out, supplicating the heavenly spirits to descend to the earth to save the earthly mortals during a time of moral chaos and suffering. Even the participants sat in their chairs and gazed at the spirits in a dreamy, trancelike state.

The ritual spirit dance and the state of spirit possession opened an alternate space for people who are excluded from social opportunities. Images and cumulative knowledge of the past—traditional customs, dance, song, and local musical instruments—are conveyed and sustained through ritual performances. Also present are the physical signs of being possessed: trembling of the body, sounds of throwing up, walking and sitting with a hunched back, speaking like an elderly person, and chewing betel nut. These bodily practices in the performative memory are essential aspects of social memory that shape individuals and groups in social ways. Through bodily practices, the "choreography of authority" expressed through the body as specific postures, gestures, and physical habit-memories used in performance of ritual provides a "mnemonics of the body" that provides codes for incorporating these practices (Connerton 1989, 74–75).

The ritual serves to transport people out of time into a timeless state of liminality. It creates a fluid, malleable situation that enables new situations to become established (Turner 1967). It achieves a collation of past and present, and by this fusion the ritual will have some bearing on social memory (Trankell 1999, 209). Through the possession of the spirits, persons become transformed. Persons are no longer unchanging entities as they are culturally constructed through the knowledge they embody (Tanabe 2002, 44). The embodied techniques and social memory are ways of knowing, negotiation, and appropriation that lead to differentiation from the dominant discourses and the possibility of contesting fields of power relations in response to the deep-seated anxiety, insecurity, and volatile contingency in the current state of flux occasioned by modernity (Tanabe 2002, 63–64).

## Constructed Hybrid Identity in Relation to Buddhism

The coming of Buddhism along with the creation of states—both the premodern state and the modern nation-state—built over the past centuries form a comprehensive cosmology with a capacity to incorporate the beliefs of the indigenous groups who worshiped the spirits in the legitimization of authority. This comprehensive cosmology can integrate other non-Buddhist beliefs into the lower hierarchical order.

In this area, the myth of the visitation of the Buddha has been a dominant narrative of Buddhist discourse. It was constructed and reconstructed by both the state and the populace through changing historical situations. According to an oral legend about Wat Phra That, this land was an ancient town in the period of the Buddha called Angkharattha. The Buddha had visited this area and predicted the eventual coming of his relics to the hill where Wat Phra That is located now.

The people said that their clan spirits comprised eight lineages of indigenous people who were Phya Angkharattha's soldiers who were assigned to take care of the relics of the Buddha. When people give the food offerings to the monks, they will put food into the baskets of each "clan spirit" and lay the baskets upon the various places in Wat Phra That where they believe that the spirits dwell. They believe that they are descendants of *kha phra that* (servants of the Buddha's relics) who have a duty to take care of *phra that*. After the temple was nominated to be a royal temple and became a Vipassana Meditation Center, the duties and services were taken over by employees hired by the temple. Though they lost their role of taking care of the temple and the power of decision-making, they still believe that their "clan spirits" dwell in the temple to take care of the Buddha's relics (Ariya 2009, 134–35).

The interpretation that the town spirit and the clan spirits have been the guardians of the relics up to the present shows the tactics of negotiation by the local people with the outsiders by redefining and constructing their hybrid identity in relation to Buddhism. The revitalization of the spirit possession of the town spirit negotiated the integration of "spirit worship" into the Buddhist cosmology. In the new spirit house, two Buddha images were placed on the higher shelf, which is normally reserved for offerings to the spirits in traditional spirit houses. Now, the offerings to the spirit were put on the food tray on the ground in front of the spirit's statue. In front of the statue is an inscription of reverential worship written in Pali script (usually used in Buddhist chants and texts). The inscription is similar to those used to honor Buddha images. The words are as follows:

*Angkharattha maha racha puchitang sirasanamami sappatukkha sappakaya sapparokha winassantu*

(Worship to the Great King Angkharattha, to protect from all sufferings, physical harm, and illness).

The town spirit coins, made to raise funds for the construction of a new spirit house, featured an image of the town spirit inscribed on one side with the words "Father Phya Angkharattha [locals call him Great Father], Guardian of the Relics of Buddha." On the other side was the image of the Buddha relics and a horoscope of the Buddha. They also distributed postcard-size photos of the statue of the town spirit to the people who attended the ceremony in honor of the statue.

In addition, two practices that had been lost or were no longer recognized as important were revived: the *dam hua* ritual (pouring water to pay respect to elders) for the town spirit during the New Year festival, and the *tan lua hing fai phra chao* tradition (burning of the firewood as offerings of warmth to the statue of the Buddha during winter). During the annual Songkran or New Year Festival on April 16, the Disciples of Phya Angkharattha Club organized a ceremony at the spirit medium's house. In the morning, they invited a monk from Wat Phra That to preach and they offered food to gain merit. This monk is the only one in Wat Phra That who was well-known as a specialist in the magical practices, such as warding off malevolent spirits or black magic. In his preaching, the monk told the story of a *thewada* (deity) who came down to earth and practiced virtues. After accumulating merit and listening to the Buddha's sermon, he was reborn as a *thewada* and lived in heaven forever. The sermon contained implications for the spirit medium. During preaching, the spirit medium listened to the monk and put the palms of his hands together in salute. After the monk returned, spirit-possession of the town spirit took place, with offering of blessings, wrist-tying, and recitation of incantations over water to provide healing. In 2013, there were around fifty men and women of all ages who participated. Some came with their families for New Year blessings. In the afternoon, they put water in buckets so that people could pour water that had been blessed by a spirit medium over their heads for the *dam hua* tradition. The water was already blessed by a spirit medium. One woman said that even though the water was placed under the sun, it was very cold; she thought that it was due to the magical power of the spirit.

Another tradition, the *tan lua hing fai phra chao* was also revived. In the past, the novice monks and the villagers brought piles of firewood for burning in front of the *bot* (ordination hall) or *wihan* (sermon hall). It is believed that the Buddha is alive and feels cold. The wood used for fuel, such as the rain tree, was peeled, dried, coated with turmeric, and tied together in bundles of eighty pieces, representing the life of the Buddha, who died at the age of eighty. This tradition had been discontinued at Wat Phra That since the temple "became modernized" (in people's words) and people lost their duties of taking care of the temple. Some said it was probably because the temple floor tiling was complete so there was no space, or due to fear of fire in the temple, or maybe because this tradition was not recognized as a Buddhist belief. Therefore, when they established the club, the group offered the firewood and brought it to the novice monks with the declaration that they were not concerned whether it was banned or not; they just wanted to carry on the tradition. The tradition was then revived and carried out annually. This shows that the constructed hybrid identity in relation to Buddhism opens the space for contestation and access to the process of decision-making with the temple management, which had been lost, through the revival of the spirit possession of the town spirit.

## Change of Gender Roles

Popular religion widely accepts as normative that men have greater roles than women in Buddhist institutions and public religious organizations.

This reflects the pattern of gender construction widely adopted and practiced in Thai society where the most active roles in the Buddhist sangha have been traditionally reserved for men, and women have long been conventionally engaged in the spirit cult (Pattana 2005, 222). Spirit mediumship, especially in northern and northeastern Thai villages, has been the traditional setting for women to express their religious authoritative voices and identities. For generations, spirit mediumship has been retained as a religious sanctuary for women's religious empowerment (see Kirsch 1977 and 1982; Cohen and Wijeyewardene 1984; Pattana 2005, 221).

This study has found some changes in the gender roles of spirit mediumship. It does not reflect the stereotype of gender roles in popular religion as aforementioned—that is, the men have a key role in Buddhism and religious organizations, as well as public spaces in general, while women play a greater role in local religious cults and in the family. In this study, the spirit medium which was chosen by the town spirit had changed from the female to the male spirit medium. However, the selection of the spirit medium of the town spirit had to be confirmed by the two spirit mediums of the soldiers of the town spirit, who are two elderly women, and without their confirmation, nobody could become the spirit medium. In this sense, the women still maintain their traditional roles inherited from one generation to the next. But in the present context, the local people who still live in the community have to encounter and negotiate with outsiders, such as representatives of state-controlled Buddhism, urban middle-class religious practitioners, business people from outside who have social and economic power, as well as those with local political power linked to the national politics. These network have weakened local power. Therefore, people need to engage in contestation and negotiation. The selection of the young male academic might be seen as counteracting the educated agency of the rationalized, state-sponsored Buddhism. And it might be a tactical adjustment to increase the bargaining power given to them in the transition to modernity.

# Conclusion

Most contemporary studies on spirit-cult practices have focused on the dramatic surge in professional spirit mediumship in Thailand as a response to individual needs prior to the collapse of the Thai economy in 1997 and during subsequent economic crises. With the breakdown of the village's sense of community and the many recent rural immigrants to the urban centers, the individualistic focus of newer types of spirit mediumship may provide a more meaningful and immediately accessible means of expression to deal with the anxieties of life among the anonymous competitive urban masses than the more collective religious forms and rituals of Buddhism (Jackson 1989, 60–61, cited in Pattana 2005, 223).

Unlike the emergent spirit mediums who are individual-based, the revitalization of the power of spirit in this study empowers the community. The study shows that the village's sense of community was revived by the group of people who still live in the community—the traditional leaders in particular—to deal with anxiety, insecurity, and uncertainty in their lives. Spirit mediumship helped to stabilize both the individuals and the collective in coping with the social sufferings associated with life's stressful conditions and shaped by powerful social forces.

In spirit mediumship, there is the transformation of the individual through embodied knowledge and practices present in actions and interactions among the participants involved. These permeable and embodied interactions enable the clients and participants to have new experiences of relief and liberation in coping with the sense of displacement and insecurity provoked by changes, especially transformations as a result of capitalism (Tanabe 2002, 44, 61–62). The possession ritual of the town spirit that has been revitalized by the traditional irrigation leaders helps create a new identity that negotiates various activities. There is hybridization of local spirit beliefs with Buddhism, whereby the structures of power have been negotiated and contested, with obvious changes in gender roles in spirit mediumship.

In revitalizing the power of the spirits, traditional representations of the locality of the spirit cult practices are used for constructing new identity, both individual and collective. Spirits are not only representations, but also more significantly "real" beings with power or potential that may affect, serve, or transform the relationships between human body and soul, between persons, and between persons and things. Spirits are power, or more precisely, a flow or a flux of power (Tanabe 2013). Worshiping the spirits and related propitiation rituals involves a series of embodied practices performed by the inhabitants and participants to reaffirm their attachment to the group and their "locality" (Appadurai 1996, 179, cited in Tanabe 2013). It opens up spaces for contestation, negotiation, selection and reinterpretation of locality, and the construction of a fluid identity. It seems to be a modern socioreligious phenomenon in an urbanizing context and could be considered an ordinary, everyday form of peasant resistance (Scott 1985).

## REFERENCES

Anan Ganjanapan. 1984. "The Idiom of Phii Ka: Peasant Conception of Class Differentiation in Northern Thailand." *Mankind* 14(4): 325–29.

Appadurai, Arjun. 1996. *Modernity at Large: Cultural Dimensions of Globalization.* Minneapolis: University of Minnesota Press.

Aquino, Karan, and Karen Lawrence. 1999. "Case Studies of Community Involvement in Forest Management: Chom Thong District, Northern Thailand." In *Communities and Forest Management in Southeast Asia,* edited by Mark Poffenberger, 98–104. A Regional Profile of Working Group on Community Involvement in Forest Management. Switzerland: World Conservation Union.

Ariya Svetamra. 2009. "Politics of Religious Space in Practical Religion: Religion in the Making of Local Identities in Peri-urban Town, Chiang Mai Province." PhD diss., Chiang Mai University.

Cohen, Paul T., and Gehan Wijeyewardene. 1984. "Introduction: Spirit Cults and the Position of Women in Northern Thailand." *Mankind* 14(4): 249–71.

Connerton, Paul. 1989. *How Societies Remember.* Cambridge: Cambridge University Press.

Irvine, Walter. 1982. "The Tai Yuan Madman, and the Modernising, Developing Thai Nation, as Bounded Entities under Threat: A Study in the Replication of a Single Image." PhD Dissertation, University of London.

———. 1984. "Decline of Village Spirit Cults and Growth of Urban Spirit Mediumship: The Persistence of Spirit Beliefs, the Position of Women and Modernization." *Mankind* 14(4): 315–24.

Jackson, Peter A. 1989. *Buddhism, Legitimation, and Conflict: The Political Functions of Urban Thai Buddhism.* Singapore: Institute of Southeast Asian Studies.

Kamala Tiyavanich. 1997. *Forest Recollections.* Chiang Mai: Silkworm Books.

Kirsch, A. Thomas. 1977. "Complexity in the Thai Religious System: An Interpretation." *Journal of Asian Studies* 36(2): 241–66.

———. 1982. "Buddhism, Sex-roles and the Thai Economy." In *Women of Southeast Asia*, edited by Penny van Esterik, 16–41. Occasional Paper No. 9. DeKalb: Center for Southeast Asian Studies, Northern Illinois University.

Pattana Kitiarsa. 2005. "Magic Monks and Spirit Mediums in the Politics of Thai Popular Religion." *Inter-Asia Cultural Studies* 6 (2), 209–26.

Scott, James C. 1985. *Weapons of the Weak: Everyday Forms of Peasant Resistance.* Yale University Press.

Tanabe, Shigeharu. 2002. "The Person in Transformation: Body, Mind and Cultural Appropriation". In *Cultural Crisis and Social Memory: Modernity and Identity in Thailand and Laos*, edited by Shigeharu Tanabe and Charles F. Keyes, 43–67. London: Routledge.

———. 2013. "Spirit Mediumship and Affective Contact in Northern Thailand." In *Duai Rak: Essays on Thailand's Economy and Society for Professor Chatthip Nartsupha at 72*, edited by Pasuk Phongpaichit and Chris Baker. Bangkok: Sangsan.

Trankell, Ing-Britt. 1999. "Royal Relics: Ritual and Social Memory in Louang Prabang." In *Laos: Culture and Society*, edited by Grant Evans, 191–213. Chiang Mai: Silkworm Books.

Turner, Victor. 1967. *The Forest of Symbols: Aspects of Ndembu Ritual.* Ithaca: Cornell University Press.

# A RADICAL ALTERNATIVE EDUCATION
## Asoke's Samma Sikkha School

KANOKSAK KAEWTHEP

From the Buddhist standpoint man must cultivate his awareness of mindfulness—to know himself in order not to exploit himself. Unfortunately most of us exploit ourselves in the name of fame, success, development or even social justice.

Only when one is less egocentric, would one become humble and natural then one would be in a true position of trying not to exploit others—not only human but animals . . . as well as being respectful to our environment.

*Sila* in Buddhism does not only mean an ethical precept for man's personal behavior to be goody goody, it in fact refers to meaning social as well as environmental relations.

—Sulak Sivaraksa (1990, 191–92)

## Introduction

The following two invaluable remarks are from a study of Santi Asoke by Apinya Feungfusakul (2010):

After more than three decades since its establishment in 1973, Santi Asoke has become well-known as Thailand's Buddhist outcast movement distinctive by its critical, continuous and relentless critiques of the mainstream Sangha's laxation. Being ex-communicated by

Thailand's Theravada Sangha Order in 1999 did not weaken its capacity, on the contrary, its demonstrating communities in various parts of the country have continuously and gradually expanded. (Apinya 2010, 1)

In the passing years, there [has] been . . . progress which I detected, namely the growth of Asoke's system of education. Samma sikkha, literally means the right education, is Asoke's system of education which offers Asoke's way of schooling to its younger members. Highly conscious of the importance of propagating its ideal to younger generation, at each . . . Asoke branch, samma sikkha schooling is offered to children of the members, but gradually children from outside the community also joined. Children here get free schooling from primary to high school level. . . . Overall number of samma sikkha students, at present, [is] around 500. Though small in number, such intense alternative mode of socialization lays a solid foundation for the growth of Asoke's next generation. (Apinya 2010, 8)

Both points above inspired me to make a study of Sisa Asoke Community but this time with a focus on Samma Sikkha School. This chapter will first examine Samma Sikkha School of Sisa Asoke as a model for alternative education, while the latter part will analyze the dynamic and rather dialectical relationship between Samma Sikkha School on the one hand and the *sadharanabhoki* principle (*lak satharanaphokhi*; Communal Property System or Cooperative System) on the other.[1]

## Samma Sikkha School at Sisa Asoke, Si Sa Ket Province

### Sisa Asoke Community

Sisa Asoke Community[2] is situated in Kantharalak District of Si Sa Ket Province in northeastern Thailand. It is one of the largest and most active centers of the Asoke group. The area of Sisa Asoke covers forty-seven *rai* (1 *rai* = 1,600 square meters or .3954 acres) and has *kuti* for about thirty monastics. The center accommodates about fifty houses and hosts the largest of the country's nine Asoke Samma Sikkha boarding schools, for both elementary and secondary levels. Sisa Asoke has similar activities to the other rural centers—rice fields, gardens, mushroom farms, a tofu factory, a cooperative Bun Niyom shop, as well as a gas station and a rice mill. They also have work bases where they produce rice from their paddy fields, tools for agricultural work, herbal products like shampoo, medicines, and tea, and more. They have been successful in rice production; Sisa Asoke sends rice once a month to Santi Asoke in Bangkok for the Phalang Bun shop and for the vegetarian restaurant.

The community structure of Sisa Asoke consists of three parts: home (*ban*), temple (*wat*), and school (*rong rian*). At the time of this field study in 2000, there were a total of 326 residents, of which the majority (about 65 percent) were students. The community area is about 123 *rai* and there are approximately five hundred *rai* of farmland outside the community. There are also forty-two work bases taking care of all activities for self-reliance in the community; these include a farm, vegetarian-food base, mechanical base, store, herbal-medicine base, media-production base, cooking base, and so on.

## Samma Sikkha School at Sisa Asoke

Literally, Samma Sikkha means "right education." The Asoke group has established community schools known as Samma Sikkha schools (*rong rian thuan krasae*, or anti-mainstream schools) all over the country. "Anti-mainstream schools" here means to give priority to applying the Buddha's teachings to everyday life and observing the doctrine strictly as well as to reject the materialistic consumerism of Thai society. "Be diligent, take initiative, dare to be poor, and endure sarcasm" is a motto which reveals the puritanical pride and reformist objectives of the Asoke communities. There are now altogether nine Samma Sikkha schools in Asoke communities.[3]

1. Sisa Asoke (Si Sa Ket Province )
2. Pathom Asoke (Nakhon Pathom Province)
3. Santi Asoke (Bangkok)
4. Sali Asoke (Nakhon Sawan Province)
5. Sima Asoke (Nakhon Ratchasima Province)
6. Ratchathani Asoke (Ubon Ratchathani Province)
7. Phu-pha Fa-Nam (Chiang Mai Province)
8. Hin-pha Fa-Nam (Chaiyaphum Province)

9. Din Nhong Daen Nue (Loei Province)

The school at Sisa Asoke has a reputation among Asoke followers for being a pioneer in many fields, a fact noted by researchers such as Kwaundin (2011) and Heikkila-Horn (1998). It was the first school opened by the Asoke group and is still considered to be a model school that other Asoke communities take as an example they strive to follow.

Formerly the school had no fixed building; Sisa Asoke later built one from community money. The students do their studies at various work bases around the community. The schedule of Samma Sikkha School differs from regular schools and is seen as an example that the other Asoke schools are planning to follow.

4:00   Wake up and individual study
5:00   Work at the mushroom farm
6:00   Work at any of the forty-two chosen bases
7:30   Breakfast
8:30   Free
9:30   Flag ceremony
10:00  Classes
14:00  Free
14:30  "Home room"
15:00  Work
16:30  Dinner
18:00  Free
19:00  Videos/TV
21:00  Silence and sleep

Students of Samma Sikkha School can stay in the community throughout the period of their studies. The community supplies food, accommodation, tuition fees, and even clothing. In case of illness, medical treatment is free of charge. For recreation they can watch videos and movies together in the common room every evening. In other words, Samma Sikkha School's students need not spend any money at all. The school has both elementary (grades 1–6) and secondary (grades 7–12) levels. At the time of this study there were altogether 210 students—fifty at the elementary level and 160 at secondary level. Tables 1 and provide further background on the students who attend Samma Sikkha School.

TABLE 1. Occupational background of students' fathers

| Occupation | Number (%) |
|---|---|
| Farmer | 85 (63) |
| Civil servant | 19 (14) |
| Merchant | 15 (11) |
| Wage laborer | 13 (10) |
| Other | 3 (2) |
| Total | 135 (100) |

Source: Kittikorn 2000.

TABLE 2. Geographical origins of students

| Region | Number (%) |
|---|---|
| Northeast | 82 (61) |
| North | 35 (26) |
| Bangkok | 11 (8) |
| Central | 2 (1.5) |
| N/A | 5 (3.5) |
| Total | 135 (100) |

Source: Kittikorn 2000.

Teachers are not limited only to those within the Sisa Asoke Community. Sometimes, outsiders who appreciate Asoke's way come to donate their time to Samma Sikkha (Apinya 2010, 8). There are three types of teachers:[4]

1. Teachers of Buddhism (monks and *sikkhamat*s—ordained females) who look after the students very closely regarding both Buddhist teachings and morality; they also advise on everyday life issues. The cultivation of a moral mind through practicing the precepts, awareness of self-control, and sacrifice is the main aim for their students.

2. Work-base teachers (*khru pracham than ngan*) are Sisa Asoke members whose duties relate to various work bases. The teaching focuses on showing students how to make a living as well as instilling indigenous knowledge for their self-reliance in the future. In these situations, the "student" is rather an apprentice.

3. Academic teachers (*khru pracham wichakan*) take care of eight academic subjects: Thai language, mathematics, science, English, arts, socioreligious and cultural studies, vocational training and technology, and health and physical education.

Tables 3–5 provide insight into the backgrounds of the teachers.

TABLE 3. Educational background of teachers

| Education level | Number (%) |
| --- | --- |
| BA and higher | 16 (43) |
| Secondary | 7 (19) |
| Primary | 13 (35) |
| No education | 1 (3) |
| Total | 37 (100) |

Source: Essen 2005.

TABLE 4. Occupational background of teachers

| Occupation | Number (%) |
| --- | --- |
| Teacher/lecturer | 7 (19) |
| Farmer | 7 (19) |
| Merchant | 5 (13.5) |
| Student | 8 (21.5) |
| Other occupation | 9 (24) |
| No occupation | 1 (3) |
| Total | 37 (100) |

Source: Essen 2005.

TABLE 5. Geographical origins of teachers

| Region | Number (%) |
|---|---|
| Northeast | 27 (73) |
| *Si Sa Ket Province only | 15 (40.5) |
| Central | 7 (19) |
| *Bangkok only | 4 (11) |
| Other | 3 (8) |
| Total | 37 (100) |

Source: Essen 2005.

Above all, all teachers devote time to teaching as well as working for the community without pay (Khwaundin 2011).

## Ideological Practice within Samma Sikkha Sisa Asoke School

What do children learn at school? They go varying distances in their studies, but at any rate they learn to read, to write and to add—i.e. a number of techniques, and a number of other things as well, including elements of "scientific" or "literary culture", which are directly useful in the different jobs in production. . . . Thus they learn know-how. . . . But besides these techniques and knowledges, and in learning them, children at school also learn the "rules" of good behavior, i.e. the attitude that should be observed by every agent in the division of labor, according to the job he is "destined" for: rules of morality, civic and professional conscience, which actually means rules of respect for the socio-technical division of labor and ultimately the rules of the order. (Althusser 1971, 132)

### Samma Sikkha School's philosophy and curriculum

The Asoke ideology[5] places a high value on proper individual behavior, so cultivating one's own thoughts, speech, and actions is considered the most important commitment of individual members. When the school in the Sisa Asoke Community was established, Bodhiraksa, the founder of the Asoke movement, directed Asoke members to apply the Buddha's teaching to everyday life and to observe the doctrine strictly. He insisted that the real aim of education is personal development by eradicating all defilements and becoming "good people."[6]

The Asoke educational philosophy is best manifested in the slogan "Strict to Buddhist precepts, efficient in working, knowledgeable in studying" (*Sin den, pen ngan, chan wicha*). So "learning while working" as apprenticeship is still maintained. Therefore, 40 percent of the curriculum is to teach and implant *sila*, 35 percent emphasizes different skills of manual labor, and only 25 percent of the curriculum is academic content (Apinya 2010, 8).

## Learning process

*1. Adhering to Buddhist Precepts (Sin den)*

Bodhiraksa's style of teaching, which is explicit, lively, and straightforward, has made the Asoke Buddhist way of life well-adapted to the modern globalized world, and at the same time the students adhere first to the old principles of the five precepts (*sin ha*). The core of the practice is present in Asoke's motto, *lot, la, loek* (reduce, refrain from, relinquish). Their technique of developing their lives is called *rabop khatklao* (human-nature polishing process). It is considered a duty of every student to self-assess his or her own development in spirit, efficiency in working, and advancement in knowledge seeking. To Asoke people, self-evaluation is for improvement rather than punishment.

What follows is how the famous Asoke precepts are established and imposed on its members, as laid out by expert on the Asoke movement Apinya Feungfusakul (2010, 6–8):

(1) Check *sila* (*Check sin*). One method of self-evaluation involves the precept-checking form. Each member must complete this form every day. The form contains lists for self-checking in the Asoke precepts. If an individual fails to observe a precept, he or she must write to explain why. Then a monk or nun will read, examine, and talk to that person if needed before signing the sheet. Such a custom enables the students to thoroughly look into themselves, conduct self dialogue, and reexamine their strengths and weaknesses. It shows that the community requires the power of religion to create social unity.

(2) Point to the treasure (*Chi kum sap*). Members are asked to point out one another's faults or weaknesses. This can be done privately or publicly, regardless of a person's status in the community. "Treasure" indicates that such occasions must be viewed positively and the one whose personal treasure is exposed must thank the other for pointing it out.

For individual student salvation, the practice of *sila* is quite possible within the constructed Asoke community, which satisfies all basic needs. The communal living provides suitable conditions for a modest everyday life, helping students as well as members to consume less, sleep less, and work harder. This can be compared with a monastic life of asceticism—devoting oneself toward personal salvation. Each student also voluntarily supports the community by contributing to collective labor and providing social pressure for other students to practice and polish (*rabop khatklao*) their *sila* in a group socialization process known as *mu klum*.

*2. Learning While Working (Pen ngan)*

Once the competence of their mind and behavior have been elevated, their work will become more creative and beneficial, not only for themselves but for their community and the society as a whole. In order to fulfill their intention of creating a self-reliant community, the Asoke members, with the community's assent, have established a number of work bases to produce products for their communities' subsistence first, as every student has to learn how to plant rice and has taken part in every step of rice production as it is one of the three types of "right livelihood" of Asoke communities—practicing organic agriculture, producing natural fertilizer, and collecting and sorting garbage. These activities have been expanded to help outsiders by selling goods of reliable quality, such as brown rice, herbal shampoos, herbal medicine, herbal teas, detergents, and more in the cooperative shop at a low price in accordance with Asoke's ideology of *bun niyom* ("meritism," which entails giving out more than is taken in), or the concept of "economics of giving" as a means for sharing resources among Asoke's members within the community as well as doing business with the society outside. In principle, *bun niyom* emphasizes the spiritual merit gained when donating goods to customers or from receiving as low profit as possible from customers, rather than money or material profit (Heikkila-Horn and Krisanamis 2002, 48).

*3. Academic Learning with Practice (Chan wicha)*
Linking both theory from academic subjects and a basic level of scientific knowledge with concrete practices and vocational knowledge has deepened students' understanding and encouraged them to gain skills from working with their own knowledge. It means not only efficiency in working but also advancement in knowledge-seeking.

All in all, the students' experiences through intensive learning processes, supervised by monks and *sikkhamats*, teachers, and community members whose good lifestyles are models for them, have raised their critical consciousness.

Of equal importance, the Sisa Asoke Community is able to reproduce both its ideology of meritism as well as labor powers from students of Samma Sikkha School through the *sadharanabhoki* principle.

In conclusion, Samma Sikkha Asoke School is quite different from regular schools in the country but rather similar to what Althusser (1971, 151) points out: "In the pre-capitalist historical period . . . it is absolutely clear that the Church . . . concentrated within it not only religious functions, but also educational ones, and a large proportion of the functions of communications and 'culture.'"

# A Dialectical Relationship between Samma Sikkha School and the *Sadharanabhoki* Principle

We shall have an association, in which the free development of each is the condition for the free development of all.

—K. Marx and F. Engels, *Manifesto of the Communist Party,* 1848

What I will examine in this last section is the role and function of the *sadharanabhoki* principle as social relations of production[7] in the Sisa Asoke Community.

As mentioned earlier, the communal living applied from the *sadharanabhoki* principle provides suitable material conditions for a modest everyday life, helping students as well as members to fulfill the Asoke ideology of *bun niyom* (meritism) by consuming less, sleeping less, and working harder. Or in the famous words of Marx (1875, 11), "from each according to his abilities, to each according to his needs." This is a rather distinctive feature of the Asoke community as a specific way of the articulation process of the *sadharanabhoki* principle and *bun niyom*. In other words, the *sadharanabhoki* principle, an abstract idea of "communal living," must be a necessary condition for and be translated into an actual system for individual members to find worth pursuing and cumulatively change toward *bun niyom*.[8]

In fact, it is worth noting here that after some years of ascetic practice, the system of sharing resources among members within Sisa Asoke has accumulated some material wealth for the community. This wealth is what ensures that Samma Sikkha School can afford to provide education for students free of charge. Therefore, it is not an exaggeration to say that all students experience the *sadharanabhoki* principle starting with their enrollment at Samma Sikkha School. From then on, for each of their school days for six years (for secondary-education level) or more, they entrust the community with their labor through various training apprenticeships. On one hand, they start their lives as consumers by consuming both material as well as mental products from accumulated wealth of the community, while on the other hand, they begin to be producers by first improving their labor capability as well as producing material products and serving the community. And with their human activities, the common wealth of the community is enlarged. It is important to note that there have been many cases of students continuing to live and work for free in the community after their graduation (Khwaundin 2011). This is one way in which students, from the Samma Sikkha School at Sisa Asoke as well as others, are able to express their gratitude to the Asoke community for supporting them both materially (food, shelter, etc.) and nonmaterially (educational knowledge, working skills, spiritual development, etc.) during their school years. In other words, this is a form of reciprocity of the "economics of giving." So, once again, free schooling from the *sadharanabhoki* principle functions as reproduction of both labor power and community capital accumulation.

The Asoke education strategy is carried out through the organization of various small groups in the community. Students' participation in these groups involves becoming better informed through discussion of many issues. They come to know of their rights, responsibilities, duties, and privileges. Within the group, they learn tolerance and the need to respect the viewpoints of others. What they practice is "real democracy" as a way of life.

In all, the basic needs in the community have to be satisfied, and exploitation of people at every level of society has to be eradicated if possible. Strategies for such individual and community (group) development can be found in Buddhist theory and practice. Sharing (*dana*) is traditionally and still the foremost virtue among practicing Buddhists. Again and again, Asoke teachings have emphasized to its members the necessity of *dana*.

In sum, Samma Sikkha School has the crucial role of promoting a sense of spiritual and mutual sharing as well as the preservation of community life in the future, or in other words, of reproducing Asoke's ideology of the anti-mainstream community.

The specific nature and context of Sisa Asoke's "communal" orientation, such as its capacity for normative integration and large-scale solidarity, should be understood as largely dependent upon its specific doctrinal and salvational content. Looking from an alternative development paradigm, with a perspective of self-reliance, it should be noted that Sisa Asoke Community has shown one example of Marx's statement given at the opening of this section.[9]

In addition, the Asoke alternative paradigm of development is not a theory imposed from above, or an academic hypothesis to be tested in the field. It is an empirical realization acquired by involving people in hard work. Bodhiraksa based his development theory on his experience of working with the people. He saw how development should be achieved as a total unified process combining economic, religious, spiritual, social, cultural, environmental, and psychological elements. It was based on human beings, treating them as the center of the total development process. Development of the individual and the development of the community are both inherent.

The Asoke group not only challenges mainstream Buddhism but also offers a Buddhist perspective on self-reliance as an alternative development paradigm. In another words, the Asoke group is a "radical conservative Buddhist utopia." Of course, this utopia, at least in terms of Rancière's view, is not the elsewhere nor the future realization of an unfulfilled dream. But it is an intellectual construction of Bodhiraksa, which brings a place in thought into conjunction with a perceived or perceptible intuitive space.[10]

# Conclusion

Beyond analyzing the religious value attained within Sisa Asoke Community, we also question how these values exist at all times in the organization, or in other words, how these values are still actualized when they work with an outside group. In this respect, the school of Sisa Asoke practices an alternative method necessary for attainment of the above values. The stance here is to promote a sense of spiritual and mutual sharing as well as the preservation of community life in the future. In this sense, the existence of the school is similar to that of the community—to exist in a dynamic process.

A new religious movement like the Sisa Asoke Community described above offers an alternative truth in the context of mainstream power. Of course, this counter- ideology threatens civic religion and offers other religious practices and doctrinal interpretations. Despite its doctrinal conservatism, the Sisa Asoke Community has displayed an intriguing capacity to coexist with and absorb heterogeneous cultural influences.

NOTES

This paper was written under the auspices of the Japan Society for the Promotion of Science, which sponsored for the research project during 2011–14. The first version of this article was presented at the international symposium "Community Movements in Mainland South East Asia" in Chiang Mai, Thailand, on March 7–8, 2014. The author is grateful for the critical reading and patient support and guidance of Professor Shigeharu Tanabe as well as the comments of participants at the symposium. Any remaining errors are, of course, my own.

    1.It should be noted that this "collective welfare" in the Pali Canon is called the *sadharanabhoki* principle, which is one principle of *saraniyadhamma 6* (Virtues for fraternal living). See Phra Rajvoramuni (1985, 233–35). See also Bodhiraksa (2007), Kittikorn, (2000, 62–63), and Apinya (1993, 117, 121). Also, under the *sadharanabhoki* principle, private property is not encouraged in Asoke. Instead, many resources are owned collectively by various foundations, associations, or organizations, such as the Dharma Santi Foundation and the Gongtub Dharm Foundation. Money is pooled together in a central office (*sadharanabhoki*) located in Santi Asoke. See for more details in Heikkila-Horn and Krisanamis (2002, 49–50).

2. This part is largely drawn from Kittikorn (2000, 87–100). See also Kanoksak (2001, 193–204).

3. Announcement for recruitment of new students for Samma Sikkha Asoke School, 2010.

4. See for more details Kittikorn (2000), Essen (2005, appendix A, table 1 and 2), and Khwaundin (2011), chapter 4.

5. Ideological practice in this section means the processes of formation and transformation of ideology at both the individual level, where an individual produces a concept of "self" through the transformation of his or her experience living in a community with certain culture and social relations of production, and the organizational level, in which the process of producing a new hegemonic ideology is generated by the collective self in order to sustain social relations. See for more details Nalinee (1994), Tanabe (1984), and Althusser (1971).

6. See Essen (2005, 45).

7. The term "social relations of production" here, taken from Godelier (1978, 763), means relations of any kind that assume one or another of the following three functions: (1) determining the social form of access to resources and to control of the means of production; (2) allocating the labor force of a society's members among the different labor processes which produce its material base, and organizing these different processes; and (3) determining the social form of redistribution of the product of individual or collective labor and, consequently, the form of circulation or non-circulation of these products.

8. For more discussion of *bun niyom*, see for example Kanoksak (2008). It is worth noting that the Asoke movement here is very close to the notion of the "new traditional economy" in which Rosser (1999) argued more than a decade ago about a new economic system emerging in the world economy. Such an economic system simultaneously seeks to have economic decision making fundamentally embedded within a traditional sociocultural framework, most frequently one associated with a traditional religion. Unfortunately, what Rosser has reviewed so far, in various parts of the world, is mostly analysis of the Islamic and neo-Confucian economic systems.

9. It should be noted that Tanabe has mentioned "association" as a reflection of his thirty-year career as an anthropologist. Though he has been influenced from Marx's work cited above, he has hoped instead for various forms of associations established from the people themselves as actors—as shown especially in his article "Buddhist Utopian Movement in Northern Thailand: The Case of Phra Pho Pan," which is also mentioned in chapter 1 of this volume—rather than focusing on the state (see, for more details, Tanabe 2007, 401–2). Therefore, inspired by Tanabe's "association," I then take it as a starting point for a critical review of the Asoke movement. In this regard, the Asoke Buddhist approach

is one channel in which community members become actors to establish an association with their collective identity—as *chao Asok* (the Asoke people)—which gives priority to community members' commitment to rigorous ascetic discipline as well as sharing their lives collectively.

10. See Rancière (2007, 15). For further discussion on this issue, see, in particular, Marx and Engels' words in *The German Ideology* (1970, 54):

> For as soon as the distribution of labor comes into being, each man has a particular, exclusive sphere of activity, which is forced upon him and from which he cannot escape. He is a hunter, a fisherman, a herdsman, or a critical critic, and must remain so if he does not want to lose his means of livelihood; while in communist society, where nobody has one exclusive sphere of activity but each can become accomplished in any branch he wishes, society regulates the general production and thus makes it possible for me to do one thing today and another tomorrow, to hunt in the morning, fish in the afternoon, rear cattle in the evening, criticize after dinner, just as I have a mind, without ever becoming hunter, fisherman, herdsman or critic.

## REFERENCES

Althusser, Louis. 1971. "Ideology and Ideological State Apparatuses." In *Lenin and Philosophy and Other Essays*, translated by Ben Brewster. New York: Monthly Review Press.

Apinya Feungfusakul. 1993. "Buddhist Reform Movements in Contemporary Thai Urban Context: Thammakai and Santi Asok." PhD diss., Universitat Bielefeld.

———. 2010. "Santi Asoke: The Buddhist Outcast Movement in Thailand." Paper presented at the international conference "Communities of Becoming in South East Asia," Faculty of Social Sciences, Chiang Mai University, March 5–6, 2010.

Bodhiraksa. 2007. *Sadharanabhoki: Sethakit chanit mai* [Sadharanabhoki: A new economy]. Bangkok: Fah Apai Publishing.

Essen, Juliana. 2005. *"Right Development": The Santi Asoke Buddhist Reform Movement of Thailand*. Lanham: Lexington Books.

Godelier, Maurice. 1978. "Infrastructures, Societies, and History." *Current Anthropology* 19(4): 763–68.

Heikkila-Horn, Marja-Leena. 1998. *Buddhism with Open Eyes: Belief and Practice of Santi Asoke*. Bangkok: Fah Apai Publishing.

Heikkila-Horn, Marja-Leena, and Rassamee Krisanamis (eds.) 2002. *Insight into Santi Asoke*. Bangkok: Fah Apai Publishing.

Kanoksak Kaewthep. 2001. "Chumchon Sisa Asok, changwat Si Sa Ket" [Sisa Asoke Community, Si Sa Ket Province]. *Warasan sethasat kan mueang* [Journal of political economy] 18 (July 2001): 191–237.

————. 2008. "An 'Imagining' Community: A Case of Sisa Asoke Community, Si Sa Ket Province." In *Imagining Community in Thailand: Ethnographic Approaches*, edited by Shigeharu Tanabe. Chiang Mai: Mekong Press.

Khwaundin Singkham. 2011. "Kan buranakan kan sueksa khong rongrian Samma Sikkha Sisa Asok puea phatthana bukkhon lae chumchon" [The integrated education for individuals and community development: A case study of Samma Sikkha Sisa Asoke School]. MA thesis, Ubon Ratchathani University.

Kittikorn Soontaranurak. 2000. "Kan phatthana chumchon phueng ton eng: korani sueksa chumchon Sisa Asok [The development of a community of self-reliance: A case study of Sisa Asoke Community]." MA thesis, Chulalongkorn University.

Marx, Karl. (1875) 1970. "A Critique of Gotha Program." In *Marx/Engels Selected Works*, Vol. 3. Moscow: Progress Publishers.

Marx, Karl, and Frederick Engels. (1846) 1970. "The German Ideology." Edited and introduced by C. J. Arthur. London: Lawrence and Wishart.

Nalinee Tantuvanit. 1994. "Ideological Practice of Thai Peasantry." PhD diss., University of Wisconsin–Madison.

Phra Rajvoramuni (P. A. Payutto). 1985. *Dictionary of Buddhism*. 4th edition. Bangkok: Mahachulalongkorn Rajavidyalaya.

Rancière, Jacques. 2007. "The End of Politics or The Realist Utopia." In *On the Shores of Politics*, translated by Liz Heron. London: Verso.

Rosser, J. Barkley. 1999. "The New Traditional Economy: A New Perspective for Comparative Economics?" *International Journal of Social Economics* 26(6): 763–78.

Sulak Sivaraksa. 1990. "Building Trust through Economic and Social Development and Ecological Balance: A Buddhist Perspective." In *Radical Conservatism: Buddhism in the Contemporary World: Articles in Honor of Bhikkhu Buddhadasa's 84th Birthday Anniversary*. Bangkok: Thai Inter-Religious Commission for Development and International Network of Engaged Buddhists.

Tanabe, Shigeharu. 1984. "Ideological Practice in Peasant Rebellions: Siam at the Turn of the Twentieth Century." In *History and Peasant Consciousness in Southeast Asia*, edited by Andrew Turton and Shigeharu Tanabe. Senri Ethnological Studies, no. 13. Osaka: National Museum of Ethnology.

————. 2007. "Kham banyai tai kan sammana" [An epilogue to the seminar]. In *Kham Khop Fa 60 pi Shigeharu Tanabe* [Across the horizon: Sixty years of Shigeharu Tanabe], edited by Kwanchewan Buadaeng and Apinya Feungfusakul. Bangkok: Princess Maha Chakri Sirindhorn Anthropology Centre.

# PRESERVING THE COMMUNITY
## The Rise of Museum Movements in Rural Thailand

KYONOSUKE HIRAI

## Introduction

Since the late 1980s, many small museums exhibiting aspects of local history and traditional lifestyles have been established throughout Thailand. Between the late 1990s and the early 2000s, these museums proliferated rapidly, and they now number over one thousand. It is not a new phenomenon in rural Thai society for objects of value within the history and culture of a community to be preserved and managed communally. This can be observed in Buddhist traditions dating back hundreds of years.[1] However, it is only since twenty years ago that some Buddhist temples have begun collecting and arranging property for public consumption, and referring to themselves as museums (*phiphitthaphan*) of some kind.

There are several specific terms for such museums. "Indigenous museum" (*phiphitthaphan phuen ban*) is commonly used among villagers, while "local museum" (*phiphitthaphan thong thin*) is more common among academics and museum practitioners.[2] In this paper, however, I shall refer to them as "community museums" (*phiphitthaphan chumchon*), because the majority of them were founded and are operated by a local community, and represent the histories and culture of that community. Here, community (*chumchon*) usually signifies the village (*mu ban*), but can sometimes mean a group of closely related villages, or else an administrative unit (*tambon*).

In this chapter it is argued that the development of community museums represents a response to social, economic, and cultural changes in rural

Thai society. There appear to be four related factors that have contributed to the development of these community museums. The first of these is the indigenous traditions, customs, and values that underlie the process of collection, conservation, and exhibition that takes place within the newly established community museums. Second, there is the state-led cultural policy and development discourse that spread extensively throughout rural Thailand during the late 1990s, which facilitated the establishment of the community museums. Third, we find that the development of community museums reflects structural changes in the rural economy that have led to the increasingly unequal distribution of wealth, a decline in solidarity and integration, the corrosion of self-identity, and the fading of local tradition and values in a community, generating common grievances among some villagers, especially those past their mid-thirties. Finally, the agency of Buddhist monks and their alignments with other parties were crucial for the rise of the museum movement.

I have used ethnographic data from more than fifty community museums, mainly in northern Thailand, in order to analyze the dynamics of the development of these rural community museums.[3] Through these analyses I intend to show that the social experiences that accompany the building and developing of community museums give rise to the creation of certain values or ethics, so we would be justified in considering this process a form of community movement. The community museums reflect and substantiate people's images of "community," thereby forming what might be seen as a cultural basis for collective political engagement. The museum phenomenon and related practices are interconnected with those practices that address people's sense of temporality, historical consciousness, and anxieties about the future (see Kreps 1998, 4).

## The Indigenous Model of Museums in Thailand

Thai Buddhist temples have long served as places where precious cultural properties and archaeological finds have been brought together and co-owned by the community. They have thereby taken on a role which could be construed as analogous to that of a museum, although the objects there were not originally accumulated for the purpose of being exhibited.

Most of the objects making up the temples' collections—such as Buddhist statues, ritual tools, lacquer ware, ceramic ware, and musical instruments—have been donated by villagers on various occasions, although others are monks' personal effects.

There are two obvious reasons why Buddhist temples store these kinds of valuable objects. In Theravada Buddhist society, making an offering to a temple or a monk is considered an important means of creating merit (*tham bun*). This is believed to bring the donor good luck in the future or in the next life. There is another reason besides merit-making for villagers to donate their own valuables to temples. In Thailand, there is the belief that supernatural forces may inhabit antiques or rare objects. Villagers believe that old objects, such as articles of unknown origin left by deceased family members, or things picked up in the rice field by chance, have the potential to contain strong supernatural forces. They may bring good or bad luck to the owner. Referring to objects having magical power as "hot things" (*khong ron*), the caretaker of a community museum said to me, "People feel nervous when they own a hot thing. For example, we don't want to keep an old weapon at home. It might have been used to kill a person. . . . If we are born as farmers, that kind of thing doesn't suit us. Therefore, we deposit it in a good temple." Buddhist temples are believed to be sacred places, protected from dangerous supernatural powers, and monks allegedly know how to handle magical objects.

Most community museums collect new objects at the time of their establishment. A large part of the community museums' core collections is made up of objects donated by villagers when the museum was established. Villagers select particular objects for donation based upon consideration of their historical value within the community rather than of their origin, artistic value, or rarity. The favored objects for donation are those that once symbolized their owner's standing or status in the village community. I found it odd to see old typewriters, televisions, sewing machines, and telephones displayed in the community museums. Having been curious objects of foreign origin some decades ago, they seemed to me not yet to be sufficiently "antique" to be exhibited in a museum. Nevertheless, these objects are common within the community museum repertoire. I speculate that this is partly because they are considered to be symbols of a certain past in the drastically changing community life, and partly because their donors are trying to illustrate their family's mark on the village history by exhibiting valuables suggestive of the owner's prestige.

Community museums rarely change their method of exhibiting objects, even after moving their collections from the temple storage into their newly built or renovated exhibition rooms. They simply clean up the room and put the artifacts in order so that visitors can survey the exhibition. It is not common within community museums for artifacts to be classified according to their function or date, or for sections to be arranged by theme. There is no sorting of the artifacts either, so it often happens that several of the same sorts of items—even those of considerable size—are shown in one exhibition. The museums simply exhibit whatever has been donated by the villagers.

Interestingly, the only principle for organizing the exhibition space is the traditional Thai symbolic order. In Thailand, the traditional notion of space is closely linked with the social order and worldview. Community museums, especially those built within a temple, organize exhibition artifacts according to this spatial order. Buddhist artifacts, recognized as having high symbolic value, tend to occupy the higher positions, and daily utensils, seen as having low symbolic value, tend to be placed lower down. The most sacred Buddhist statues are often exhibited at the highest locations, while women's sarongs are often laid out, covered with dust, on the lowest tables, even though they are of apparent value as artistic handicrafts. Some community museums are situated beneath the floors of the monks' cells. In such museums, only Buddhist statues are exhibited separately, above the floor or in the main building.

The relation between museum artifact and donor is comparable to the one between object and donor within the Buddhist tradition. A donated object is preserved in the museum as common property of the community, yet even after the donation, the donor continues to behave as if he or she has some personal connection to the object. Customarily, the name of the donor and the date of the donation are written on the bottom of the object or a tag attached to it. Although it is quite difficult to speculate as to how much the donor would maintain a sense of ownership over that object, there are two occurrences—which I heard of at several community museums—suggesting that personal relations between the object and the donor are maintained to a considerable degree. First, as has been mentioned previously, community museums tend to exhibit several artifacts of the same type. This is inconvenient, given the small exhibition space. However, caretakers say that they cannot do away with any of these duplicates; each artifact in the museum represents the honor of its donor, so they cannot choose one particular artifact from among many of the same type. Second, caretakers say that a donor can reclaim an object from the museum even several years after its donation if it is felt that the object is not being treated properly or that it is in danger of being stolen. If an object is treated improperly or stolen, it is believed that the donor might have bad luck through the supernatural force of the object. I heard from several caretakers similar stories of an object's original owner, now deceased, appearing in a dream to a family member, asking him or her to retrieve the object from the museum because it was not being treated properly there. Surely, then, it is believed that the individual donor or family keeps a certain inalienable right to the object donated. In this way, community museums have the role not only of preserving objects physically but also of maintaining harmonious relationships between villagers and supernatural beings, just like temples in the Thai Buddhist tradition.

## Local Culture and Development

Since the mid-nineteenth century, the Thai ruling elite have put much energy into spreading the discourse concerning the common cultural feature of "Thainess" (*khwam pen thai*) or Thai identity (*ekkalak thai*) in the country of Thailand (Thongchai 1994; Reynolds 2002a). During the period when neighboring countries had become colonized, they believed that they could prove the legitimacy of Thailand as an independent state by showing its unique distinguished culture. Moreover, after Thailand became a nation-state in the early 1930s, the ideology of Thai culture as the national culture was used to mask cultural and ethnic heterogeneity within the county. This ideology took the Thai culture born out of the Bangkok elite—supposedly unchanged by the process of modernization— as its essence, while at the same time eschewing regional cultures, such as northern, northeastern, or southern Thai, and minority cultures such as those of Muslims or hill tribes, by labeling them obstacles to progress

(Keyes 1989; Thongchai 1995). National Museums have been utilized as a powerful apparatus for spreading this ideology.

Nevertheless, in the mid-1970s, regional cultures began to be found worthy of positive recognition. The revolution of 1973 aroused political consciousness throughout Thailand and created a surge of interest in local history and identity (Thongchai 1995, 110). With the end of the Cold War in the 1980s, Thailand achieved political stability and economic development, and cultural diversity became tolerable. The central government encouraged the development of local history, in part as a bid to promote tourism. However, there was a common recognition that this kind of local history should not disrupt national integration. Autonomous local identities were celebrated predominantly in art, literature, and local traditions, and they were selected depending upon whether they contributed to the story of national history or culture (Thongchai 1995, 113). Thus, local cultures were depicted only as variations on the national culture.

There was another discourse about Thainess that arose from the influence of the 1973 revolution, a school of thought among intellectuals about what they called "community culture" (*watthanatham chumchon*). According to leaders of this school, Thainess is deeply rooted in the ways of living and wisdom of rural people, especially peasants, and its existence is founded upon the village community (Chatthip 1991; Thongchai 1994; Reynolds 2002b; Delcore 2003). They insisted that cultural features of Thai village society, such as generosity, kindness, and mutual aid, should be regarded as positive Thai values rather than signs of backwardness, and that Thai society was in danger because the village community which maintained this Thai culture was on the verge of collapse owing to the neoliberal government policies and Westernization. Within their discourse, community culture was defined as a foundation for sustainable development strategies that were both modern and uniquely Thai. This simplified, idealized image of community provided Thai NGOs in villages with the necessary conceptual framework with which to protest against the state-led bureaucratic, capitalistic development discourse and to support the sustainable and grassroots development discourse.

In the late 1990s, state agencies started to make use of the vocabulary of cultural diversity, local wisdom, and community-based development (Connors 2005a; Sirijit 2013). The 1997 constitution defined for the first time the provision of "the rights of community," whereby people's participation in the political process was encouraged. The Eighth National Development Plan (1997–2001) specified the building of strong communities as one of its tasks. During the financial crisis of 1997, ideas like "community," "subsistence economy," and "local wisdom" became political buzzwords. In the 2000s, the Community Organization Council Act and the Community Forest Act were enacted, both of which aimed to support communities in securing self-management. Another example of the state commitment to community development was the state-led promotion of community business (*setthakit chumchon*), such as One Tambon One Product (OTOP). Abandoning the idea that the central government would bring progress to communities through bureaucracy, these policies called for the reorientation of development toward local initiatives, although they should be recognized as an instance of social control as well as a process of community empowerment.[4]

As these state-led community-development programs were implemented, people in rural villages became more interested in their own local culture. This was not because they shared the intellectuals' and NGO activists' sense of crisis about Thai identity, but rather because they found local traditions and cultures worthy of recognition as resources for tourism or community development. During the economic boom of the mid-1980s in Thailand, domestic tourism started to be given the status of a major leisure activity among the urban middle classes, and the Tourism Authority of Thailand was increasingly devoted to the promotion of domestic tourism by supporting tourist events and advertisements (Peleggi 2002, 64). In the 1990s, there began to be a growing interest in tourism among people in rural villages also, thanks to the increase in cash income, the improved transportation infrastructure, and changes in the pattern of consumption. In 1994, various policies were implemented by the state in the Thai Culture Promotion campaign with the slogan "Conserve Thai Culture" (*Anurak watthanatham Thai*), which boosted the consciousness of cultural heritage in rural villages. This was the first time when politically aware rural villagers, chiefly led by Buddhist monks, realized that their everyday objects and customs might be viewed as cultural property worthy of preservation. Their festivals, dances, and costumes soon came to be described as indigenous (*phuen ban* or *phuen mueang*) and often used with words such as "heritage" (*moradok*) and "conserve" (*anurak*). The term *boran* also entered common usage to mean "traditional," in addition to its original meanings of "old-fashioned" or "ancient." Tourist guidebooks for each province and illustrated magazines targeted at working-class tourists were published from the late 1990s onwards. They played a prominent role in promoting domestic tourism by introducing not only national-level historical heritage but also regional- and local-level present-day culture, customs, and arts and crafts. The Thai national tradition was no longer understood as something owned exclusively by the urban elite, but as something that could also be found in popular or rural everyday life.

The promotion of community culture as a kind of development ideology facilitated the development of community museums throughout Thailand. The abbot of a temple told me about his reasons for building a community museum:

> It first occurred to me when I attended a seminar organized by the *tambon.* Then, I became interested in community museums. It costs less than five hundred thousand baht to build a community museum in total. But once it is established, tourists will come, and students will come. . . . Villagers can sell things. They will be well provided for.

The institution of the museum attracted villagers' initial attention not as an apparatus to salvage the vanishing community culture but as a tool to promote economic development. In fact, many of those involved said that since establishing the community museum, more people have visited their temple and joined their rituals and festivals. However, most of the visitors were either villagers or their kin or friends who lived in Bangkok or other cities. In this sense, it cannot be said that community museums contributed to attracting tourists or developing the local tourism industry.

However, there are a few community museums that have succeeded in significantly developing local economies by linking the image of the local tradition and culture symbolically with local products. For example, a Tai Lue village started a revival movement of traditional handicrafts at the same time that a community museum was established. The Tai Lue were widely known for their beautiful folk costumes and refined weaving techniques. They almost lost their own tradition when modernization meant the village's way of life became similar to that of the majority of the northern Thai villages. The Tai Lue language was changing rapidly as younger speakers used more northern or standard Thai in schools or workplaces. By collecting what few traditional textiles were within the community, they established a museum where they exhibited their traditional tools, techniques, and knowledge. Moreover, a weaving class for the women's society was organized in the temple, where local women learned the traditional skills from a few elderly women. Those local women now demonstrate the traditional weaving techniques to museum visitors and sell their products in the museum shop. Although they are quite limited in number, successful museums such as this one garner a lot of attention from those interested in museums. This contributes to generating exaggerated images and expectations of successful community museums.

It is worth noting that the cultures and identities represented by community museums are defined with reference to their place in the wider Thai national culture. Community museums tend to emphasize this fact. For example, the boundaries of the communities represented by community museums are often the same as those of the administrative unit as defined by the national government, and there is a strong tendency for diversity or disparity among community members to be ignored. Community museums categorize different periods of history according to the monarchy at the time (e.g., "Rama IV era") and use the same system for categorizing art history as that which is commonly prescribed by the National Museums. In a manner clearly designed to attract the visitors' attention, most community museums proudly display at their entrances items such as photographs depicting members of the royal family visiting local temples, royal gifts, medals or certificates awarded by the government, national newspaper articles about local events, and photographs of local women who have won national beauty contests. Moreover, the community museums run by ethnic minorities who have migrated from foreign countries provide an illustration of how these minorities have integrated into the national culture. While referring to their historical links with their country and region of origin, they tend to emphasize how they have developed their own unique culture in Thailand. For example, the community museum in a Phuan village depicts the origin of their culture in Laos, while also emphasizing the differences between their current language, culture, and way of life in Thailand from their peers' in Laos.

These people call themselves Thai Phuan, a national identity quite distinct from Lao Phuan. Moreover, although Thai Phuan villages occasionally exchange information with one another when exhibiting their difference from the mainstream Thai culture, they tend to recognize their village as a part of a *tambon* (subdistrict) or *amphoe* (district) rather than a part of the ethnic group. This is because they insist that their cultures are variations on the diversified Thai national culture. In other words, community museums help to situate local communities in the Thai national culture. While people try to reconstruct local differences within the exhibits and find ways of cementing the sense of community, these variations are becoming standardized as this movement spreads over the country. The activities associated with elucidating cultural differences led toward a movement that generates feelings of national identity.

## Growing Uncertainties in Village Life

In the 1990s and 2000s, many northern Thai villages experienced significant economic and structural changes. Although these changes generally improved the standard of living, they affected people in the villages differently, leading to anxieties and grievances among some villagers. These villagers bemoaned the increasingly unequal distribution of wealth, the decline of solidarity and integration, the corrosion of self-identity, and the fading of local tradition and values in the community. In this section I argue that these anxieties and grievances constitute a background against which it was possible for community museums to develop.

Until quite recently, it was *ngan* activities that were responsible for forging social relations, values, and group identity in rural Thai villages. *Ngan* in northern and standard Thai means "work," such as rice cultivation, wage labor, or housework, as well as communal work and certain kinds of rites (Hirai 1998). Let us take an example of Lai Hin Village in Lampang.[5] Villagers there have traditionally cultivated rice and sugar cane for their subsistence. The village was regarded as a conglomerate of independent houses, and each villager had to become a legitimate member of the village through *ngan* activities. Through these activities, villagers learned about particular aspects of the culture, attached various symbolic meanings to the village facilities and natural surroundings, and became moral members of the village (see Hirai 1998). Participation in *ngan* was the process whereby the moral members of the village, the physical space, and the community as a whole were reproduced.

Significant structural changes occurred when many young villagers started working outside Lai Hin Village. In the 1980s, men in the village started working in foreign countries—first Saudi Arabia, Libya, and Lebanon, and then Singapore, Taiwan, and South Korea. The village became affluent through the remittances from these migrant workers. Many of the workers' families built new houses, bought cars, and started businesses, although the majority of villagers still maintained their traditional lifestyle to a certain extent. From the 2000s, villagers in their twenties and early thirties began working in industrial parks established within commuting distance of the village. This resulted in two simultaneous changes that disrupted the traditional community life. The first of these was the decline in agriculture. As households got financial support from family members who worked in factories or other jobs in cities, they tended to stop or reduce their involvement in rice cultivation. This economic trend weakened the traditional sources of social cohesion and integration, because cooperation in rice cultivation had constituted a means of integrating socially and forming patterns of association in community life. Second, the disruption of community life was facilitated by the increased freedom to develop social ties outside the community. For many young villagers, the village where they lived was now physically separated from their place of work, where they spent most of their day. Away from parents, kin, and neighbors, they enjoyed more freedom in many aspects of their lives and reorganized their social activities. One result of this was the decrease in the number and scale of rites in the village, which represents the waning of the local community as a place where relationships of trust and mutual support originated. While villagers became better off and their lives more convenient, their way of life became more individualistic and they had less opportunity to cooperate with one another. While young villagers recognized these changes as empowerment or development, those over forty tended to feel a sense of crisis in cultural identity caused by the intrusion of consumer goods and urban culture, and also to feel that their sense of security was threatened.

Community museums provide a place where these villagers can savor a sense of nostalgia for their old communities. It is the elderly that visit the community museums most frequently. Most of the objects displayed there are familiar to them from their childhood or youth. When kin or friends come to visit them from far away, the elderly take them to the museum and, while pointing at objects, tell tales about the community life in the past and their old days, with a sense of yearning. For example, they might tell of how their farming was supported by mutual aid, or else the numbers of people that gathered for village festivals in those days, and what kind of events took place. The exhibited objects mainly represent the communal activities of *ngan* in the village, which were farming and various rites, as well as also mutual aid, and the generosity and solidarity arising from them. "Tools that were once instrumental extensions of the body now extend their makers (users) imaginatively into the past and socially into the world" (Kirshernblatt-Gimblett 1989, 335). As Connerton (2009, 50) argues, "the identity of place is always embedded in the histories which people tell of them, and, most fundamentally, in the way in which these histories were originally constituted in processes of labour." Bringing back the memories and emotions shared by villagers, the objects used in *ngan* allow people to remember that their community was founded on everyday *ngan* practices, thereby stimulating them to recollect a wider spectrum of experiences and feelings. Especially in those who feel left behind by the rapid modernization and who have lost the prestige they enjoyed in their traditional community, this evokes nostalgia for the relationships, values, and beliefs that accompanied the traditional rural way of life. Since this evocative power derives from the associations that have accumulated with these objects over time, they would be unlikely to have such an effect on outsiders.

Museum activities can be considered a movement in which people seek to revive a lost communal ethos. For village elders, the community museum is an object of passionate attachment because it symbolizes the possibility of a moral life characterized by mutual aid, generosity, and solidarity. This idealized image of a simple Thai rural life is juxtaposed with the nature of their actual life in the recent past. In fact, creating an ideal image of the community provides an ideological backdrop against which to challenge the recent changes in the community. Although they were established as a tool for the development of tourism, the success of community museums depends partly upon how much they appeal to the villagers who feel distressed by the rapid transformations in the community and are critical toward the modernization of the community life.

## The Agency and Alignments of Monks

Now we shall consider an agency that assembles these diverse practices and discourses and makes connections between them. The majority of community museum administrators and caretakers I met were monks and educated men (former monks, retired teachers, local council members) who were eager to support museum activities and cooperate with local governments, academics, and donors from outside the village to engage in local projects designed to develop community museums.

Let us take the case of Lai Hin Village again. In about 1960, a community museum was established in Lai Hin temple by rearranging the antiques and religious objects that were stored in the temple quarters (*kuti*). According to a leaflet, the museum was established by villagers to "collect and preserve the traditional local objects that illustrate the long-lasting identity and culture of the community." However, according to the villagers, the museum was little more than the temple's storage facility. In 1989, the present building was constructed, paid for by donations of villagers and those who respected the abbot of the temple. Nevertheless, according to Mr. S, the present caretaker of the museum, it remained as it had been for more than ten years.

It was after Mr. S became caretaker of the museum that things began changing. In 1999, elected as a member of the *tambon* council, he was also charged with the management of the museum. When he first entered the museum in 1999, he found it "full of mice and insects." In 2004, he raised funds by organizing a big merit-making ritual (*pha pa*), and renewed the exhibition. Also, Mr. S learned how to create a collection database at a seminar organized by the Chiang Mai National Museum. In 2007, jointly with the Princess Maha Chakri Sirindhorn Anthropology Centre (SAC),[6] the museum started the Local Museums Research and Development Project. Since then, Mr. S has attended various seminars, exchanged information with monks and other museum caretakers, and conducted workshops at the museum in which the museum exhibited old photographs of the community with comments from elderly villagers. In 2009, obtaining financial support from the *tambon* council, and technical assistance from SAC, Mr. S opened a new room displaying scenes from community life, such as rice cultivation, housework, rituals, and the local market. Mr. S said:

> In the past, [the museum] used to be a storeroom. . . . SAC came and helped us to improve the exhibition. It took five years for villagers to become able to manage [the museum]. At first, villagers didn't understand its importance. Little by little, elders began to tell their experiences to children [at the museum]. It also happened that some villagers talked about their working experiences in foreign countries at the museum. Then, [villagers] began to think that our village has its own precious history. The museum is not just a storehouse, but a place to collect emotional stories.

Mr. S is just an ordinary villager, with a fascination for the village history and culture. Working principally as a *tambon* council (*ongkan borihan suan tambon*) member, he is not stationed at the museum. At the museum there are two cleaners and one temporary museum guide, but in practice it is Mr. S that manages the museum almost singlehandedly, with support from the temple monks.

As the museum is part of the community temple, the community has maintained legal rights as well as moral claims to it. Mr. S must consult the community when he makes decisions about workshops or collection management. When he wants to organize a workshop, he first seeks the permission of the village temple committee. When he plans to renew the exhibition or repair the building, he must get the approval of a village meeting. The foundation of these decision-making procedures is the villagers' recognition that the museum is run as a part of the temple that is shared by the community. In the management of the community museum, consensus within the whole village is always given priority in regard to making decisions about the museum's activities, its role as a public establishment, and the overall administration of the museum. Forging links with the villagers is an essential component for community museums in general, but this process can be quite a fragile one, as it is in this particular case. The community is internally divided by age, gender, status, education, and other personal experiences, and its members typically have many different perspectives on heritage, development, culture, and the museum. Moreover, they have different expectations from the museum, tourism, and related local industries. Mr. S is always looking for ways to ensure his proposals are compatible with the villagers' diverse demands.

The agency of monks and temples plays a crucial role in the development of community museums. Buddhist temples used to be the epicenter of art and education—the prototype of the museum or archive center—in Thai communities. Since the 1980s, the relation between religion and society has changed significantly, and temples have a weakened influence on communities when it comes to culture and morality. In Thai rural society that was becoming rapidly more secular, those involved with the temples felt that they were on the verge of losing their role as intellectual leaders or cultural experts and wished to legitimize or restore their authority and identity by reaffirming the significance of Buddhist traditions and morality. Thus, community museums attracted the attention of the monks and temples as an apparatus to recover the roles and prestige that they had enjoyed before. When I asked one monk the reason that he established a museum, he replied, "Nobody was interested in this temple. So, I established the museum." The essential elements of the ways of life, customs, and aesthetics in traditional communities originated from Buddhism. Exhibiting these traditional ways of life, customs, and aesthetics within a museum context would therefore urge villagers to rediscover the importance of Buddhism and allow monks to reestablish privileges to which they believe they are entitled. Monks are likely to win cooperation in the development of community museums from the elderly. This is especially true of older former monks, because they share with the monks the sense of regret that their prestige as a source of knowledge has been undermined as a result of the spread of the modern education system and the secularization of village life. How much monks and their collaborators take an interest in community museums, how profitable they regard community museums as being, and how much they help to develop community museums reflect the material or symbolic gains they can justifiably expect to receive by participating in community museum activities. While the community is rapidly changing, representing the image of the community in the past can be considered an attempt to rebuild a community in which their privileged positions are secured and to reclaim religious authority.

Monks' strategic alignment with interested, supportive external parties has contributed to the development of community museums. One kind of external party in this case has been local governments. They have offered resources to improve exhibitions, although the stipulated uses for these resources were quite limited and often quite different from local demands because local governments usually have little knowledge about museums and museum practices. Also, some local governments invited monks and museum practitioners to seminars they had organized as a part of their program to enhance rural development. Another external party was academics and cultural experts who believed that local museums were important for the conservation of cultural heritage in the Thai nation. Provincial National Museums and the Department of Fine Arts of the Ministry of Culture devised policies that sought to conserve national treasures. They conducted research on major community museums in order to record objects of cultural heritage. This implied their recognition of the legitimacy of these objects as cultural property. Provincial National Museums also organized multiday training seminars concerning museum practices, although they tended to draw upon theories about museum activities and cultural property that were strongly influenced by Western museology, emphasizing the necessity of expert assistance to conserve the collection and denying indigenous museum practices.

Among the academics and cultural experts who supported community museums, the SAC was especially important. Recognizing the important role of community museums in the protection of cultural heritage, the SAC conducted the Local Museums Research and Development Project between 2003 and 2008. In this project the SAC created a digital database of community museums in Thailand and promoted the formation of a museum network through publications and seminars. One of their findings from this project was that Thai community museums have developed within the traditions of Thai popular Buddhism (Paritta 2006). It is since the SAC began a comprehensive project to survey, support, and form a network of community museums in Thailand that an understanding of the museums has been developed among practitioners, monks, and the public. Although its scope and resources were quite limited, I would assert that the SAC made three important contributions to the development of community museums: building a network among interested parties, providing national publicity for community museums, and raising the awareness of monks and museum practitioners.

Finally, the development of community museums would have been much more difficult, and perhaps even unlikely, without the network of linkages among Buddhist monks and temples in Thailand. Monks frequently exchange information through meetings, seminars, casual visits, and, increasingly, mobile phones and the Internet in order to find ways of contributing to their local communities. Such networks serve as a conduit for the distribution of material and technical and intellectual resources, and many monks said that it was through such a system that they first came up with the idea of establishing a community museum. Monks have helped each other learn how to run museums, mutually corroborated one another's knowledge and self-identity, and motivated one another to carry out various activities based around the museum. This web of connections between monks has facilitated the spread of ideas, differing viewpoints, and tactics in the development of community museums.

## The Community Museum Movement

Since the late 1980s there has been an explosion in the number of community museums in rural Thai temples. These community museums emerged as part of a changing Thai community, reflecting its new needs. Villagers use these community museums differently according to their class, gender, age, urban experience, and individual dispositions, producing different discourses and conceptualizations surrounding the community. These ideas have developed through interaction with people who view the history and culture of the community from diverse standpoints, such as museum practitioners, local governmental officers, NGO workers, and the mass media. The community museum has thereby become a location in which competing understandings of community, tradition, and social change are produced, reproduced, and transformed. Founded on indigenous Buddhist traditions, Thai community museums have grown out of an entanglement of different practices. Various individuals in different positions have tried to utilize them creatively, with different aims and views about the meaning of the museums, all against a backdrop of changing relationships in Thai rural society and the state-led development discourse.

The community museum forms a medium for thinking about and mobilizing the community and for stimulating the vitality of its culture. It provides resources to think of shared experiences, relationships, and histories, which allow some villagers to feel longing for a past sense of attachment and place or even to feel a sense of security that they now rarely feel when the kind of lifestyle they are accustomed to is rapidly disappearing. With the community museum, people are not just affirming their existing community but rather seeking an alternative community in the past while recognizing that the kind of cultural model they long for is generated by a social context that has already expired.

The family of activities pertaining to the development of community museums can be considered a form of community movement. They are collective enterprises designed to defend or revive existing structures and systems of authority, and to resist indirectly sociocultural changes. Forming loosely connected networks and alliances, those involved with the museums engage as a whole in a series of activities that exert influence on individuals or society with some degree of continuity. The phenomenon of the community museum is not just a reflection of existing ideas and emotions among villagers, or the influence of the state or capitalist ideology, but a dynamic agent that produces, reproduces, or transforms people's views through interaction with other external agents, ideas, and materials.

NOTES

I would like to thank the numerous people in Thailand who provided me with their help during my fieldwork. Paritta Chalermpow Koanantakool, the former director of the Princess Maha Chakri Sirindhorn Anthropology Centre, gave me much help and advice. I also had many thought-provoking and enjoyable discussions with Nitaya Kanogmongkol, the Director of Chiang Mai National Museum. Some of the material was collected with the help of Kanokwan Jayadat and Jutamas Limrattanapan.

1. Of the 1,052 museums that the Princess Maha Chakri Sirindhorn Anthropology Centre (SAC) found in their 2008 research, 314 were operated by

temples (SAC, n.d.). Many of the other museums had close relationships with temples. Some of them were established within a temple compound, while others originated from collections of objects in a temple.

2. Some museums called themselves "culture centers" (*sun watthanatham*), "local culture centers" (*sun watthanatham thong thin*), or "indigenous culture centers" (*sun watthanatham phuen ban*). This may be because they placed more emphasis on the community activities facilitated by the museum than on its display of objects, or because they put more of their energies into the revival of culture than into the conservation of cultural heritage.

3. Fieldwork for this study was conducted for eight months in total between 2008 and 2014, with financial support from JSPS KAKENHI (grant numbers 20520721 and 23401050).

4. As Connors (2005a, 264; 2005b, 534) argued, there seem to be two major factors that influenced this trend. On the one hand, there were political struggles over democracy and political reform during the 1990s that resulted in a fusion of liberal democratic politics with local and communitarian ethics. On the other hand, the need to find alternative policies after the financial crisis of 1997 accelerated the entrenchment of this trend, especially under the influence of the king's speech on sufficiency economy and policy formation backed by international agencies like the World Bank.

5. Lai Hin Village is about seven kilometers from the center of Ko Kha District in Lampang Province. It is a relatively large village, consisting of four hundred households, or a population of about 1,500.

6. The Princess Maha Chakri Sirindhorn Anthropology Centre is a Bangkok-based independent organization committed to supporting the development of anthropological research, the accumulation of anthropological materials, and the promotion of public education.

REFERENCES

Chatthip Nartsupha. 1991. "The Community Culture School of Thought." In *Thai Constructions of Knowledge*, edited by Manat Chitakasem and Andrew Turton, 118–41. London: School of Oriental and African Studies.

Connerton, Paul. 2009. *How Modernity Forgets*. Cambridge: Cambridge University Press.

Connors, Michael K. 2005a. "Democracy and the Mainstreaming of Localism in Thailand." In *Southeast Asian Responses to Globalization: Restructuring Governance and Deepening Democracy*, edited by Francis Loh Kok Wah and Joakim Ojendal, 259–86. Singapore: NIAS Press.

Connors, Michael K. 2005b. "Ministering Culture: Hegemony and the Politics of Culture and Identity in Thailand." *Critical Asian Studies* 37(4): 523–51.

Delcore, Henry D. 2003. "Nongovernmental Organizations and the Work of Memory in Northern Thailand." *American Ethnologist* 30(1): 61–84.

Hirai, Kyonosuke 1998. "Women, Family and Factory Work in Northern Thailand: An Anthropological Study of a Japanese Factory and Its Workers' Villages." PhD thesis, University of London.

Keyes, Charles F. 1989. *Thailand: Buddhist Kingdom as Modern Nation-State.* Bangkok: Duang Kamol.

Kirshernblatt-Gimblett, Barbara. 1989. "Objects of Memory: Material Culture as Life Review." In *Folk Groups and Folklore Genres: A Reader,* edited by E. Oring, 329–38. Logan, Utah: Utah State University Press.

Kreps, Christina. 1998. "Introduction: Indigenous Curation." *Museum Anthropology* 22(1): 3–4.

Paritta C. Koanantakool. 2006. "Contextualizing Objects in Monastery Museums in Thailand." In *Buddhist Legacies in Mainland Southeast Asia: Mentalities, Interpretations and Practices,* edited by Francois Lagirarde and Parrita C. Koanantakool, 149–65. Bangkok: Princess Maha Chakri Sirindhorn Anthropology Centre.

Peleggi, Maurizio. 2002. *The Politics of Ruins and the Business of Nostalgia.* Bangkok: White Lotus Press.

Reynolds, Craig J. 2002a. "Introduction: National Identity and Its Defenders." In *National Identity and its Defenders: Thailand Today,* edited by Craig J. Reynolds, 1–32. Chiang Mai: Silkworm Books.

———. 2002b. "Thai Identity in the Age of Globalization." In *National Identity and its Defenders: Thailand Today,* edited by Craig J. Reynolds, 308–38. Chiang Mai: Silkworm Books.

SAC (Princess Maha Chakri Sirindhorn Anthropology Centre). n.d. *Local Museums: Research and Development Project.* Bangkok: Princess Maha Chakri Sirindhorn Anthropology Centre.

Sirijit Sunanta. 2013. "Negotiating with the Center: Diversity and Local Cultures in Thailand." In *Rights to Culture: Heritage, Language, and Community in Thailand,* edited by Coeli Barry, 163–88. Chiang Mai: Silkworm Books.

Thongchai Winichakul. 1994. *Siam Mapped: A History of the Geo-Body of a Nation.* Honolulu: University of Hawai'i Press.

———. 1995. "The Changing Landscape of the Past: New Histories in Thailand Since 1973." *Journal of Southeast Asian Studies* 26(1): 99–120.

# PART III

# EXPERIENCE AND ALLIANCE

# IDENTITY POLITICS AND RELIGIOUS EXPERIENCE
## Female Movements in Theravada Buddhism in Contemporary Thailand

APINYA FEUNGFUSAKUL

## Introduction

At present, the attempt to open up religious space for women in Theravada culture in Thailand can be realized through various forms, namely female lay practitioners or the ordained roles of *mae chi* (lay nuns in white robe observing eight precepts) and *bhikkhuni* (fully ordained nuns in yellow robe observing 311 precepts). Each identity is related to different codes of conduct, different levels of social status and recognition, and different spatial strategies. The revival of *bhikkhuni* ordination a decade ago spurred intense debate about the legitimacy of the *bhikkhuni* ordination ritual and led to increased public attention and debates about the different ordained status of women.

Viewed from a postmodernist perspective, women's efforts in spiritual fields also share the ironic crisis of identity politics, namely the pitfall of identity fixation and essentialization as well as the tendency to marginalize other identities. Identity always requires difference in order to exist and conveys marginality onto otherness in order to secure its own identity borderline. Moreover, identity politics in the spiritual realm faces further complication since the final goal of spiritual practice, especially in Buddhism, is the total eradication of the sense of self. But as a social movement, it is necessary to make society recognize the meaningfulness of "our struggle" and "our goal." Would it then lead to the contradiction between the strategic necessity to create the movement's identity (be it a process or a performance) and the spiritual goal to get rid of it? This chapter aims to lay out how women with different religious identities perceive and address this problem and to compare their strategies of identity politics. The community to which they belong is an important part of their spatial strategies. We will see how the environment of the religious community helps shape their sense of self, and how their sense of religious self is manifested in and guides the direction of their constructed community.

Another important point is the relationship between identity and religious experience. This chapter focuses on three prominent women with different social backgrounds and religious roles—one *bhikkhuni*, one *mae chi*, and one lay practitioner. Comparison of their life stories will help us to understand how their sense of religious self is expressed in and related to gender ideologies in Thai society.

## Ven. Dhammananda

Chatsumarn Kabilasingha was born in 1944 into a middle-class family in Bangkok. Her father came from a well-to-do family and engaged in a political career as a parliament member of the southern province of Trang. An ancestor of her father used to be a royal page of King Rama VI. Her exceptionally strong mother, Mrs. Voramai, was a teacher and writer and raised Chatsumarn alone in Bangkok. Mrs. Voramai's avant-garde characteristics left a deep imprint on her daughter. Mrs. Voramai's religious interests led her to become ordained, first as an anti-mainstream *mae chi* wearing a light yellow robe and later as a Chinese *bhikkhuni*. In order to maintain her independence, Mrs. Voramai had a monastery built at her house and actively engaged in various social welfare activities as well as pursuing her esoteric meditation practice.

Under her mother's guidance, Chatsumarn studied for a bachelor's degree in philosophy from Visva-Bharati, the university founded by famous Indian philosopher Rabindranath Tagore, then got a master's and PhD in religious studies from McMaster University in Canada. While teaching at Thammasat University in Bangkok, she wrote and translated many books and articles about Buddhism for both Thai and English journals. She helped establish and became the head of Sakyadhita, an international association for Buddhist women, from 1991 to 1995. At the age of twenty-eight, under her mother's management, she got married to a soldier and went on to have three sons. After years of career success and householder life, she decided to become ordained as a Theravada *bhikkhuni* and went to ordain first as *samaneri*, or female novice, in Sri Lanka in 2001. She received the higher ordination as *bhikkhuni* in 2003.

At her monastery, at the time of my interview in April 2013, there were six *bhikkhuni*s and three *samaneri*s. One important activity there is the annual *samaneri* ordination, which is a crucial occasion not only to recruit temporarily new members, but also to train and teach young girls about the significance and social role of ordained females. The teacher-disciple relationship is quite strong and close. A *bhikkhuni* who has been ordained for eight years and is in charge of public relations described the socialization process. She said Luang Mae (Respectable Mother) is full of compassion but is very strict and sometimes quick to scold her students. She teaches them by making them do hard work. Monastery dwellers must do every kind of hard manual labor traditionally known as men's jobs, such as digging up soil or dredging the pond. One of the *samaneri*s wrote, "Many times, she did not teach us through words but through her deeds. . . . She made us realize that all of us are part of the problems we create. We have to realize this and begin to solve the problem by scrutinizing inside ourselves and changing ourselves from within" (Phimpan 2011, 187–88).

At present, apart from writing regularly, she engages in various types of welfare activities since she made a vow to follow the path of *bodhisatta* (one destined to buddhahood).

## Mae Chi Kaew Sianglam

Mae Chi Kaew is well known and revered as a female saint of the Northeast. She was born in 1901 into the Phu Thai minority ethnic group in Mukdahan province. Her ancestors were of the elite class in the village, and her father had the title of local magistrate. She lost her mother in childhood and never attended school; therefore she could not write or speak the central Thai dialect, though the family's economic status was quite secure. Since childhood, she had the inborn faculty of seeing *nimitta* (meditative visions) of events from her past lives.

At the age of seventeen, Achan Mun, known as the greatest master of the northeastern forest monk tradition, arrived in her village with a group of disciples. He showed great compassion toward her and prophesized that she would achieve spiritual greatness in the future. Then, her father arranged a marriage for her, and she did not have any children. At the age of thirty-seven, she decided to become a *mae chi*. Her husband's discontentment displayed the traditional bondage that confines women to the domestic sphere. Through negotiation, she was allowed to be ordained but had to disrobe after three months. When the disrobing time came, she returned home wearing a black tube skirt over a white one. Wearing the white skirt inside indicated her determination to maintain *mae chi* status, while her husband wanted her to resume the role of a wife. This enraged her husband, who eventually divorced her. Then she practiced meditation intensively in a mountainous area thirty kilometers from her village. During that time, a lot of extraordinary meditative experiences occurred, such as purported encounters with *naga*s (legendary serpents), ghosts, and celestial beings. In 1945, she returned to her village and established a nunnery despite a lot of physical hardship. There were eight nuns altogether. However, the need for teachers compelled them to travel on foot through the jungle, sometimes to stay with Achan Mun or with other monks in his school. In 1950, she met Luang Ta Bua, who was widely revered as a living *arahant* (fully enlightened one). Under his guidance, she was able to advance in the practice until she achieved her full awakening.

When she passed away in 1991, after the crematory ritual, the remains of her body became relics. This was a decisive factor that boosted public veneration. According to Thai popular belief, this is an indicator of her arahantship. Buddhists hold that an enlightened person's ashes and bones will transform, after cremation, into small particles like pebbles or tiny beads in various colors, crystal clear or ivory white, red or brown or yellow. Under Luang Ta Bua's initiation, funds were raised and a hexagonal shaped stupa was constructed in her nunnery to venerate her relics. The ground floor of the stupa has her statue in walking meditation posture and bilingual placards on the wall telling her life story. The place has attracted visits from tourists and pilgrims from all over the country.

## Ouyporn Kheunkaew

Ouyporn Kheunkaew was born into a peasant family in Chiang Mai in 1963, the youngest of six siblings. She was raised within the cultural environment of northern village life. Her parents, apart from being farmers, were also local musicians. Her father had a lot of minor wives and children, which caused bitter quarrels in the family. Ouyporn remembered well the violent scenes at home. Unlike her brothers and sisters who seemed to accept their father's violence, Ouyporn chose to escape, returning to help her mother with everyday chores in order to lessen her mom's bitterness. When one of her sisters was scolded by her Bangkokian middle-class husband in front of her parents, who just stayed silent, Ouyporn, then in her teens, shouted to her brother-in-law to respect her sister (Ouyporn, interview, Feb. 2014).

She was socialized within the northern village syncretistic belief system. The combination of Buddhist and magical beliefs resulted in a gender ideology which suppressed femininity. "A few months after my first menstruation, I went to a temple festival and among the crowd, somebody pushed me into the compound of the sacred building where women were not allowed to enter. For many years, I felt very bad and guilty, assuming I had done something very sinful" (Ouyporn 2010, 2).

Ouyporn was the only one in the family who earned a bachelor's degree. After graduation, she worked in a refugee camp that had been set up in a central province. After being married to a German governmental advisor for some years, she ended her married life and pursued her career helping marginalized people, such as HIV patients, sex workers, women from ethnic minorities, and people of the third sex. In the course of her work, she became acquainted with prominent leaders in the circle of socially engaged Buddhism—Sulak Sivaraksa, Pracha Hutanuwatr, and Phra Pisal Visalo, to name but a few. She read Buddhadasa in her teens, went to practice Zen with Ven. Thich Nhat Hanh in France, and took spiritual healing courses from Quakers in Philadelphia. She has also had close relationships with feminist groups in India, the United States, and Canada that combined spiritual concerns with feminist principles. In 2002, she set up a center called the International Women's Partnership for Peace and Justice (IWP) in the village where she was born. The center offers different workshops and retreats on topics like diversity of gender, violence against women, sexuality, nonviolent action, and engaged Buddhism.

## Identity Politics and Spatial Tactics

Though Ven. Dhammananda is known as a *bhikkhuni* in the Theravada tradition, her monastery displays a hybrid religious disposition and outlook. Near the front gate is a huge Chinese-style statue of Phra Mahagajayana, one of the Buddha's enlightened disciples. Near the eating hall is a central Thai–style big spirit house. The main Buddha hall has a Tibetan-influenced roof. Inside the hall, the main Buddha statue, in deep blue, is Mahayana's Bhaisajyaguru, or medicine Buddha. On the wall, there is a Tibetan *tanga* painted by Ven. Dhammananda's son. Some religious rituals here also belong to Mahayana beliefs. Every full moon night, the temple's members gather to chant a prayer dedicated to the medicine Buddha. On New Year's Day, there is a special confession ritual that includes the Mahayana Bodhisatta resolution. The main ritual object is a *tanga* of thirty-five Tibetan confession Buddhas, each of which helps to purge a particular kind of sin. Participants are asked to carve a piece of turnip into the object or person to whom they want to apologize. They pray asking for forgiveness, and vow not to repeat the sin. The hybrid religious symbols and rituals, on the one hand, display Ven. Dhammananda's religious preferences and taste. On the other hand, they convey a spiritual message that *dhamma* essentially transcends all kinds of duality and categorization. Theravada or Mahayana, it does not matter since they all bring people to the same goal of liberation. It can also be interpreted as a criticism of both sects' rigidity in judging the other sect as lower.

Choice of word for the place also manifests identity politics. In referring to the temple, the word *watr* (วัตร) is used instead of *wat* (วัด), the usual term for temple. *Watr* literally means observance or practice. Such phonetic correspondence despite significative difference between these two words seems to serve two functions. One is to avoid legal problems since the present ecclesiastical law of Thailand does not recognize the existence of *bhikkhuni*; hence, she does not have any legal right to establish a monastery. However, the identical pronunciation of the two terms suggests that *watr* serves a religious purpose like *wat*. This is an indirect insistent claim to an alternative religious space. Another hidden and more polemical implication is that the word *watr*, with its emphasis on observance, can also become an indirect criticism of the laxity of many mainstream male monks living in *wat*s.

Apart from the word, daily routine in the *watr* also displays body politics. Going out for alms rounds, wearing the yellow robe, using ecclesiastic terminologies: all these activities used to belong exclusively to male monks. Therefore, when women began to perform these activities, it implies that they are quietly and resolutely asking for a legitimate share in the sacred space. Such spatial challenge was, during the early phase of this female community, accompanied by enthusiasm and stress. When the ordained women went on their alms round for the first time, lay supporters followed them in a car for fear that people who did not understand would cause problems (Varaporn 2006, ch. 6).

Having domestic and international networks is indispensable for launching identity politics. At the international level, apart from founding the Sakyadhita movement, in 2004 she was chosen by the UN as one of the distinguished Buddhist women of the year. In 2005, her name was among female nominees for the Nobel Peace Prize. Her close relationship with the Dalai Lama is well known. At home, she has tried to establish connections with local and central authorities. In 2013, she invited influential monks and lay authorities of the province to the opening ceremony of a new building in the *watr*. Their presence displayed indirect acceptance of *bhikkhuni* status. An interesting communication strategy is to set up an exhibition booth in big shopping arcades in Bangkok during certain religious festivals and have a well-trained *bhikkhuni* to answer questions and explain the meaningfulness of *bhikkhuni* to passers-by. Another more active and insistent form of communication is to launch a campaign for legal revision of the Ecclesiastical Act to make *bhikkhuni* legal status valid. They issue pamphlets, write articles, hold seminars, and undertake legal proceedings to appeal for the revision of the law.

When asked about the possible conflict between identity politics and religious goals, she said these two goals are not necessarily in conflict. The spiritual goal is to transcend duality whereas the social goal is to change structural obstacles. These two different levels necessitate each other. If the ordained life form is unimportant, the Buddha would not have tired himself establishing the sangha (the ordained community) or taking more risk to allow women to join it. Precisely because he knew that this particular form of life is a path to reaching the final goal, he finally decided to let both men and women join the sangha. In this sense, the structural form of the sangha community supports the transcendent goal. Insofar as the campaign and movement are pushed forward with spiritual awareness, it is possible to launch a selfless movement. It is precisely the life form of the ordained that helps to reduce the sense of attachment to the movement itself.

Comparing Mae Chi Kaew to the other two women under study, it seems that Mae Chi Kaew herself neither had an intention to lead a movement nor to launch an identity politics for women. She could not speak the central-Thai dialect and did not have a big group of disciples. Her prime concern was practicing meditation. Then how can we claim a movement under her name? What is her significance from the perspective of identity politics?

Her distinctiveness lies in the fact that within a male-dominated forest monk tradition, a humble yet resolute *mae chi* came to be revered as a female *arahant*. This is a rare case if we consider the social context that marginalizes women in sacred space (Keyes 1984; Falk 2002). Modernity seems to offer a better chance for female participation in meditation practice (Seeger 2010; Apinya 2013), and some of them did succeed in becoming meditation teachers—for example, Mother Siri Karinchai or Achan Naeb Mahathiranon. However, they are from the middle class, and this fact makes Mae Chi Kaew's rural origin even more distinct.

The decisive factor that enables her to transgress gender barriers in Theravada culture is twofold. First is what A. Sponberg (1992, 8) called "soteriological inclusiveness"—the idea that, in principle, Buddhism holds that a person, regardless of sex, social status, or class, can be able to achieve the final goal. Therefore, there is no barrier in terms of capacity to attain liberation. This is the only reason why the Buddha allowed women to be ordained as *bhikkhuni*. Second is the popular belief about the source of transcendental power. Here, we can consider Mae Chi Kaew's transcendental achievement as her crucial means of spatial tactics. Her practice and its result were acknowledged, accepted, and praised by the great masters. According to Buddhist meditative theory, when practitioners achieve the level of *jhāna* (meditative absorption),[1] they can possess extraordinary mental faculties, such as clairvoyance or seeing past lives and future events. When mixed with indigenous beliefs in magic and spirits, the outcome is the popular craze for miracles. Such trends are manifested in the tradition of magico-religious monks called *phra kechi*. Though the Buddha did not praise or allow monks to display such transcendental faculties, people love to see and hear about the miraculous power of monks. Such religious disposition and tastes make room for a female practitioner who possesses that faculty to be venerated and accepted. The narrative of Mae Chi Kaew's biography follows the pattern of hagiography of forest saints. Inborn miraculous power and *nimitta* during childhood were followed by resoluteness in practice, an enlightening moment, and extraordinary encounters with supernatural beings, some of which were converted to Buddhism after a miraculous fight with the master.

Another rapid and far-reaching turning point which spurred Mae Chi Kaew's posthumous movement of worship came after her crematory ritual when her remains were found to be relics. Recently, worship of relics has become a very popular cult. During important Buddhist holidays, many temples organize a public display of relics of the Buddha and enlightened disciples. Sometimes, relics are borrowed from India or China to be displayed and venerated. Relics are said to be able to multiply, arrive or disappear by themselves depending on the moral quality of the possessor, and cause a radiant light in the place. Ven. Nandiyani, a *bhikkhuni* living in Chiang Mai, organized a public veneration of the Buddha's relic at her temple, inviting a high-ranking monk to preside over the ceremony. This was an interesting spatial tactic, using relics to legitimize a female movement. Strange events during the construction of Mae Chi Kaew's stupa confirmed public belief in her posthumous transcendental power. Before the construction began, her followers failed to buy land for the construction site from a landlord. A monk then prayed and asked Mae Chi Kaew for help. The next day, the owner came to offer the land himself. The most miraculous event occurred near the end of the construction process. The light bulb at the tip of the stupa switched on by itself, despite the craftmen not having finished the connection of electric cords (Moradok Tham 2010, 167–70). On a tablet in the stupa, a big plate displayed Luang Ta Bua's words, "She knows what I know, and has achieved what I achieved."

A huge crowd participated the opening ceremony, and now the place has become a site of popular veneration. Commemorative amulets are sold at the nunnery and online.

Hence, in terms of spatial tactics and body politics, it is her spiritual body rather than her gendered body that legitimizes and makes room for her. Moreover, within the worldview of magical belief, the female gender is considered dangerous since her menstrual blood can destroy even the most potent magic. According to this popular perspective, men's magical power comes from acquiring or learning from teachers whereas women's negative power to nullify magic is inborn. Even though the Buddhist Pali canon did not consider female menstrual blood an obstacle to spiritual achievement, the mixing of Buddhism with indigenous beliefs has resulted in the discrimination of women as the more magical perspective has dominated the Buddhist view. Therefore, for example, women are not allowed into the inner space of a pagoda where relics are located. In this light, Mae Chi Kaew's achievement has reversed the power relationship of the mainstream belief. Instead of being barred from the inner pagoda space, a woman can strive to have her own relics put in a stupa. If magical belief has dominated Buddhism regarding the fear of menstruation, now her case also reversed the position; Buddhism believes in a person's moral strength rather than a person's ascribed gender.

Ouyporn's identity politics involves reinterpretation of Buddhist core concepts. Her discursive strategy combines Buddhism and feminist values, using the strong points of each to compensate for the weak points of the other.

> Feminism offers structural analysis, making us see structural roots of the problem, especially the entrenched gender ideology. But feminists are usually trapped in their anger, using it to justify their movements. Buddhism on the other hand is trapped within its extreme individualism, being unable to address structural problems, but it offers insight into individual suffering and has a very powerful method to overcome it. (Ouyporn, interview, Feb. 2014)

She reinterpreted the Buddhist Four Noble Truths to incorporate social suffering, namely suffering which is caused by systematic oppression and violence against marginalized people. She saw the root cause of social suffering in patriarchy that created social injustice and proposed the path to end the suffering through collective actions to change legal, social, and ideological conditions.

When I asked her whether identity politics would contradict the spiritual goal of eradicating the sense of self or not, she took out a pen and drew a picture of an onion, and said, "Look, if you peel off the onion layers after layers, at the end, in the middle, what will you find? Nothing. It's like the self." From a Buddhist perspective, there are two kinds of truth, which coexist: provisional truth, determined by convention or social law, and transcendental truth, which corresponds to the law of nature. Though there is a social goal to strive for, if one keeps the transcendental goal in mind, one will always be able to let go of attachment to one's own self. Both Ven. Dhammananda and Ouyporn seem to be well aware of these two levels of truth and the pitfall of attachment. For them, identity politics in the spiritual realm entails regular self-reflection and self-criticism.

Ouyporn's challenging attitude was observed attentively by the government. During the early phase of her activity at the center, an officer from the government's security office came to spy on her. She invited him into the course and let him observe the training activities. Her direct exposure strategy and her deliberation not to expand the center in terms of size led to lessened suspicion. Moreover, the success of the previous trainings has drawn in more people, and many governmental offices have sent their employees to be trained with her.

Small but meaningful steps and self-reliance underpin her organizational strategy. Different from most NGOs whose growth and development desperately depend on foreign funds, she tries to be as independent as possible. At present, a large part of training courses come from various projects under a state agency called the Thai Health Promotion Foundation. Other NGOs dealing with gender also bring in trainees, and some NGOs workers also help in organizing the course. Running the center in her own home, she benefits from kinship ties in the village. Her sister gave her a piece of land in which she had a cozy clay house built to serve course trainees. A neighbor also offered a place with a very low annual rent to build a clay library and meditation hall.

Women and relatives in the village come to cook, do laundry, and take care of the facilities.

These three women used different spatial tactics. Mae Chi Kaew's success came from her inborn spiritual faculty and Thai society's enthusiasm for miraculous power. The movement inspired by her spreads within the network of the male-dominant forest monk tradition. Ven. Dhammananda and Ouyporn both combine feminism with Mahayana and Theravada tradition. However, Ven. Dhammananda's choice of *bhikkhuni* form has compelled her to strive from within the sangha. In order to have relative independence, she created her own physical space and used both traditional legitimation techniques and a legal campaign. In this light, Ouyporn's lay status seems to be of great advantage since she enjoys relative independence, so much so that she can launch her own reinterpretation of Buddhist core concepts without much criticism from the sangha.

## Religious Form and Religious Experience

Religious studies in the tradition of William James have emphasized the "ineffable and mystic" kind of religious experience which rarely occurs in an individual's life. However, this study seeks to emphasize the aspect of religious experience in everyday context that is closely related to a specific religious "form of life" of an individual. Each of the women profiled here chose a particular form of religious identity, and that specific religious form yielded certain kinds of religious ethos and forms of life which crucially shape the sense of self, legitimize the chosen path, and lead to serious commitment in religious practice.

Ven. Dhammananda said in an interview that it seemed she had the determination to become a *bhikkhuni* in her DNA. She remembered well the day of her mother's ordination. Seeing her mother's hair falling on the ground and witnessing her receiving the eight precepts, Chatsumarn at age eleven got an unforgettably strange feeling. Her mother's choice of light yellow robe also caused criticism from certain conservative monks since it deviated from the ordinary white robe of *mae chi*. However, her high-ranking preceptor protected her. A home-monastery atmosphere and her mother's esoteric practice deeply shaped Chatsumarn's sense of ordained self. Later, after finishing her dissertation comparing *bhikkhuni* codes of conduct, she persuaded her mother to go to Taiwan to be ordained properly as Mahayana *bhikkhuni*. Therefore, *bhikkhuni* was naturally the only form she chose when she decided to be ordained (Phimpan 2001, 204).

> The goal of an ordained person is drastically different from that of the lay. Once ordained, we cannot eat according to our own preference. We have to eat what laypersons present to us. While eating, we should make a wish to transfer merit to the lay who offers the food. If people offer ten dishes, we should take a bit from every dish, and cannot just choose them at will. All our gestures must be made for the sake of preserving the religion. I could not grasp it fully while being a lay, but now it is so clear to me. How beautiful the ordained life is! (Ibid., 48–49)

For her, religious experience is encapsulated in every meticulous detail of the *bhikkhuni*'s form of life. It is precisely this ideal form of the fully ordained person that gives her a sense of self.

In Mae Chi Kaew's case, her inborn faculty of mystic experience and the encounter with Achan Mun were determinant factors that made her choose the religious path. During childhood, she had a past life *nimitta* seeing herself as a hen trying to protect her chicks. When she first met Achan Mun, she had a vision of her own body becoming a corpse and consumed by worms. Achan Mun appeared pointing his cane to it, causing a huge flame that turned the corpse into a heap of ashes. Traditional belief in the potential of *nimitta* to convey religious message directed and shaped her religious resolution, which did not waver during the interval years of marriage. When allowed to be ordained, *mae chi* was the only possible form of female renunciant she could become since her immediate context ruled out the being a *bhikkhuni*. After returning to householder life, she refused to eat with her husband and ran away when he held her hand. Luckily, her brother calmed his fury and persuaded him to let her go. After the separation, she was able to pursue her religious ideals in the white robe again.

Life as a *mae chi* in the northeastern forest monk tradition was very hard. The area she stayed in was short of water, and renunciants had to dig a deep well. There was also no toilet. In 1945, they cut back the thick jungle to build a nunnery. Basic and necessary utensils were scarce. They used dry betel nut husks to make shoes, and used bamboo for cups and utensils. Each day, nuns went into the jungle searching for young bamboo shoots or mushrooms for cooking. However, she said it was much easier to put up with physical hardship as *mae chi* than to be without a good teacher (Ariya Savika 2010, 16). For this reason, from time to time she would go on foot with a small group of nuns through thick jungle for eleven or twelve days to seek advice from Achan Mun. Frugality, patience, and hardship were at the core of the religious ethos and form of life of the forest monk, which molded Mae Chi Kaew's sense of ordained self. Being accepted and supported within the network of Achan Mun, her meditative practice gradually advanced.

Compared to those two cases, Ouyporn's layperson status does not impede her religious practice. However, she made her intentions very clear: "I don't have any intention of becoming ordained, not now or in the future. As a laywoman, I can do so many things that I could not do as an ordained person. Mother Dhammananda told me a laywoman can attain liberation as a householder. This was so revealing." Insofar as her chosen way of life allows her to practice meditation and insofar as she can realize her religious ideals in her social work, ordained form does not matter to her.

## Mahayana and Theravada Meditation Practice

Opinions differ between Mahayana and Theravada practitioners. Mahayana tradition, according to the *bodhisatta* ideal, gives priority to social welfare activities; therefore contemporary practitioners of this tradition tend to emphasize mindfulness meditation within an everyday context. They often view Theravada's seclusion and tendency to separate serious practice from other daily activities as egoistic, aiming only at individual liberation, whereas adherents of Mahayana, which literally means "great vehicle," aims to liberate all beings from suffering.

Theravada tradition tends to focus more on the necessity of practicing in a secluded environment, though it does not repudiate the incorporation of the practice into everyday life. The argument is that the mind has a very subtle nature working at incredible speed. In order to observe the process clearly, it is necessary to stop doing other activities and just focus intensely and continuously on one's own body and mind. The separatist method can thus enable one to experience the very refined process of self-creation in the stream of thought, and only then can one find the way to detach oneself from it.

Globalized contexts have led to various attempts to rationalize and make Buddhist ideals and practice relevant to everyday life experiences. The rapid increase of mass meditation centers throughout Thailand displays the blend of traditional seclusion strategy with everyday urban logic (Apinya 2013). The renowned Buddhadasa Bhikkhu combined Zen Buddhism with Theravada tradition, which helped to lessen the well-known gap between religiosity of the layperson and monk in Theravada culture. The rational attempt to anchor *dhamma* in everyday life can also be seen in the popularity of the Vietnamese meditation master Ven. Thich Nhat Hanh, who has garnered overwhelming enthusiasm among Thai middle-class practitioners. Ven. Dhammananda and Ouyporn's meditation practice must be grasped within this context.

Ven. Dhammananda has spoken on the tension between solitude and engagement:

People usually expect a good monk to live in seclusion. However, seclusion is impossible for me as an abbess. I try instead to make every action in daily activities a form of *dhamma* practice, trying to observe my own mind all the time. Alone in the forest or mountain, there won't be interaction with people which arouses greed, anger or ignorance. In short, there is no challenge. On the other hand, the environment of the temple often compels us to have a test . . . to see how far the mind can transcend its emotions and ego. (Phimpan 2011, 58–59)

Though her preference for awareness practice in daily life is clear, she does not altogether neglect Theravada's seclusion practice. She inherited esoteric meditation from her mother. At the age of eight, she followed her mother to learn *samatha* (concentrative meditation) from Luang Pho Sod, one of Thailand's foremost meditation masters famous for his miraculous power; then she learned *vipassanā* (insight meditation) from Luang Pho Lee, another famous master. Her mother, after being ordained, is said to have learned advanced meditation directly from "the masters in the above realm." Such mystical inclination significantly influenced Ven. Dhammananda. However, she once told a reporter,

> For beginners, meditative visions can easily mislead them, but for advanced ones, they know how to make use of them. I myself blend many techniques together. Normally, I use *phuttho* [recitative word which means Buddha] and if any *nimitta* occurs, I ignore it, but don't push it away. In meditation, when thought occurs, we neither push it away nor attach to it. This is how to see things from insight meditation perspective. (Phimpan 2001, 153–54)

Thus, she blends many techniques together, both Mahayana's emphasis on everyday life practice and Theravada's concentrative and *vipassanā* technique.[2]

In Mae Chi Kaew's case, she followed the traditional seclusion method of forest monks. Her accounts of meditative experience were full of miraculous phenomena. Why do life stories of meditation masters always have such a narrative pattern? What is its cultural significance? An answer might be that ordinary people have no way to prove whether a master can really achieve the final liberation or not. For them, an indicator of achievement in transcendental states is the faculty of miraculous power. Though the Buddha forbade monks to display such faculty for fear of misleading people, the masses are always drawn to such a thing. Miraculous power is simply a marker of transcendence. Mae Chi Kaew seems to have viewed her inborn miraculous faculty as significant in two ways. First, it was one of the markers that directed her future choice of a white robe. The vision of her body being completely burnt at the time she first met Achan Mun assured her that she belonged to the world of the ordained person. Secondly, miraculous power was related to her sense of ego, making her stubborn in the eyes of her teachers. During her stay with Achan Kongma, a member of Achan Mun's school, her meditation became stagnant. Analyzing deeply, she discovered her own conceit and her antipathy toward Achan Kongma's guidance. She resorted to a harsh measure, contemplating unceasingly her own conceit until the mind was tamed, and progressed further into a transcendental state (Chomrom 2010,

22). Later, under the guidance of Luang Ta Bua, she was able to progress in her *vipassanā* practice until her crucial moment occurred. "When she was going to lie down, she heard a very loud noise as if lightning was hitting the platform where she stayed. In that moment, she heard a voice saying, 'Thy births have come to an end!' Her tears of joy were flowing." (Chomrom 2010, 34–35). Continuous and relentless practice led to a radical self-transformation.

Though this success is an individual achievement, such individual pursuit was possible through strong support of the *dhamma* community— namely, her meditation teachers, their network, and the companionship of other nuns who accompanied her. Achan Mun redirected her physical and spiritual life, and connected her to other teachers. Luang Ta Bua, though using harsh words with her, always displayed compassion and offered patronage. When she got sick, he sent a female doctor to take care of her, and monks in his lineage paid visits. After her death, he presided over her crematory ritual, leading the donation campaign to have a stupa built to consecrate her relics. Seen in this light, individual seclusionist achievement is enhanced and progressed through group support.

In Ouyporn's case, her religious practice is grounded in her career as an NGO worker. She learned Theravada meditative method from the center of master Goenka, an Indian teacher in the Burmese meditative tradition. She also visited Ven. Thich Nhat Hanh in France to train in the art of deep listening, which is an aid in practicing meditation in everyday busy working life. Deep listening is the art of listening carefully and intensely without judging. To achieve this goal, one must constantly focus on how one's mind reacts and becomes angry or sad in the course of interactions with others. Only after one realizes that suffering comes from the mental tendency to judge and react can one detach from such entanglement and listen to others with deep understanding. In group training, she teaches breathing meditation and awareness of the body while trying to build trust among participants until they tell their own stories. Getting them to open up is crucial. In order to heal the wound, the wound itself must be directly addressed and accepted by its bearer. To tell one's own story is an important part of self-analysis and healing that arouses sympathy and compassion within the group.

However, there are often cases in which, during the first few days, certain participants belittle or hurt others. In those cases, Ouyporn constantly observes her own thoughts, refraining from negative feeling, and does not try to intervene immediately. Instead, she talks about deeply entrenched gender bias or negative judgment toward marginalized people in Thai society in later sessions. She lets participants gradually ponder it and come to understand by themselves that their seemingly personal problems are but a mere manifestation of gender, class, or ethnic ideologies in Thai society. If certain participants cannot come to the conclusion, there will always be some participants who get the point and voice it out loud. In short, deep listening enables trainees to come to terms with their own wounds while structural analysis leads them to realize the social and cultural roots of their misery. This group dynamic is thus a path to healing; for Ouyporn, the process empowers her and helps her progress spiritually.

## Gender and Religious Experience

The relationship between gender and religious experience is a part of the wider debate concerning the nature of the mind in religious practice. The universalist view holds that the characteristics of our mental structure, including the ineffable moment of transcendental experience, are the same everywhere despite different religions and meditative techniques. On the other hand, historians and anthropologists alike emphasize the contextualized nature of religious experience, which is shaped by cultural values, differences in sex, age, and ethnic group, and historical periods. These two perspectives seem not to be mutually and necessarily exclusive. A study comparing meditative experiences of enlightened male and female monks in the Buddha's time found that though their liberated experiences were similar, there were significant differences regarding their attitudes toward relationships with others and the use of certain meditative technique dealing with bodies (Blackstone 1998).

This chapter aims to discuss how gender concepts in Thai society and gendered relationships within the immediate environment of the women under study affect their religious attitudes. How does each woman view the relationship between gender and religious experience?

Ven. Dhammananda's feminist leaning is shaped greatly by her mother's exceptionally strong character. Mrs. Voramai was the first Thai woman who showed her judo (a Japanese martial art) skill in public, and also the only woman who joined the male scout team bicycling from Thailand to Singapore. "Mom was very strict, her words were the law of the house. No one dared argue with her." The strength of motherhood that she absorbed from her mother manifests itself when she became mother of her three sons. She explained that motherhood is closely related to the female religious experience:

> In a Buddhist sacred text, there is a part describing women's woes, and giving birth is one of them. The sacred book was written from a male perspective, seeing such a duty as negative. For me, the experience of giving birth was overwhelmingly wonderful and the joy from giving birth is beyond words. Through being a mother, woman learns to sacrifice her own happiness for the sake of her kids. She is trained to become selfless. (Ven. Dhammananda, interview, April 2013)

However, she also admits that the state of enlightenment transcends all kinds of dualism.

Mae Chi Kaew, on the other hand, was born into the context of northeastern rural customs, and the network of forest monks also displayed traditional gender hierarchy. Achan Mun's compassion towards her made people gossip that the great master fell in love with the young village girl. Later, after her ordination, she used to express the limitation of teacher-disciple relations due to gender difference. "We are *mae chi* in white. Though staying not far from our teacher, he seems so far away since we cannot go near him" (*Moradok tham* 2000, 39). The traditional gender hierarchy also is manifested in the stupa built in her honor. Her relics were placed at a level below that of male saints (Seeger 2010, 580–81). Despite being accepted and included within the sacred space, her place in that space must be located below that of the monks. However, she did not perceive the gender hierarchy to be an obstacle: "We should not feel discouraged or sad. Our teacher does love us; his *dhamma* loves us" (*Moradok tham* 2000, 40).

Regarding the ineffable moment of transcendence, she shared a similar attitude with the other two women of our case that "[the transcendental] mind has no sex" (*Moradok tham* 2000, 145). When compared to Ven. Dhammananda's comment on the uniqueness of a mother's experience, though Mae Chi Kaew never had the direct experience of giving birth during her marriage, she did have visions of miraculous labor. More than once, in her visions, celestial beings asked to become her children. In one of the visions, she flew into the sky and gave birth there.

> No blood, not dirty like ordinary labor. . . . It was a boy with gold radiant skin. . . . While he was inside me, my womb was transparent. After coming out, he bowed to me and said, "In order to achieve moral perfection, I'd like to become your child. (*Moradok tham* 2000, 56–58)

After that, she prophesized more than once that such-and-such a couple living in such-and-such a village would have a son. Her prophecies came true, and the boys in these cases later became her students. These episodes combined her motherhood instinct with meditative experience, and displayed her charisma as a meditation teacher.

In Ouyporn's case, sexuality and spirituality do not exclude each other. She wrote about her experience of discovering her own sexual identity as a lesbian:

> It was one of the happiest self-discoveries. I found that sexuality is such a core of my life. It was a fortunate experience because we are both feminists so we did not suffer from internalized homophobia. The spiritual foundation that I nurtured a few years earlier was a major support for rediscovering my sexuality. Feminism and my Buddhist spiritual awakening were the strong foundations that helped me embrace my sexuality. (Ouyporn 2010, 4–5)

However, during the early phase of self-discovery, she also experienced certain moments of inner loneliness since her attempt to fuse sexual and spiritual awakening together could hardly find any support or sympathy within conservative Theravada culture. Unlike Tibetan tradition, Theravada Buddhism regards sex and religious practice as antithetical to each other. Among friends of the third sex, both Thai and foreigners, Ouyporn found out that most of them had turned their backs on religion. She resorted to books of certain Western authors who followed Tibetan masters using sexuality as a method of meditative practice. According to her, Khemananda, a famous activist monk, was the only Thai Buddhist intellectual who acknowledged such a combination (Ouyporn, interview, Feb. 2014). When one combines sex and religion together, it helps to cultivate an ethics of care in an intimate relationship. It makes the couple attend to each other's emotions, which in turn enhances and deepens self-understanding. In her training program, her sexual experience has gained strategic importance since she uses it to induce trust and courage of other participants making them feel more comfortable about sharing their own long-suppressed pain, fear, and sorrow.

## Conclusion

Religion is seen in this chapter as a mediated space between an individual practitioner and the community. Even though religious practice is a private action, we have seen how the achievements of the women in this study were possible within the environment of a community that shaped each one's sense of self, and the special characteristics of each community that helped them express their religious identity. Ven. Dhammananda, who grew up in an alternative home-monastery environment, continued to expand the legacy of her mother in building a hybrid communal sanctuary for *bhikkhuni*. Mae Chi Kaew had been molded in the religious framework of the northeastern forest monk ethos. The stupa housing her relics not only symbolizes her distinct meditative achievement but also reproduces the popular reverence for forest monks' miraculous power. In sum, her personal achievement helps to sustain the cultural value crucial to the forest monk community. Ouyporn's gradual discovery of her own alternative gender preference was a part of her spiritual growth and all activities at the center she established manifest clearly her strategy of identity politics.

At present, the politics of religious form has made the status of *mae chi*, *bhikkhuni*, and female lay practitioner into opposing positions. Conservative groups hope that the improvement of *mae chis'* status will discourage women from becoming *bhikkhuni*, and maintain, with reference to Buddhist sacred texts, that active lay persons can attain the first three steps of enlightenment (*sotāpanna, sakādagāmī, anāgāmī*). Some feminists see such views as spatial tactics to exclude *bhikkhuni* from sacred space (Seeger 2010, 558).

This chapter proposes that we should not let the politics of form antagonize women toward one another. We have seen how women in our cases, with different cultural capital, religious dispositions, and religious forms, invented different spatial tactics in their own ways to open sacred space for themselves. At the societal level, forms have strategic significance as a part of tactics utilized by women and by those who want to marginalize them. At a spiritual level, the Buddha created the sangha, the community of ordained persons, and later allowed women to join it, precisely because he knew that religious identity is closely related to spiritual progress. Women in different forms, therefore, should hear and pay attention to one another rather than perceiving one another as threat.

NOTES

1. *Jhāna* refers to a special state of consciousness in which there is a complete, though temporary, suspension of five-fold sense activities and of the five hindrances (sensual pleasure, aversion, drowsiness, doubt, and wild thoughts). The mind in this state is full of alertness and lucidity with very high degree of one-pointedness.

2. There are two meditative methods in the Theravada tradition. *Samatha* (concentration) binds the mind to just one object. The result is various *jhāna* states with overwhelming one-pointedness, deep tranquility, and extraordinary mental power. *Vipassanā* (insight meditation) contemplates the three characteristics of body and mind (impermanence, suffering, and nonself). The result is total eradication of defilement. In order to reach final liberation, a practitioner needs both methods.

REFERENCES

Apinya Feungfusakul. 2013. "Prasopkan thang sasana nai thana pheunthi roi to: kanpatibat tham klum nai prathet Thai patchuban" [Religiosity as mediated space: Mass meditation in contemporary Thailand]. In *Duai Rak: Ruapruam botkhwam nai okat satsatrachan kittikhun Doro. Chatthip Nartsupha ayu 72 pi* [With love: Collection of essays in commemoration of professor emeritus Dr. Chattip Nartsupha at 72]. Bangkok: Sangsan.

Blackstone, Kathryn. 1998. *Women in the Footsteps of the Buddha: Struggle for Liberation in the Therigatha*. London: Curzon.

Chomrom Kalayanatham. 2010. *Ariyasavika: Khun mae chi Kaew Sianglam* [Enlightened female disciple: Mother Kaew Sianglam]. Bangkok: Chomrom Kalayanatham.

Keyes, Charles F. 1984. Mother and Mistress but Never a Monk: Buddhist Notions of Female Gender in Rural Thailand. *American Ethnologist* 11(2): 223–41.

*Moradok tham khun mae chi Kaew Sianglam* [Mae Chi Kaew Sianglam's dhamma legacy]. 2010. Bangkok: Prima Publishing.

Ouyporn Kheunkaew. 2010. *Sexuality and Spirituality: A Connection for Transformation*. Paper presented in the International Symposium on Women's Health, Well-Being between Culture and the Law, January 28–29. Bangkok, Thailand.

Phimphan Hansakul. 2001. *Dr. Chatsumarn Kabilasingha: Phu phlik fuen phiksuni song* [Dr. Chatsumarn Kabilasingha: The one who revived the tradition of the *bhikkhuni* sangha]. Bangkok: Phra Athit.

———. 2011. *Dhammananda: Bon senthang phiksuni phothisat* [Dhammananda: On the path of bodhisattva *bhikkhuni*]. Bangkok: Amarindhamma.

Seeger, Martin. 2010. "Against the Stream: The Thai Female Buddhist Saint Mae Chi Kaew Sianglam (1901–1991)." *South East Asia Research* 18(3): 555–95.

Sponberg, Alan. 1992. "Attitudes toward Women and the Feminine in Early Buddhism." http://www.nku.edu/-gartigw/teaching_files/sponberg.

Varaporn Chamsanit. 2006. "Reconnecting the Lost Lineage: Challenges to Insitutional Denial of Buddhist Women's Monasticism in Thailand." PhD diss., Australian National University.

Voramai Kabilasingha. 2003. *Phiksuni Phothisat: Vipassana ha baep* [Five types of vipassana practice]. Bangkok: Bhuda Savika Foundation.

# MAKING SENSE OF A BUDDHIST MONKS' NETWORK AS A COMMUNITY MOVEMENT IN CONTEMPORARY THAILAND

MAYUMI OKABE

## Introduction

In Thailand, many Buddhist monks have recently been engaged in worldly affairs that are meant to improve the lives of people, such as road construction, credit unions, buffalo banks, care for people living with HIV/AIDS, treatment for drug addicts, environment conservation, and so on. The scope of their activities ranges widely throughout the country. These activities have been labeled "community development" activities and the monks "development monks" (*phra nak phatthana*).[1] It might be inferred that development monks are far different from the image of ideal Theravada Buddhist monks who devote themselves to ascetic practices in pursuit of otherworldly goals or enlightenment.

Development monks are expected to engage in community development activities rather than just devote their energies to worldly affairs or social engagement. However, we cannot easily distinguish the work of "development monks" and the "community development activities" of other monks. This is because, aside from ascetic practices, Theravada Buddhist monks have also been inevitably involved in worldly affairs in local communities in Sri Lanka and mainland Southeast Asia. They have had various roles, such as performing religious rituals and ceremonies, applying traditional knowledge of astrology and herbal medicine, giving advice to the villagers on naming infants, arbitrating in family or village conflicts, and so on. In this regard, the terms "development monks" and "community development" are socially constructed discourses used in the process of implementing development policy by the Thai government and in the expansion of alternative development led by NGOs (nongovernmental organizations) opposing it since the late 1970s in Thailand (see Escobar 1995).

Yet the narratives of some development monks raise another question. One monk said, "The monks can no longer stay in their temples and only preach." Another said, "We need to play social roles more actively." This illustrates that the monks do not just accept their traditional roles uncritically, but that they are passionate about being engaged in worldly affairs or, as they call it, community development.

Moreover, the monks have not only been individually engaged in community development activities but have also constructed networks beyond localities in order to exchange information about their activities. This trend has gradually taken hold throughout the country since around the end of the 1980s and the beginning of the 1990s. There are many different networks, such as the Sekkhiyatham Group, the Lanna Community Development Sangha Group, and the Community Development Monks' Network in Northern Thailand (*Khrueakhai phra nak phatthana chumchon phak nuea*), which will be the focus of this chapter.[2]

This chapter addresses why some Buddhist monks have expressly engaged in community development and constructed networks during these decades in Thailand by paying particular attention to the case of the Community Development Monks' Network in Northern Thailand. As will be examined later in detail, this network consists of a variety of monks who pursue life-changing transformations in a rapidly shifting society. They do not share any collective identities peculiar to this network, but they have constructed communality by discussing their experiences in community development.

This study regards this network as neither a static, substantial, and homogeneous community nor a part of modern social movements since the nineteenth century in Europe. Rather, this paper sees it as a community movement, constructed through a newly emerging community in the context of globalization in late modernity (Tanabe 2008, 1–12). In order to understand such a community movement, it is necessary to explore how an assemblage[3] appears as a dynamic and contingent configuration through the articulations of the actors—monks and multiple forces— involved in a movement in the midst of ongoing sociopolitical changes in contemporary northern Thailand. Therefore, first, this chapter will focus on the construction process of the network by reviewing the life stories of three monks who played significant roles in this process. Next, this chapter examines the kinds of features that can be found in this movement led by Buddhist monks. The values, images, and communality that were pursued by the monks in the network will be the focal points.

The data that this paper deals with is based on my continuous and ongoing fieldwork, mainly in Chiang Mai and northern Thailand, from 2004 to the present.[4]

## Networking Development Monks: The Community Development Monks' Network in Northern Thailand

### Sociohistorical aspects of the construction of the network

In order to understand how the network was constructed, we will briefly look at the life stories of the three monks who played leading roles in this construction process. They are given the pseudonyms of monks X, Y, and Z.

### 1. Monk X

Monk X, a Tai Yai[5] monk who is forty years old and from a Thailand-Myanmar border village in Wiang Haeng District, Chiang Mai Province, has dwelled at a Buddhist temple in Doi Saket District, a suburb of the city of Chiang Mai, since 1989. Though he was ordained as a novice in his hometown, there were few opportunities for higher education. At that time, the temple school for novices in Doi Saket was quite famous for its high rate of successful examinees for *palien*[6] from 1987 to 1989. For this reason, he decided to move to this temple, even though he had no acquaintances in Doi Saket. After his move there, he kept studying *palien* and *naktham*,[7] and finally obtained *palien* level six. He studied secular subjects at the novice school of this temple and entered Mahachulalongkorn Buddhist University, Chiang Mai campus, for his bachelor's and master's degrees in Buddhist studies. During his pursuit of higher education, the abbot of this temple, monk P,[8] ordained him as a *bhikkhu*.[9]

At the same time, monk X had started to engage in health-care activities in the local communities around this temple since the beginning of the

1990s. Monk P had been engaged in providing care for people with HIV/AIDS by implementing his home visit project in Doi Saket District soon after the HIV pandemic in the end of the 1980s.[10] Monk X followed the abbot and helped with his activities as one of his disciples. For the abbot, monk X seemed to be more interested in health-care activities than his other disciples. However, after the abbot was assigned to the position of head of the Doi Saket District sangha, he became too busy with administrative work within the sangha organization to spend time on community development himself. Instead, monk X gained opportunities to be engaged in home-visit projects and teach meditation to people with HIV/AIDS. As monk X's eager involvement deepened, he was also increasingly invited to seminars and workshops on HIV/AIDS held by NGOs, mostly in Chiang Mai and Bangkok. Accordingly, it became harder for monk X to attend classes regularly at the university.

Although he eventually had to give up studying for his master's degree, he seemed to be satisfied with his choice to be more actively engaged in community development rather than only focusing on his pursuit of higher educational achievement. He said that even though he did not get his master's degree at that time, there was more to learn from the local community than from textbooks. He also said that enlightenment was the highest goal only for monks, particularly those who devote themselves to ascetic practices, but it was not for him. His goal had been to help those who were suffering in this world. It was the salvation of others that made him happy with his life.[11] This clearly indicates that community development activities were an important part of his life and purpose as a Buddhist monk.

At one seminar in Chiang Mai, monk X encountered an unexpected question when a lay participant asked where and how many monks have been engaged in the HIV/AIDS issue. Although he tried to respond to the question, he was unable to give a clear answer. This experience helped him recognize the lack of communication about monks' involvement in the HIV/AIDS issue and made him want to contact other monks who had been engaged in this issue. After this episode, monk X was able to gradually expand his network among both monks and lay people.

## 2. Monk Y

It was not monk X's individual experience alone that drove the monks to construct the network. Monk Y was another important instigator whose leadership influenced the network.[12]

Monk Y was a Lisu[13] monk from a farming family in a mountainous area in Mae Sot District, Tak Province. In his youth, he obtained his education without ordination as a novice. After his study in Phitsanulok Province, he returned home to help with his family's farm. He decided to become ordained as a monk in Tak in 1992 and soon moved to Wat Sri Soda in Chiang Mai city, the temple where the headquarters of the Thammacharik[14] project in the north is located.

At that time, a new project had just been launched by the Department of Public Welfare and Chiang Mai Rajabhat University[15] in line with the Thammacharik project. It aimed to encourage the monks to engage in spreading *dhamma* among the non-Buddhist ethnic minorities in the mountainous areas in northern Thailand, and to obtain a higher education. After monk Y joined this project, he moved to a hut in his hometown in order to be engaged in community development activities. He attended classes at Chiang Mai Rajabhat University only once a month. After he obtained his bachelor's degree, he moved to Wat Sri Suphan in Chiang Mai in order to pursue a master's degree in educational studies at Chiang Mai University.

What is most important is that in the process of his educational pursuits he became acquainted with many development workers in NGOs. Some invited monk Y to join their organizations, such as the Foundation for Northern Thai Society (*Kong thun phuea sangkhom phak nuea*), the Foundation for Children of a Green World (*Munlanithi luk lok si khiao*), and so on. Moreover, his selection as an Ashoka Fellow[16] in 2002 enabled him to expand his network of both monks and lay people who were interested in community development. He also started to invite younger monks to engage in community development activities.

Not only did monk Y have a great influence on the construction of the network, but so did the sociopolitical context. In this case, it was a protest movement among the farmers. After Thailand's newly revised constitution was adopted in 1997, many groups of poor farmers gathered to protest against the Thai government in front of the Chiang Mai Provincial Office.

These people came from rural and remote mountainous areas where land conflicts had been caused by the development policy of the government.[17] Four Buddhist monks,[18] including monk Y, were invited by the protesters to perform religious rituals and preach about the importance of using nonviolent (*ahingsa*) means to solve problems.

At this event, those who invited these four monks were the development workers who had worked with Phra Thep Kawi, an outstanding development monk of Wat Pa Dara Phirom in Mae Rim District, Chiang Mai.[19] Most of them were from the central region of Thailand and initially started to work as development workers sent from the Thai Volunteer Center to the Foundation of Education and Development for Rural Areas (*Munlanithi kan sueksa lae phatthana chonnabot*), which was founded by Phra Thep Kawi. When a land-use conflict occurred in Ban Chan[20] in Mae Chaem District, Chiang Mai, these development workers brought young monks to learn what was happening in the local community from an active development monk who was also a disciple of Phra Thep Kawi and one of the four monks invited to the protest movement. Both the active development monk and the other young monks were members of the Lanna Community Development Sangha Group,[21] founded with support from both Phra Thep Kawi and the YMCA of Chiang Mai.[22]

Indeed monk Y was neither a disciple of Phra Thep Kawi nor a member of the Lanna Community Development Sangha Group. He started to engage in community-development activities after his encounter with the Thammacharik project during his pursuit of higher education. This enabled him to extend his network of both monks and lay people. Yet it was the farmers' protest movement that directly motivated him and the other three monks to construct a small group of monks around Chiang Mai, naming it the Monks Network for the Poor (*Khrueakhai phrasong phuea khon chon*) (*Krungthep thurakit* 2002). After the protest movement calmed down, the monks of this network gathered repeatedly under monk Y's leadership to discuss their roles in solving the problems impoverished farmers faced in a rapidly changing society.

### 3. Monk Z

Monk Z was the person who attracted monks X and Y. He was also one of the four monks who were invited to the protest movement in 1997, and he played a significant role in the construction process of the network after this event.

Monk Z was a Khon Mueang (northern Thai) monk from Phayao Province. He was the youngest son of six children in a farming family and ordained as a novice in his hometown to pursue educational opportunities. He then moved to Nakhon Ratchasima Province in northeastern Thailand, where his relative lived, and enrolled in Mahachulalongkorn Buddhist University in Bangkok to continue his studies until he obtained a master's degree. He went on to study at Delhi University in India for his doctoral degree in Buddhist studies, and finally came back to Thailand to teach at the Chiang Mai campus of Mahachulalongkorn University, where he still teaches today. Thus, he is a highly educated monk both in religious and secular studies. Monk Z became familiar with monk X after his entering the university.

When the protest movement took place in Chiang Mai in 1997, monk Z was invited to the movement as the representative of his university. In fact, he had been strongly interested in monks' engagement in worldly affairs for a long time.[23] In addition, he had presented an article on this topic in a magazine published by the Sekkhiyatham Group. For these reasons, he was invited to join the protest movement. This was also an opportunity for him to start working with monk Y.

After that, in 1999, some monks and lay people gathered twice for meetings at the temple in Doi Saket District where monk X lived, to exchange and share information about community development activities and the social roles of monks. Then, they invited about one hundred fifty monks from northern Thailand to meet at a temple in Nan Province to introduce themselves and exchange information and opinions about their activities. At this meeting, they agreed to construct a network among them in the near future, and then organized a small committee for the preparation of their new network at Wat Suan Dok, Chiang Mai, in April 2000. Finally, in March 2001, they held a meeting at the temple in Doi Saket again to found the Community Development Monks' Network in Northern Thailand with more than a hundred attendees from all over northern Thailand.

However, this network drastically declined around 2005 because of monk Y's disrobement in 2004, the expiration of the financial aid to a nonprofit organization supporting this network, and some troubles inside the network. According to my fieldwork in 2012, most of the monks recognized that the network no longer persisted at a collective level but had not entirely disappeared. They explained that the network had temporarily fragmented into innumerable parts, depending on the issues they dealt with, such as HIV/AIDS, alcoholism, or the environment. Some monks recalled with nostalgia the past activities of the network.

## Organizational features of the network

The purpose of the network was: (1) to improve the potential of development monks in northern Thailand, (2) to support and encourage community development activities by individual monks, groups of monks, and community-based organizations, (3) to increase the awareness of administrative monks in the sangha as well as lay people in regard to community development, and (4) to advocate new directions for and models of community development based on Buddhist *dhamma* (Kiattisak 2004).

This network had no firm membership, except a small committee of about ten young monks. For this reason, each time the network held a meeting, it was difficult to estimate the number of monks that attended. Monk X, Y, and Z, who took central roles on the committee, always attended the network meetings, though only a few of the other committee members attended the meetings.

A noteworthy fact is that outside development agencies acquired influence over this network, both economically and organizationally. The network received financial aid from the Social Investment Fund (*Khrongkan kong thun phuea kan long thun thang sangkhom*).[24] This enabled them to found the Phothiyalai Institute (*Sathaban phothiyalai*), whose office is located on the campus of Mahachulalongkorn University in Chiang Mai. The foundation of the Phothiyalai Institute enabled them to have a common place for their meetings. Of greatest importance was the fact that they could afford to have permanent staff at this office who could be take care of paperwork and logistics, such as coordinating with monks and arranging transportation. There were approximately ten people on staff, including both monks and lay people from 2004 to 2005. Comparatively young, these monks were current students or graduates of Mahachulalongkorn

University; the lay people were former monks studying at the university, or development workers in NGOs, including women.

The Phothiyalai Institute had its own advisory board and committee, which consisted of many senior development monks in northern Thailand, such as monk P, academic researchers, and well-known development workers, primarily around northern Thailand. Thus, it cannot be overlooked that lay development workers, NGOs, and external forces had an important influence on the network.

## Collective activities of the network

The main activities of the network at the collective level were meetings facilitating the exchange of information and discussion of experiences related to community development activities. Additionally, members sometimes visited other monks around northern Thailand to encourage one another.

The network had a relatively large meeting at a temple in Nan Province on August 25–26, 2005. There were about thirty monks from at least four provinces[25] in the North and seven lay people from the Phothiyalai Institute. The abbot of this temple, monk N, is famous for tree ordination (*buat ton mai*) across the country,[26] and was a part of the network from its inception. Because the other participants were highly interested in monk N's activities, they visited his office within the compound. In this way, a meeting of the network gave the monks an opportunity to encounter in an informal way others who shared an interest in community development activities.

On the first day, the meeting commenced with monk N's remarks, and then monk Z explained the goals of the meeting, which was to mark the fifth year of the network and review past activities thoroughly.[27] On the second day, they discussed their individual experiences in community development activities. During this discussion, a few senior monks, such as monk A and monk S, also spoke about their individual experiences with difficulties they faced while conducting community development activities.

First, they discussed the social roles of the Buddhist monks in contemporary Thailand. Monk A, who had been engaged for a long time in forest conservation and watershed management activities in Fang District, Chiang Mai, told them, "We monks should not make the villagers' matters worse. . . . We need to provide awareness (*sati*) to the villagers."

He insisted that monks should take the middle ground when they are engaged in community development activities. In fact, he had previously been caught in a conflict between the villagers and the developer of a large-scale orange-farming project in the local community. Monk A was regarded as an obstacle for the developer seeking economic profit because he had been engaged in protecting the community forest together with the local villagers. As the other monks had been interested in environmental issues or community development in general, they gave some questions to monk A and proceeded to discuss the experiences of each monk.

Another senior monk at the meeting, monk S, told them:

> As ordained monks, we have been dependent upon the villagers for everything to eat, wear, and live in. So, we monks have to repay their giving by helping to solve the problems they face. The villagers' hardships, which might occur from a lack of solidarity (*samakkhi*) among them, are also our hardships. That is why we monks are engaged in development works. Community development (*phatthana chumchon*) by the monks should help villagers lead better lives based on Buddhist morality and self-reliance.

Monk S had been engaged in poverty reduction for over thirty years in a rural area of San Sai District, a suburb of Chiang Mai city. The points that monk S emphasized were derived from his long-term activities that addressed the social problems the villagers faced in a rapidly changing local community. Young monks especially listened to his messages with great interest.

The ideas and thoughts about community development put forward by the senior monks of this network are found widely throughout the country. For example, the idea that the monks should give back to the villagers is also advocated by Luang Pho Nan,[28] the most famous development monk, and P. A. Payutto, the most renowned intellectual monk in Thailand. P. A. Payutto, the director of the Mahachulalongkorn Buddhist University, asserted in an article that "Monks are dependent upon the villagers for everything material. In order to repay the villagers for supporting the monks, monks should help the villagers to solve the problems in their everyday lives. The monks should play active roles in the contemporary world" (Phra Maha Prayut Payutto 1968).

These ideas are quite similar to the thoughts of other influential development workers, such as Prawet Wasi and his arguments about community culture based on Buddhist teachings (Prawet 1985, 91–92; 1988).[29] Prawet emphasized the role of Buddhism in community development, and his thoughts are primarily antistate, advocate the promotion of the community, and based on religious principles (precepts, meditation, and wisdom) (Chatthip 1991, 124–26).

Although monk A and monk S did not use the same words as P. A. Payutto and Prawet, they emphasized the importance of restoring solidarity among the villagers, and also the social roles of Buddhist monks as leaders who could promote morality in the local communities. Instead of referring directly to these development monks or development workers, they prefer to legitimize their community development activities with reference to the Buddha's teachings in the Tripitaka.[30] They usually explain their activities as the duties of monks that were given by the Buddha.

For most of the monks who joined the network, it was important to neither become disciples of any particular monk nor obtain any distinguishing collective identity of their own. Rather, they exchanged and shared their individual experiences in relation to community development activities through repeated discussion on the image of how an ideal monk should live in a changing society. On this point, the Phothiyalai Magazine (*Chulasan phothiyalai*), which is a small-sized magazine regularly published by the Phothiyalai Institute, also helped monks stay aware of the community development activities of other monks and rethink their own activities.

## Considerations

Having explored the case of the Community Development Monks' Network in Northern Thailand above, we will return now to clarifying the features of the network as a movement among the Buddhist monks in contemporary northern Thailand.

First, it is clear that this movement was constructed through the articulations of the internal and external actors of the network, the monks and multiple forces; in this movement the assemblage appeared as a dynamic and contingent configuration. The assemblage depicted in the case studied in this chapter is also far beyond the concepts of totality and essences, as DeLanda (2006, 9–10) and Escobar and Osterwiel (2010, 191) have written about.

All the monks who joined the network are from remote villages, and most were ordained as novices or monks in order to pursue opportunities in higher education. Both monk X and monk Y are from ethnic minorities in the Thailand-Myanmar border areas. The other monks can be roughly categorized into two groups. One is elder monks who are well known as veteran development monks in northern Thailand. Most of these are not as highly educated, but they have lengthy experience in community development activities. The other group is younger monks who have just graduated from or are currently studying at university. Some are from ethnic minorities from the border areas or from neighboring countries such as Laos and Myanmar. Monks of this group were also ordained to obtain higher education, and they have moved to the downtown or the suburbs of Chiang Mai city. Unlike the elder monks, they spend much of their time studying and so have less experience with community development activities.

Monks X, Y, and Z exemplify the variety of monks who got involved. No particular lineage of a certain monk or temple could be found among them. They had not shared any previous experiences, such as being brought up within the same village or in the same ethnic group, living at the same temple, or studying at the same school. They individually became engaged in community development activities, such as when monk X succeeded to his master's HIV/AIDS care activities, when monk Y joined the Thammacharik project in pursuit of higher education, and when monk Z began teaching at the Buddhist university. They had encountered each other by chance through the lay development workers or NGOs involved in the community development activities of each monk.

The factors influencing the composition of the network include not only younger monks and elder monks but also development workers, NGOs, ethnicity, the Thai government's policies, development projects, the farmer's protest movement, and others. These different components were gradually formed into an assemblage during the construction process of the network. These parts are, to use the words of Escobar and Osterwiel (2010, 191), "contingently obligatory."

Thus, the construction process of the monks' network should be understood in relation to the NGOs and the farmer's protest movement in northern Thailand in the late 1990s. Although this chapter does not deny the significance of vertical relationships between the monks, such as the master-disciple (*luksit-achan*) or senior-junior (*phi-nong*) relationships, which Tambiah has pointed out, we need to reconsider the reasons why the monks attempted to construct a new network beyond their traditional community, the sangha, and beyond their existing relationships.

Second, what enabled monks to construct the network through the assemblage consisting of multiple forces? This question brings us back to the life stories of the three monks, especially monk X.

As indicated earlier, community development activities have been part of the purpose of monk X's life as a Buddhist monk. When he recalled earlier days, from about ten years ago, he said that the only development monk he knew was his master, monk P. Although monk X succeeded to monk P's health care activities, he knew little about how to work with people with HIV/AIDS, villagers, and development workers in NGOs. He said, "Luang Pho[31] is my master, and also a good example to me of a development monk. . . . Yet, I do not have as much religious power [*barami*] as Luang Pho." He explained that this fact motivated him to join a variety of seminars and workshops held by NGOs relating to HIV/AIDS and other issues.

By joining these activities, he learned the importance of honing the skills to encourage villagers to express and discuss individual opinions and construct their own solutions to the social problems they faced. However, he also realized that such a skill was not available in the local community, because it neglected to take into account the differences in the local community: social class, economic status, ethnicity, and so on. The longer he was engaged in community development activities, the more he realized this fact. The problem, it seemed to him, was the lack of solidarity in the local community.

Participating in the collective activities of the network was meaningful to such monks. It allowed them to construct an ideal image of what it was to be development monks and also to be Buddhist monks in a rapidly changing society. In the cases of monks A and S, their discussions included these points. The monks of the network were not the disciples of any particular monk, so their conceptions of development monks differed. Yet they tried to understand the experiences of the others, both monks and lay development workers. They repeatedly discussed not only their concrete and individual experiences in community development activities but also their social roles in the contemporary world.

During this process, the monks of the network had come to identify themselves as community development monks who were devoted to solving the social problems people faced in the local community and to leading the people to live in a community based on Buddhist teachings and morality. According to monk X's explanation, he and the monks who joined the network were not development monks in general but were "community development monks." He meant that community development monks should be clearly distinguished from development monks, who emphasized material development such as building new facilities and restoring old temples.

Thus, each monk of the network could imagine a development-monk ideal that would share a situation or experience but not an identity (McDonald 2004, 589). Through their discussions with multiple groups, the monks seemed to patch together some fragmented ideas and thoughts on their community development work; these ideas were those of veteran development monks, well-known but never-seen development monks, influential development workers, and so on. The monks sometimes reflect on such knowledge, accessible through their joining the network, in their everyday practices in each local community, and they go on struggling to find their identities as Buddhist monks in this social world.

The emergence of the assemblage put together and shaped by both community-development monks and multiple other forces might be understood as an example of what McDonald (2004) calls "experience movements." Significant forms of experience movements cannot be analyzed in terms of collective identity, reflecting a social identity, but must be analyzed in terms of one's relationship to the other, in which the self becomes another (McDonald 2004, 590). Likewise, the network of monks featured as an experience movement does not represent any existing group, such as the sangha or an ethnic group, but represents a new way of constituting the social world for the monks in contemporary Thailand. This alerts us to reconsider the increasingly visible practices of those who struggle with globalized modernity and look for new spaces in which to share a situation and experience in today's world.

## NOTES

1. For sociological analysis on the emergence of development monks, and their social positions in northeastern Thailand, see Somboon (1977; 1981), Seri (1988), and Phinit (1986; 2007; 2012).

2. The Sekkhiyatham Group (*Klum sekkhiyatham*) was founded in 1989 by development monks in northeast Thailand with the support of Sulak Sivaraksa and the Inter-religious Committee for Development, organized on his initiative. Phra Phaisal Wisalo, a revered monk in Chaiyaphum, became the leader of the group. Others include the Lanna Community Development Sangha Group (*Klum sangkha phatthana chumchon Lanna*) in Chiang Mai, the Khorat Development Sangha (*Sangkha phatthana Khorat*) in Nakhon Ratchasima, the Mae Chan Monks Group (*Klum sangkha phrasong Mae Chan*) in Chiang Rai.

3. As Escobar and Osterwail (2010, 191) explain, "Assemblages are wholes characterized by relations of exteriority; the whole cannot be explained by the properties of components but by the actual exercise of the components' capacities."

4. During 2012–14, I conducted fieldwork mainly in Chiang Mai (Mueang, San Sai, Doi Saket, Mae Rim, Samoeng, and Wiang Haeng Districts) and in some other provinces, such as Chiang Rai, Phrae, Nan, and Tak. The subjects were eight monks and seven lay people (including former monks) who were a part of this network.

5. Tai Yai, one of the Tai-speaking ethnic groups, is the second-largest ethnic minority in Thailand.

6. *Palien* is a grade of *Pali* studies in Thailand. It has nine levels.

7. *Naktham* is a grade of *dhamma* studies in Thailand. It has three levels: primary, intermediate, and advanced.

8. Monk P was born in Nan in northern Thailand in 1945. He was ordained as a novice and a monk there, and then moved to Wat Buppharam in the city of Chiang Mai to pursue educational opportunities. He was one of the disciples of Monk W, the abbot of Wat Buppharam and as the head of Chiang Mai Provincial Sangha until 2009. Monk W is famous for a variety of community development activities around Chiang Mai, and Doi Saket in particular, from the early 1970s (Gosling 1981; 1983).

9. A *bhikkhu* (*phiksu* in Thai) is a monk over twenty-one years old. *Samanera* (*samanen* in Thai) is a monk under twenty-one years old. A *bhikkhu* is distinguished from a *samanera* in terms of the number of precepts kept.

10. See Chiranut (1999) and Seri (1996).

11. Per interviews with monk X conducted on March 22, 2005, and September 1, 2007.

12. The data on monk Y is based on an interview with him on March 4, 2011, in Bangkok. The other publications are used here complementally. Unfortunately, he suddenly passed away in a traffic accident in July of 2011, when he was only forty-one years old.

13. Lisu is one of the non-Tai-speaking ethnic minorities in Thailand, as well as the Karen, Hmong, Akha, Lahu, and so on. Most of them follow Christianity and live in the mountainous area in northern Thailand, Laos, and southwest China.

14. Thammacharik is a project run by the Department of Public Welfare, Ministry of Interior, since 1965. *Thammacharik* means "traveling to disseminate the *dhamma*." This comes from the Buddha's teaching that "all monks must travel to teach *dhamma*, for the sake of happiness, to people all over the world." Yet the Thammacharik project was an extension of the many programs and organizations set up by the government to "develop" the hill tribe people (Kwanchewan 2003, 247–48). The program's objectives were (1) to develop a belief in Buddhism, and (2) to strengthen the sense of Thai nationality among the hill tribe people (Somboon 1977, 104).

15. This is the former Chiang Mai Teacher's College.

16. The Ashoka Fellowship is a project of the Ashoka Innovators for the Public, a non-profit organization founded in the US. This provides financial support to outstanding social entrepreneurs who give solutions to social problems and have the potential to change patterns across society. There are about three thousand fellows in over seventy countries around the world.

17. This movement was partly derived from a nationwide protest movement called the "Assembly of the Poor," which sought to solve the problems faced by poor farmers after the economic crisis and the implementation of the "people's constitution" in 1997. See Baker (2000).

18. The others were Karen and Khon Mueang monks from Chiang Mai and a Khon Mueang monk from Phayao. All of them dwelled at temples in the city of Chiang Mai and its suburbs .

19. Taken from interviews with with three lay development workers on February 22, February 26, and March 6, 2012, respectively. All of them worked in community development with Phra Thep Kawi. For more on the philosophy and activities of Phra Thep Kawi, see Darlington (1990).

20. This is a village dominated by the Karen, the largest ethnic group among the non-Tai-speaking ethnic minorities mainly living in the mountainous areas of Thailand.

21. Regarding the details of the group's activities, see Somchai (1995).

22. The YMCA of Chiang Mai was founded in the late 1950s.

23. For example, the idea was the focus of his PhD dissertation submitted to Delhi University in 1997, entitled "Role of Monks and Monasteries in Social Affairs of Thailand."

24. This was a kind of poverty reduction program that existed from the late 1980s until 2001 and provided about $3.5 billion from the World Bank to fifty-eight different countries. The Thai government promised to implement Social Investment Fund initiatives in 1998 in order to solve the problems caused by the economic crisis in July 1997. The fund was distributed through NGOs.

25. The participants list from this meeting indicated twenty-eight monks from four provinces: ten from Chiang Mai, one from Chiang Rai, two from Phrae, and thirteen from Nan. The origin of the other two monks is unknown because they did not register at the meeting.

26. This is a Buddhist ritual performed by the monks to protect trees from being cut down. See Darlington (1997; 1998; 2003).

27. Until that time, the network seems to have had countless activities carried out by individual monks all over northern Thailand. The monks intended to set up translocal zones depending on the issues that each monk dealt with.

28. See Phitthaya (1993).

29. It can be supposed that Father Niphot Thianwihan, the director of the Catholic Council for Development of Thailand, also has great influence on the ideas and thoughts of this network. He is a prominent development worker who has engaged in community development activities, mostly in the mountainous areas of northern Thailand. His activities are based on his own philosophy about "community culture," which stems from his faith in Christianity. He was a member of the advisory board of the Phothiyalai Institute as well.

30. Tripitaka (Pali: Tipitaka) means three baskets: the Sutra Pitaka, Vinaya Pitaka, and Abhidharma Pitaka. These are the categories of various Buddhist canons containing the Buddha's teachings.

31. *Luang pho* is a general noun and demonstrative pronoun in Thai that is used to refer to monks who belong to the same generation as the father of the speaker. In this context, "*luang pho*" was meant to refer to monk P.

REFERENCES

Baker, Chris. 2000. "Thailand's Assembly of the Poor: Background, Drama, Reaction." *South East Asia Research* 8(1): 5–29.

Chatthip Nartsupha. 1991. "The Community Culture School of Thought." In *Thai Constructions of Knowledge*, edited by Manas Chitakasem and Andrew Turton, 118–41. London: School of Oriental and African Studies.

Chiranut Wonguthai. 1999. "Botbat phrasong nai kan songkhro chumchon panha rok et: Karani sueksa Phra Khru Sophonpariyattisuthi Wat Doi Saket Changwat Chiang Mai" [The role of Buddhist monks in community social work on the

AIDS problem: Case study of Phra Khru Sophonpariyattisuthi of Wat Doi Saket in Chiang Mai Province]. Master's thesis, Chiang Mai University.

Darlington, Susan M. 1990. "Buddhism, Morality and Change: The Local Response to Development in Northern Thailand." PhD diss., University of Michigan.

————. 1997. "Not Only Preaching: The Work of the Ecology Monk Phrakhru Pitak Nantakhun of Thailand." *Forest, Trees and People Newsletter* 34:17–19.

————. 1998. "The Ordination of a Tree: The Buddhist Ecology Movement of Thailand." *Ethnology* 37(1): 1–16.

————. 2003. "Buddhism and Development: The Ecology Monks of Thailand." In *Action Dharma: New Studies in Engaged Buddhism*, edited by Christopher S. Queen, 96–109. London: Routledge Curzon.

DeLanda, Manuel. 2006. *A New Philosophy of Society: Assemblage Theory and Social Complexity*. London: Continuum.

Escobar, Arturo. 1995. *Encountering Development: The Making and Unmaking of the Third World*. New Jersey: Princeton University Press.

Escobar, Arturo, and Michael Osterweil. 2010. "Social Movements and the Politics of the Virtual: Deleuzian Strategies." In *Deleuzian Intersections: Science, Technology, Anthropology*, edited by Casper B. Jensen and Kjetil Rödje, 187–217. New York: Berghahn Books.

Gosling, David L. 1981. "Thai Monks in Rural Development." *Southeast Asian Journal of Social Science* 9(1–2): 74–85.

————. 1983. "Redefining the Sangha's Role in Northern Thailand: An Investigation of Monastic Careers at Five Chiang Mai Wats." *Journal of the Siam Society* 71:89–120.

Kiattisak Muangmit. 2004. "Kansueksa lae phatthana sakkayaphap khueakhai phrasong: Karani sueksa phra nak phatthana chumchon phak nuea" [The study and development of potential of monks' networking: Case study of the Community Development Monks' Network in northern Thailand]. Report. Community Organizations Development Institute.

*Krungthep Thurakit*. 2002. "Chut prakai: Rueang phiset" [Flashpoint: Special story].

Kwanchewan Buadaeng. 2003. *Buddhism, Christianity, and the Ancestors: Religion and Pragmatism in A Skaw Karen Community of Northern Thailand*. Chiang Mai: Sprint.

McDonald, Kevin K. 2004. "Oneself as Another: From Social Movement to Experience Movement." *Current Sociology* 52(4): 575–93.

Phinit Laptananon. 1986. *Botbat phrasong nai kan phatthana chonnabot* [The role of Buddhist monks in rural development]. Bangkok: Social Research Institute, Chulalongkon University.

————. 2007. *30 Phrasong nak phatthana den nai phak Isan 2546-2547* [30 outstanding development monks in northeastern Thailand, 2003-2004]. Bangkok: Social Research Institute, Chulalongkorn University.

————. 2012. *Development Monks in Northeast Thailand*. Kyoto: Kyoto University Press.

Phitthaya Wongkul. 1993. *Luang Pho Nan: Sangop ning phuea sang san* [Luang Pho Nan: Calm to be creative]. Bangkok: Muban.

Phra Maha Prayut Payutto. 1968. "Problems, Status and Duties of the Sangha in Modern Society." *Visakha Puja* B.E. 2511: 58–71.

Prawet Wasi. 1985. *Satharanasuk kap Phutthatham* [Public health and the Buddha dharma]. Bangkok: Komonkhimthong Foundation.

————. 1988. "Sasontham kap kan phatthana muban" [Buddhist teachings and village development]. In *Thitthang muban Thai* [Directions of Thai villages], edited by Seri Phongphit. Bangkok: Village Foundation, Rural Development Institute.

Seri Phongphit. 1988. *Religion in a Changing Society: Buddhism, Reform and the Role of Monks in Community Development in Thailand*. Hong Kong: Arena Press.

————. 1996. *23 Prasopkan kan thamngan kiaokap rok et phak nuea khong Thai* [23 experiences of working with AIDS in northern Thailand]. Bangkok: Ministry of Public Health.

Somboon Suksamran. 1977. *Political Buddhism in Southeast Asia*. London: C. Hurst & Company.

————. 1981. "Religion, Politics and Development: The Thai Sangha's Role in National Development and Integration." *Southeast Asian Journal of Social Science* 9(1–2): 54–73.

Somchai Lekphet. 1995. "Wikhro ngan khong phrasong nai thana thi pen phu nam phatthana chumchon" [An analysis of the work of Buddhist monks as leaders of community development]. Master's thesis, Chiang Mai University

Tambiah, Stanley J. 1976. *World Conqueror and World Renouncer: A Study of Buddhism and Polity in Thailand against a Historical Background*. Cambridge: Cambridge University Press.

Tanabe, Shigeharu, ed. 2008. *Imagining Communities in Thailand: Ethnographic Approaches*. Chiang Mai: Mekong Press.

# DETOXIFICATION
## A Practice to Reform Medical Knowledge

MALEE SITTHIKRIENGKRAI

## Introduction

Over the last two decades, the social movement in the health domain could be divided into two movements: one involving medical personnel and another undertaken by the people themselves. During the 2000s, the most significant contribution of the first movement was health reform. During this initiative, civil society took part in this attempt for health-care reform with the aim of boosting heath awareness among common people as well as helping them to better understand how to take care of their own health so that they do not have be dependent on health services. In other words, it is a strategy of *sang nam som* (literally "prevention before cure"). This movement supported the push for a new law, the National Health Act of 2007 (Kritaya and Kulapa 2008). An earlier movement, led by people and patients, emerged in 1992. It encompassed various approaches to health care—for instance, the HIV/AIDS network which demanded the right to self-care, the network of cancer patients which gradually formed the Cheewa Jitr Group under the guidance of Dr. Sathit Indharakamkaeng, as well as several other alternative health-care initiatives which included natural healing, macrobiotic treatment, vegetarian food consumption, and so on. Both movements can be conceptually seen as "new social movements" that provide social space for people to choose alternative ways to take care of their own health. This entails a radical change of power—from medical doctors and experts to common people—in caring for health. Even though the first movement allows some space for people to participate, it has its own collective identity. It is regulated and controlled by law; it has an institution, and it obviously needs a political mechanism to push for reform (Mills 1997; Komatra 2004).

This chapter analyzes a detoxification group in Thailand. I joined this group for a detoxification training workshop in October 2012 at Sisa Asoke Community in Kantharalak District, Si Sa Ket Province. Through participant observation, I discovered that detoxification is not only alternative health care but is also a kind of social movement that is different from other health movements like those mentioned above. This detoxification practice renders a new perspective toward health and body different from the contemporary modern medicine. This study benefits from the concept of "new social movement," or what McDonald (2004) calls "experience movement," in explaining the social movement represented by the detoxification group. I will begin by explaining the concept, and then describe the activities in the detoxification training workshop as a process of social movement which changes our understanding of body and illness.

## Experience Movement

According to McDonald (2004), the social movements during the 1960s–1980s were largely linked to political activism as well as leading to collective identity. Each individual who joined the movement transformed his or her own identity to take on the identity of the movement, as in the case of labor movement, which struggled against the state and then transformed into a socialist movement. This process can be called a "movement of identification," which is a concept that is often used to reflect a group's potentiality. This collective identity is meaningful and important for the group because it renders power to the group and makes available for the group a social position that can bring about social change. On the other hand, "experience movement" has a different meaning because it puts an emphasis on the exchange of experiences, information, situations, or what is understood as "movements of expression." The exchange of experiences is not meant to find a collective identity for those who join the movement because their individual experiences differ from one another. They join the movement out of their own interest and do not necessarily participate in the movement continuously. McDonald gives two examples to illustrate his concept of experience movement: Falun Gong and the antiglobalization movement.

The website of Falun Gong in Thailand (www.falunthai.org) describes the movement as involving high-level meditation practice that allows an individual to integrate three basic principles: truth, benevolence, and forbearance. It is a process of self-transformation from within, and regular practice will enable development of the mind. McDonald draws upon Farquhar (1996), who claims that the practice has healed both sufferers and the healers leading them, spurring them to become decent individual beings who have a good and responsible conscience or "intensified personhood." The characteristics of these individuals are rather different from those of people in the nineteenth century, when rationality was emphasized. Falun Gong has spread quickly since 1992. It has more than 100 million members in more than eighty countries. However, it has not been recognized by the Chinese government.

The antiglobalization movement, on the other hand, is a new political movement focusing on emerging issues that are sometimes neglected, such as cross-border trade, women, and the environment. The nature of the movement is more or less like a network rather than a group or community. McDonald uses the case of the Quaker activists who were against nuclear proliferation in 1970s as an example. The antinuclear movement came from a genuine concern for human life and resources which might be harmed and lost. Two of the highest-profile activists, an American husband and wife, drew upon Quaker ideas in their campaign against nuclear weapons, making the antinuclear ideals spread widely. Crucially, the relationships within the antinuclear group were based on group affinity; however, the group was not formed as an organization. Most importantly, it did not aim to topple the government but was a group of people who shared a common interest or a concern about a common problem. Once their mission was completed, they disbanded. Members of the group worked together based upon each individual's different capacity and skills, which were not related to their former status (McDonald 2004).

In his article, McDonald asserts that he does not want to describe in detail nor deeply analyze both movements. He only wants to point out a new trend among social movements, which emphasizes exchange and sharing of experiences rather than trying to search for collective identity. It is my contention that the detoxification practice can be understood as an experience movement as described by McDonald. However, I will go further to analyze some case studies that show how detoxification practice transforms the individual self.

## From Alternative Community to Alternative Health

The birth of the Santi Asoke Community Network around the mid-1970s came from belief in the teachings of Phra Bodhiraksa or Samana Phothirak, or Pho Than as he is called by the Asokians. From the gathering of the Yatidham (Dhamma relatives) at Pathom Asoke Community in 1980 until the present, Santi Asoke has sown the seeds of their teaching in such a way that nine communities have been established, in Nakhon Pathom, Bangkok, Si Sa Ket, Nakhon Ratchasima, Nakhon Sawan, Chiang Mai, Ubon Ratchathani, Chaiyaphum, and Trang. These communities follow a common lifestyle with a unique identity. For example, women are supposed to wear short hair. Both men and women dress in indigo, wear no shoes, and do not use any cosmetics. They have polite manners, they abstain from eating meat, and they strictly observe five or eight Buddhist precepts. For their self-sufficient livelihood, members of the community practice organic farming. Besides, they uphold social mechanisms of checks and balances between the clergy and the lay people, with Pho Than as the spiritual leader unifying all the members together. The formation of Santi Asoke during this time can be seen as a community movement with a collective identity that emphasizes "we-ness."

Detoxification was pioneered by the Sisa Asoke Community, but the detoxification group is not limited only to Santi Asoke members, the Yatidham. I observed that some participants had not known of Santi Asoke before. Once they attended the detoxification program, they began to reflex upon their way of life and the diseases they were encountering. In attending the detoxification program under the supervision and care of Santi Asoke, the participants did not come to experience the "we-ness," but their purpose was to improve their health situation. However, each individual's definition of good health varies a great deal. For those who have severe health problems, good health means an ability to help oneself. In some cases, good health means longevity or just being free from chronic illness and ailments.

## Detoxification Training Program and Movement of Expression

Generally, detoxification is an effort to get rid of waste or foul elements from the body system. It is not a new health remedy but was used before the emergence of biomedicine. However, this chapter will not examine detoxification in the past but will focus on detoxification provided by Sisa Asoke Community in Si Sa Ket Province.

The people who played a vital role in developing and implementing the detoxification program were Achan Khwandin and Achan Kaenfa. The former gave an account of the detoxification program beginnings in 2005. A member of the Santi Asoke community came to ask for a reimbursement for detoxification and intestinal cleaning. Since such expenses were not included in community welfare, the request was rejected. That was the beginning of Khwandin's curiosity. During the time, Achan Kaenfa became ill and began to experiment detoxification with other Yatidham. Upon seeing that the health of some Yatidham improved after detoxification, Achan Khwandin decided to try it herself and accumulated knowledge about detoxification. From 2006 until 2008, detoxification became widely known in Thai society and it was better received than other activities carried out by Sisa Asoke with the surrounding communities, such as a campaign in support of organic farming and others to reduce or eliminate the consumption of alcohol and tobacco. People increasingly participated in detoxification. Many of those who attended detoxification programs with Santi Asoke used the knowledge gained through their experiences to help set up eighty-one independent detoxification centers.

The training workshop took five days. The course which I took began on October 22, 2012. When I arrived at Sisa Asoke, it was about six in the evening. I had not anticipated seeing so many people there. Later, I learned that a total of ninety-four people were attending this course. When I looked around, I noticed that most people were over forty years old. A few teenagers were among our group. Interestingly, one teenage girl came from Korea.

Activities on all five days were similar: waking up in the morning without brushing teeth followed by oil pulling, exercise, foot soaking, covering the face with curcuma powder, and detoxification twice daily— before drinking Lidtox, an herbal drink for cleansing the intestine, in the morning, and around five or six in the evening. Lidtox was drunk three times a day, around 9:00 a.m., noon, and 3:00 p.m. During some afternoons, participants who were knowledgeable about alternative health care would share their knowledge on body massage, how to balance body systems by affixing seeds to specific acupuncture points on the ear, making herbal balls for hot press, Chinese martial arts, and so on. In addition, a few participants with professional skills also provided services for other participants. For instance, a participant who was a beautician did hairdressing for other participants, while another who has some experience in using universal energy for healing also provided services free of charge.

The fifth day of the training program was the preparation day for liver detoxification. Each would drink Lidtox juice only twice and refrained from drinking anything after 3:00 p.m. in order to be ready for liver detoxification with a mixture of olive oil and lemon juice. The toxin sweeper was virgin olive oil, the taste of which I found nauseating. The lemon juice was meant to make it taste better. Around 10:00 p.m., everyone was anxious, waiting for the moment the resource person would ask them to hold a bottle of olive oil and stand outside their room. A few seconds before 10 o'clock, the resource person started to count down and then asked participants to shake the bottle all at the same time and drink the oil immediately. I intended to drink it all at once but I could not. I wanted to vomit, so I paused briefly and then finished the whole bottle. I had to take some tamarind to reduce the nauseated feeling.

That night, everyone went to sleep with much anxiety because the resource person told us emphatically that in the previous courses several participants could not sleep, felt fidgety, and vomited around two in the morning. In addition, after this, we would have to release from our system into small buckets for Achan Khwandin to examine in the morning. I was very apprehensive and uncertain about what would happen. But everything went well. Some participants woke up in the middle of the night and vomited. For me, I could see clearly the feces I discharged. I realized how bad the smell was. However, Achan Khwandin, who had to examine every participant's feces, did not show any dislike; she investigated it and explained how its characteristics indicated the abnormality of the owner's body.

When all the detoxification activities were completed, everyone was ready to go home. But before we parted, we ate one last vegetarian meal together. This meal was most delicious after having not eaten for a few days.

During the five days of the detoxification training workshop, Achan Khwandin and other resource persons always reminded us that what they did was an act of merit-making. At the same time, participants also came to make merit or to receive merit as well. The acts of merit-making began with fasting, wearing comfortable clothing, and transforming the original self to a new self, constructed within the workshop. Everyone must collect merit regardless of social or economic status. From dawn, everyone must help each other with preparing herbal beverages, cleaning toilets, cleaning the floor, collecting herbs, cleaning waste buckets, and other chores.

All of these activities cultivated friendship among the participants and reduced social and occupational cleavages among them, leading to exchanges of experiences and creating social space where they could discuss. I noticed that during the first days of the workshop, the participants hardly spoke to one another. But during the last day, they worked together without any segregation. They interacted and shared, as in the case of a university lecturer who was responsible for filling a basin with hot water for the foot soaking of a farmer. This cannot happen in the larger society outside. But this detoxification program made the participants transcend their selves and become new selves who accepted others.

Besides, I noticed that Achan Khwandin and other Yatidham showed to us that they came to make merit as well. Achan Khwandin stayed with participants and took part in the training until 10:00 p.m. She woke up at 4:30 a.m. and thereafter would be busy all the time. Even though she was busy, she would meet with anyone. When she met other people, she would smile and greet each politely. She ate only one meal a day and wore no shoes. Her personality made the participants admire her act of merit-making, especially during the last day when she examined the feces of all participants. Achan Khwandin did not show any of her dislike. She told us,

> When we think we want to give, we must really give without any condition. The foul smell and the dirtiness teach us to realize the

reality. Nothing is permanent. If we do not have any attachment, we wash it out, and it will go away. Whether it smells badly or not, it depends upon our mind. Everything is in fact a supposition. If we train ourselves regularly, we will feel that it is wonderful; it is wonderful in the sense that we possess nothing at all. There is nothing real for our life. But we can find happiness—happiness comes from giving.

The philosophy of merit-making is upheld by the Santi Asoke followers. It has been used in the detoxification program as well. This is what makes the Santi Asoke detoxification program different from other programs—it is not only a detoxification of the body but a detoxification of the mind as well.

Detoxification practices have incorporated some existing principles found in Santi Asoke—that is, the principle of *bun niyom* as seen in how a certain action is interpreted as merit-making. What merit is—and it cannot be empirically observed—must be realized through, and within, oneself. When one makes merit, one will feel happy, similar to Qigong exercise, which basically is a form of body training through the control of breathing and also a training of the mind done in a group. The practice of merit-making teaches us the meaning of giving, helping, and sharing based upon our own capacity. It changes an individual's attitude and perception toward how to lead one's life and relationship with the outside world. It is essentially a transformation from within that an individual can realize and act out differently. This kind of social movement is developed from diversity and from people of different backgrounds. It is a movement of expression.

## To Understand the Body and Illness

Illness is not an enemy and is not always bad. It is a signal for a person to know that there is a disorder in their life, attitude, or other area. It is a warning for people to change something to balance their life again.

This message was posted in the training room. The attitude behind this message is a different approach from Western medicine, which looks at illness as an enemy: germs are enemies that come to attack and destroy the body; cancer cells are abnormal cells that exploits the organs. To make a person healthy again, cancer cells, germs and abnormal cells must be killed or their growth stopped by strong chemicals. In contrast, the message above perceives illness only as a warning signal for the patients to balance themselves again.

The training course at Sisa Asoke repeatedly mentioned toxins in the body's alimentary canal and digestion system. Achan Khwandin and other speakers explain that the system collects all refuse from what we eat. To be healthy, we need to take it all out. They use pictures, multimedia, and research findings from Thailand and abroad to bolster the scientific credentials of detoxification.

The organs mostly mentioned in the detoxification course were the liver, gallbladder, and intestines. Undigested food, foods with chemical addititves, carbonated soft drinks, and junk food all change the body's balanced state to be more acidic. This increased acidity will erode body organs and become toxic.

Another topic was the biological clock, a concept which helps participants understand how each of the twelve organs works together during each day. They include the liver, lungs, large intestine, stomach, spleen, heart, small intestine, urinary bladder, kidney, pericardium, the thermoregulatory system, and the gallbladder. One point that is emphasized is being able to make lifestyle changes at a fitting time for each organ; for example, eleven o'clock at night is said to be the time of the gallbladder, while one to three in the morning is the liver time. That is why we needed to drink olive oil at ten o'clock at night, as we were told that is the time the gallbladder is most open to draining toxins and gallstones, and the liver can get rid of toxins more easily. Understanding the biological clock can help in scheduling lifestyle changes to achieve balance and a healthy life.

To convince participants that their bodies have toxins, the speakers showed academic data. This was confirmed again with the evidence from each participant's stool defecated after the liver detoxification during the last day, as this stool was an indicator of each person's health. Achan Khwandin is the one who examines stool on the last day of the detoxification training programs. In general, she will just look and stir with a stick but in special cases, such as stool with blood clots or an unusually strong smell, she will squeeze it with her hand and smell closely. The detoxification training course gave new knowledge of the body and illness to participants, explaining that illness comes from meat and other unhealthy food that causes toxins to accumulate inside the body. Therefore, treating illness by defecating toxins out of body and seeing toxins come out in their own stool makes participants understand the relationship of their health to the food they eat. So they start to review their eating habits and become more willing to change themselves.

As mentioned earlier, detoxification is not new at all; it has been practiced for more than a thousand years. In the case of the detoxification at Sisa Asoke Community, the incorporation of the principle of balanced systems, which is the foundation of Oriental medical science, has made it more reliable, allowing for a new interpretation and making the new knowledge more empirically verifiable with photographic evidence. This process leads to new scientific knowledge accepted by the middle class, who differentiate it from other alternative medicines which are largely lacking of scientific evidence. The detoxification process, which has been widely recognized, comes from the way in which illness is explained from feces of the patients. The fact that each patient sees his own feces as the deposit of poison from his or her body system enables close reflection on the vulnerabilities caused by all kinds of food contaminated by poison as well as danger from air pollution, all related to the fast pace of life or what Beck (1992) calls the "risk society." Confronted with evidence, participants of the training workshop gain agency and become more reflexive and mindful about their risky lifestyles.

## Illness and Relationships

This part will explain the personal reflections of some participants, demonstrating how some individuals reflect differently despite all receiving the same training.

One participant was a forty-year-old male who became acquainted with the Sisa Asoke group during political activities in 2006. He admitted his eating habits were not punctual; he slept late and was a workaholic. When he was twenty-seven years old, he got migraines and coughed blood clots. He was treated by Western medicine for a long time and had to take more and more medicine. He was admitted to the hospital when in too much pain. He also had asthma as a congenital disease, for which he took medicine all his life. When he was grown up, he often had a fever (every two weeks). He switched between being treated by doctors and self-medicating. He had to take antibiotic medicine for a sore throat, and the more medicine he took, the sicker he became. The doctor told him that he must complete the prescribed antibiotic dose or otherwise the disease would become resistant. He had other illnesses and had to take medicine constantly. Then he found that he had high cholesterol and high blood sugar despite his age and healthy weight. Later on, he had blood tests to find the cause of his asthma and allergic reactions. His blood was tested with five hundred types of foods, revealing that he is allergic to milk, eggs, and twenty-seven other types of food. He stopped eating the allergy-causing food and his migraine headaches improved. He got to know alternative treatments and researched the body. He decided to try detoxification as one alternative treatment. He explained, "Illness caused by our habits means we need to improve these habits."

This led him to understand more about his body and its working system, such as how during a high fever the white blood cells will work faster to protect the body from disease and bacteria. Taking medicine will make white blood cells lose the opportunity to work. He used his body to try alternative treatments and became a facilitator to conduct research on detoxification and alternative health care.

Another man, a fifty-year-old university academic, was diagnosed in 2011 with a blocked heart blood vessel and was told that he needed an operation to enlarge the blood vessel, which would cost 600,000 baht. He would be able to get reimbursed for the cost, but he thought it was too much and also that he may not be cured by the operation. Furthermore, he thought he was not that sick. When his older sister, who had cancer, felt better after attending a detoxification course, she recommended that he join the training in Sisa Asoke. He was treated as a special case and received one-on-one treatment. During his first detoxification, he passed twelve big pieces of stool, which is unusual. The second time, he filled the bucket with his stool and blood. The third time, he passed stool with gallstones, blood clots, and fat. After a stay in the hospital, he continued his fourth and fifth courses. Achan Khwandin made herbal tea for his detoxification; his bruised skin improved and he had more energy. He strongly criticized conventional treatments for not allowing patients to undergo herbal detoxification or other alternative treatments. The doctors scoffed at him and other patients when they found that patients used other treatments. With Sisa Asoke, he was pleased to let the center use his body to try alternative treatments and detoxification to avoid the expensive conventional treatment. He also thinks health knowledge, like recognition of detoxification, has changed, but health workers, doctors, and nurses are still far behind.

One of the women there was a fifty-eight-year-old school administrator from the northeast. Her parents died of cancer, so she was looking after her younger siblings and their children, which made her stressed because the children did not listen to her and she had conflicts with the new school director. With a large body, she did not look ill but she told of suffering from chronic constipation, causing pain in her abdomen and affecting her appetite, for five years. She liked to eat meat and starchy food. She tried treatments in many places. She was afraid of having cancer like her parents, so she agreed to a private hospital's plan to undergo blood detoxification for over one hundred thousand baht, but it did not treat her problem. Her health problems made her lose confidence and worry when she traveled. She is a school friend of Achan Khwandin and reconnected with her after a long time. Achan Khwandin suggested an anal detoxification and that she attend the detoxification training course. She said that the detoxification course at Sisa Asoke was different from other places as this place taught each participant to change their lifestyle and to exercise and eat vegetables and fruits. She was very attentive to speakers, and she woke up early to exercise, walking around Sisa Asok Community. She said, "I never knew a community like this existed—small house, no TV and electronic appliances."

These three cases represent the variety of motivations participants have in attending the detoxification training. All the participants in the detoxification training workshop essentially want to get out of Western medicine, even though such treatment has an influence upon their lives and illnesses. These individuals also try to resist the hegemony of the differentiated Western medicine. Participants can be classified into three groups.

The first group seeks new knowledge and includes people like Achan Khwandin and Achan Kaenfa. During the detoxification training workshop, I observed that some patients agreed to participate in trials of different formulae. Achan Khwandin told me that she is not a medical doctor but has been interested in finding a new body of knowledge. She has tried to access a large amount of information through the Internet, books, and articles, as well as learning from medical doctors and other resource persons. This has enabled her to apply what she has learned to each individual patient. Achan Kaenfa, on the other hand, after he discovered that he had contracted hepatitis B and was told by his doctor that he had a high likelihood of getting cancer, has tried to find out ways to care for himself. He began to undergo detoxification by himself, experimenting with various formulae, trying different herbal medicines and in different combinations until he discovered the formula that is being used at Sisa Asoke Community. Such acquisition of knowledge based on experience is quite common among traditional healers and practitioners of Oriental medicine. It is a learning process from actual and empirical problems; it is an evidence-based, not theory-based, type of learning, unlike the process of learning in modern Western medicine.

The second group does not want to develop new knowledge but is looking to participate in experimentation. As with the male university academic discussed above, in Western medicine, the self of a patient in this group becomes an "object" which has no individual voice. However, in the detoxification process, the relationship between the healer or the experimenter and those who lend their bodies for experimentation is reciprocal. It is collaboration in the production of new knowledge.

The third group consists of general participants; those who belong to this level can be exemplified by the female school executive. They are the ones who try to find alternative ways to care for themselves; they are not patients with any serious health problems, although some had been afflicted by cancer and received Western medical treatment that stopped the growth of the cancer cells. They came for detoxification in order to get rid of the residual poisonous elements in their body.

To summarize, those in the first group search for new knowledge in order to resist the dominant medical knowledge, individuals in the second group lend their bodies for the construction of new knowledge, and those in the third group are searching for different health-care systems. If the latter individuals find detoxification suitable for them, they may change to be in the first or second group. In contrast, if they find a better health-care system, they will be ready to adopt it. However, the three groups are related to one another and aid the construction of new knowledge, based on exchanges and interactions, which leads to a change of knowledge about the body and illness.

One important feature of the change is group affinity. Individuals are not connected to one another by kinship relation, but they show concern for one another as if they were related by blood. Such relationships can be observed in the way they help each other in keeping the venue of the training workshop clean and in their willingness to participate in experimental techniques. McDonald (2004) explains that this type of social movement is not continuous. He claims that the group affinity exists for the period of action and then dissolves, only to come together at the next action. Similarly, the detoxification group also comes together and then dissolves; however, it continues as a group for information exchange and developing and sharing knowledge. The group solidarity is based upon mutual trust, cooperation, and social obligation toward one another.

## Conclusion

At the surface level, detoxification is often seen only as an alternative health-care practice. As a result, the state's health-care development scheme often tries to integrate it into mainstream health services. Such an attempt tends to look for a structural space within the mainstream medical system for alternative health care, and the importance of the individual's potentiality is neglected.

In this chapter, I have tried to explain the potential of the individual in the detoxification group, who tries to maintain personal control and attain improved health—the "subject" who works together with other individuals to establish a new "community." This new community differs from the community commonly defined by social scientists, and can be called a "community of practice" (Wenger, 1998), which is constructed based upon the knowledge of experiences of its members' illnesses. The process of knowledge production is not from experts or professionals; such a process is often criticized by the mainstream medicine as nonscientific or illegitimate knowledge.

Another interesting feature of this community of practice is that the Sisa Asoke detoxification group is developed out of the Santi Asoke community, which has a highly distinguished collective identity. The community has established its own regulations, prohibiting meat consumption and controlling the body and behavior. But the detoxification group is flexible and open to a multiplicity of membership. At the same time, it adopts the *bun niyom* concept of the Santi Asoke community as its own principle. For example, it prohibits meat consumption, encourages a simple and modest livelihood, and emphasizes devotion of oneself toward collective ends. All activities help raise new awareness of living together in society. Detoxification in this sense is therefore a process of balancing one's body and mind at the same time.

The potential of the individual may decenter the mainstream medical knowledge to some extent, but it enables individuals to gain a new understanding of the body and health. The "subject" both maintains control and comes from the collective experience of the movement.

## REFERENCES

Beck, Ulrich. 1992. *Risk Society: Towards a New Modernity*. London: Sage.

Chen, Nancy. 2003. *Breathing Spaces: Qigong, Psychiatry and Healing in China*. New York: Columbia University Press.

Farquhar, Judith. 1996. "Market Magic: Getting Rich and Getting Personal after Mao." *American Ethnologist* 23(2): 239–57.

Komatra Chuengsatiansup. 2004. *Sam pi bon sen thang pathirup rabop sukkhaphap haeng chat* [Three years on the path of national health system reform]. Nonthaburi: National Health System Reform Office.

Kritaya Archavanitkul and Kulapa Vajanasara. 2008. *Bot samruat watthakam lae kan muang rueang samatcha sukkhaphap.* [Exploring discourse and politics on the health assembly]. *Warasan sangkhomsat mahawitthayalai Chiang Mai* [Journal of the Faculty of Social Science, Chiang Mai University] 20(1): 113–42.

McDonald, Kevin. 2004. "Oneself as Another: From Social Movement to Experience Movement." *Current Sociology* 52(4): 575–93.

Mill, Anne. 1997. "Current Policy Issues in Health Care Reform from an International Perspective: The Battle between Bureaucrats and Marketeers." In *Health Care Reform at the Frontier of Research and Policy Decisions*, edited by Sanguan Nitayarumphong. Nonthaburi, Thailand: Office of Health Care Reform, Ministry of Public Health.

Wenger, Etienne. 1998. *Communities of Practice: Learning, Meaning, and Identity.* Cambridge: Cambridge University Press.

# CONTRIBUTORS

TOSHIHIRO ABE is associate professor at the Department of Literature, Otani University (Japan). His research interests focus on community-level mediation in the multinational urban milieu and reconciliation in transitional justice projects with specific reference to the cases of South Africa and Cambodia. His recent works include "Perceptions of the Khmer Rouge Tribunal among Cambodians: Implications of the Proceedings of Public Forums Held by a Local NGO" (*South East Asia Research*, 2013) and "Reconciliation as Process or Catalyst: Understanding the Concept in a Post-conflict Society" (*Comparative Sociology*, 2012).

APINYA FEUNGFUSAKUL is assistant professor at the Department of Sociology and Anthropology, Chiang Mai University. She has conducted research in anthropology of religion with an emphasis on religious movements in Thailand—especially women's movements. Some of her recent works include "Urban Logic and Mass Meditation in Contemporary Thailand," in *Global and Local Televangelism*, edited by Pradip Thomas and Philip Lee (Palgrave Macmillan, 2012) and "Art and Culture in Thai Cultural Movements," in *Some Thoughts on Northern Thai Cultural Research*, edited by Anan Ganjanapan (Department of Sociology and Anthropology, Chiang Mai University, 2015, in Thai).

ARIYA SVETAMRA is lecturer at the Department of Women's Studies, Faculty of Social Sciences, Chiang Mai University. Her recent works include "Politics of Religious Space in Practical Religion: Religion in the Making of Local Identities in Peri-urban Town, Chiang Mai Province" (PhD diss., Chiang Mai University, 2009), *Narrative Experience of Daraʼaang Ethnic Women in Access to Justice* (Law Reform Commission of Thailand, 2014, in Thai), and *Knowledge and Meaning of Underground Lottery in Women's Perspective* (Center for Gambling Studies, 2014, in Thai).

KYONOSUKE HIRAI is professor of anthropology at the National Museum of Ethnology in Japan and is also teaching social anthropology at SOKENDAI (Graduate University for Advanced Studies). His recent publications include two edited volumes: *Social Movements and the Production of Knowledge: Body, Practice, and Society in East Asia* (National Museum of Ethnology, 2015) and *Community as Practice: Mobility, State, and Movement* (Kyoto University Press, 2012, in Japanese).

KANOKSAK KAEWTHEP is associate professor and works at the Political Economy Centre, Faculty of Economics, Chulalongkorn University. His publications include an article in Shigeharu Tanabe's edited volume *Imagining Communities in Thailand* (Mekong Press, 2008), *The Economics of Giving* (Pab Pim Press, 2009, in Thai) and, with Kanjana Kaewthep and Anan Ganjanapan, *The Political Economy School* (Chulalongkorn University Press, 2006, in Thai).

NOBUKO KOYA is research associate at the Research Institute for Languages and Cultures of Asia and Africa, Tokyo University of Foreign Studies. Her recent works include "Herbal Medicine as a Medium for the Relationships between Northern Thai Folk Healers and Their Clients," in *Anthropology of Time: Affect, Nature, Social Spaces*, edited by Ryoko Nishii (Sekaishiso Sha, 2011, in Japanese).

KWANCHEWAN BUADAENG is assistant professor at the Department of Sociology and Anthropology, Faculty of Social Sciences, Chiang Mai University, Thailand. Her recent works include "Changing Familial Relations and Practices of the Karen People in Chiang Mai, Northern Thailand," in *The Family in Flux in Southeast Asia: Institution, Ideology, Practice*, edited by Yoko Hayami et al. (Kyoto University and Silkworm Books, 2012) and "Religious Space of Migrants and State Control at Thai-Burma Borderland," in *Society in Transition/Transforming Society*, edited by Wasan Panyakaew (Faculty of Social Sciences, Chiang Mai University, 2014, in Thai).

MALEE SITTHIKRIENGKRAI received her PhD in Medical and Health Social Sciences from Mahidol University (Thailand). She is affiliated with the Center for Ethnic Studies and Development and is lecturer in the MA program in ethnicity and development, Faculty of Social Sciences, Chiang Mai University. Her recent works include "Long Life of People Living with HIV/AIDS and the Practice of Medical Power," in *Socio-Ecological Dimensions of Infectious Diseases in Southeast Asia*, edited by Serge Morand *et al.* (Springer, 2015).

RYOKO NISHII is professor at the Research Institute for Languages and Culture of Asia and Africa, Tokyo University of Foreign Studies. She is an anthropologist who has studied Buddhist-Muslim relationships in southern Thailand for many years. Her recent works include *Ethnography of Affect* (Kyoto University Press, 2013, in Japanese), and an edited book *Anthropology of Time: Affect, Nature, Social Spaces* (Sekaishiso Sha, 2011, in Japanese).

MAYUMI OKABE is associate professor at the School of Contemporary Sociology, Chukyo University (Japan). She published her first book, *Buddhist Monks Engaging in "Development": An Ethnographic Study on Development Discourses and Religious Practices* (Fukyo Sha, 2014, in Japanese). Her recent works also include "Beyond Localities: Community Development and Network Construction among the Buddhist Monks in Northern Thailand," in *Contemporary Socio-Cultural and Political Perspectives in Thailand*, edited by Pranee Liamputtong (Springer, 2014).

SHIGEHARU TANABE is professor emeritus at the National Museum of Ethnology in Japan and currently teaches social anthropology at the Center for Ethnic Studies and Development and the Japanese Studies Center, Chiang Mai University. Recent works include "Spirit Mediumship and Affective Contact in Northern Thailand," in *Duai Rak: Essays on Thailand's Economy and Society for Professor Chatthip Nartsupha at 72*, (Sangsan, 2013) and *Anthropology of Spirits: Politics of Communality in Northern Thailand* (Iwanami Shoten, 2013, in Japanese).

# INDEX

revivalism in, 35, 37–38, 40n14
socially engaged, 191–92
utopian ideas in, 25, 27–28, 33–34, 44, 160
*See also* monks
*bun niyom* (meritism), 151, 157–59, 162n8
Burmese, 10, 43, 46, 48–49, 50–52, 54, 58, 107, 113–25, 203

capacity
of component parts, 45, 58, 64–65, 108, 150, 160, 161
individual, 3–4, 14, 22, 36, 38, 55, 56, 65, 71, 73, 79, 80, 194, 233, 238
*See also* potential
Center for Cambodian Civic Education (CIVICUS), 99
Center for Justice and Reconciliation (CJR), 99
Center for Social Development (CSD), 88, 96, 98–99, 101–3, 104n9, 104n10
*chan. See jhāna*
Cham, 90, 94
Chamathewi, Queen, 28, 37
Chao Regina, 34–35
Chao Suphan Kanlaya, 34
Chao Dara Ratsami, 34
charisma, 25, 50, 59n5, 60n8, 206. *See also under* monks
Chhang Youk, 88, 89, 93–94, 102
Chiang Mai, 9, 21, 25, 36–37, 43, 45–46, 54, 65, 67–71, 111–12, 115, 125n5, 126n6–7, 125n9, 129, 151, 177, 213–20, 222, 226n15, 226n18, 226n22, 234
civil party, 88
cofunctioning, 4, 8, 9, 12, 15, 35, 40n10
collectivity, 6
Cohen, Paul, 33
commodification, 3
communal ethos, 8
communality, 1–2, 12, 86, 212–13
utopian, 30
*communitas*, 9–10, 12, 14, 38
affectual, 9
collective, 30
model, 14

community
alternative, 2, 11
business, 171
communitarian, 6, 183n4
development, 12, 170–71, 211–24, 225n8, 226n19, 227n29
of *dhamma*, 203
empowerment, 145, 171
of practice, 10, 244
as a process, 14
reflexive, 11
religious, 13, 44, 188
sense of, 137, 145, 174
traditional, 11, 175–76, 179, 223
utopian, 21, 32, 34–36, 59
*See also under* culture; museum; Muslim
Community Development Monks' Network in Northern Thailand, 12, 212–13, 221
community movements, 1, 3, 5, 7, 8, 9, 11, 13, 15, 15n1, 38, 166, 182, 234
models of, 14
Connerton, Paul, 140, 176
Connors, Michael, 183n4
contagion, 9, 35
contestation, 129, 143–44, 146
contingently obligatory, 6
cultural pragmatics, 12
culture
community (*watthanatham chumchon*), 170, 172
regional, 169–70
Thai, 169, 171
cure, 25–26, 28, 37, 80, 135–36, 231, 241

Dalai Lama, 39n1
*dam hua*, 66, 138, 142–43
*dana* (sharing), 11, 157, 159, 160–61, 163n9
deity (*thep, thewada*), 29–30, 133, 142
DeLanda, Manuel, 4–5, 15n3, 44, 64, 222
Delanty, Gerard, 14
Deleuze, Gilles, 3–4, 9, 15n2, 16n8, 33, 35, 40n6, 64, 107
Democratic Kamphuchea (DK), 87, 89, 90–91, 93

Democratic Karen Buddhist Army (DKBA), 49, 51, 57
Department of Fine Arts, 180
depression, 29
desire, 12, 15n5, 22, 36, 38, 49, 53, 55–56, 90, 98, 122
deterritorialization, 10, 38
detoxification, 2, 10, 13–14, 231–45
  as a new social movement *See* new social movement.
  and the potential of the individual, 244
  training program of, 235–42, 244
  and understanding of the body and illness, 232, 238, 241, 245
  and Western medicine, 238, 242–43
*dhamma* (Buddhist moral principles), 10, 22, 25–26, 31, 32–34, 36, 60n12. *See also under* community
Dhammananda, 188, 192, 197–98, 200–202, 205–7
dhammic practice, 21–22, 32, 38
diaspora, 85
  returnee, 85–86, 88, 90, 100, 102
difference, 3–4, 58, 70, 82n5, 94, 103, 117, 173–74, 187, 192, 204–5, 223
divination, 25–26, 28, 39, 65
divine prescription (*ongkan*), 31
Documentation Center of Cambodia (DC-Cam), 88, 90, 92, 94, 102, 103n6, 104n7
Doi Suthep, 36, 39, 46, 58
Doi Tao District, 56, 59
dream, 27, 39, 48, 133, 136–37, 160, 169
Duch, 87, 95, 99

Ecclesiastical Act, 192–93
*élan vital*, 9
embodied knowledge and practices, 145
emergent property, 8, 39
encounter, 5, 8, 13, 29, 36, 39, 60, 89, 112, 144, 190, 195, 199, 214, 216, 219, 222, 234
Escobar, Arturo, 4, 45, 108, 222, 225n3

essence, 4, 14, 108, 169, 222
"event relations," 8

exorcism (*lai phi*), 35, 37
experience, 12, 13, 212, 214–15, 219–22, 224–25
  personal, 2, 12–13, 49, 179,
  religious, 198–99, 204–5
exteriority of relations, 5, 45, 64, 108, 225n3
Extraordinary Chambers in the Courts of Cambodia (ECCC), 86–88, 92–94, 97–102, 103n1

femininity, 34, 191
feminism, 6, 191, 196, 198, 206, 208
fetishism, 39
filiation, 9, 13
flight, 38
fluidity, 3
"folded" environments, 32, 38
folk medicine (*kan phaet phuen ban*), 2, 7, 14, 63–65, 67–68, 70, 74–77, 79–81
forest monk, 190, 194, 198–200, 202, 205, 207
fortunetelling (*du chata chiwit, poet kam*), 29, 39
Foucault, Michel, 14, 16, 21, 25
friendship, 14, 237

Ganesha, 23
gender, 197, 204
  bias, 204
  concepts, 204
  hierarchy, 205
  ideology, 188, 191, 196, 204
  role of, 36, 143
global capitalism, 4
goddesses, 23, 34
Guattari, Félix, 3, 35, 40n6, 64

Habermas, Jürgen, 13
Harvey, David, 34, 39
healer-patient (client) relationship, 66, 78
health care
  alternative, 232, 234, 236, 241, 244
  public, 63, 66
  and understanding of well-being, 232, 238, 244–45

museums
  in Buddhist temples, 165, 166–67, 168, 172, 177, 178–79, 181, 182n1
  community/local, 1, 8, 11–12, 14, 165–69, 172–74, 176–82
  indigenous, 165
  National Museums, 170, 177, 180, 182n1
Muslim
  communities, 2, 10, 90, 107–8, 115, 119–20, 124
  Burmese, 10, 107, 114–15, 117–18, 120–24
  Thai, 10, 107, 117–20, 122–23
Myaing Gyi Ngu, 43, 49, 51, 55, 60n10

nation-state, 3–5, 9, 11, 15, 125, 130, 141, 169
networks, 1, 5, 11, 36, 37, 38, 39, 212–24, 225n4, 227n27, 227n29
  interpersonal, 2, 5, 58
"new space-time," 33
ngan (work, rite), 174–76
NGO (nongovernmental organization), 7, 65, 212, 214–15, 219, 222–23, 227n24
nimit, nimitta (meditative visions), 23, 25, 27–29, 36, 39n2, 40n11, 189, 195, 199, 202, 206
nirvana (nipphan, nibbana), 27
normative structure, 12, 14
Norodom Ranariddh, 87
Northern Coordination Center for Thai Traditional Medicine, 69–70, 79
northern Thai. See Khon Mueang
NorthNet Foundation, 68–69, 79
nunnery, 31, 34–35
Nuon Chea, 87, 101

Omkoi District, 45, 48, 59n3
oracle, 36
order
  alternative, 15, 16n8, 25
  Buddhist, 26, 27, 35, 38
  modern, 15
organismic whole, 6
Osterweil, Michal, 4, 45, 108
Ouyporn Kheunkaew, 191, 196–98, 200–201, 203–4, 206–7

Pa-an, 46, 47, 59n2, 59n5
pagoda, 7–8, 23, 43–44, 46, 48–54, 56–58, 59n4, 60n8, 196
Panchasila Herbal Club (Chomrom samunphrai panchasila), 68, 74, 76, 78
Paris Peace Accords, 87
Parnet, Claire, 4, 15n2
Patton, Paul, 3
peasant, 10, 33, 21, 81n4, 170, 191
  resistance, 146
Pha Nam, 45, 47
Phnom Penh, 87, 94, 98, 100
pho kae mask, 30, 40n8
Phra Anan, 37
phra kechi (magico-religious monk), 195
Phra Naresuan, King, 31, 34
Phuan, 173–74
Phue Khaw Taw, 43–45, 47–59, 59n7, 60n9, 60n10
phuttha thet (buddhadesa), 27
Pol Pot, 86
potential, 1–4, 7, 9, 15, 22, 35–36, 38, 81, 102, 108, 125, 145, 167, 199, 218, 226n16
  group, 232
  individual, 12, 14, 244
  transformative, 2
  See also capacity
power relations, 5, 140, 196
precepts (phra winai), 13, 26, 44, 149, 153, 156, 187, 198, 221, 225, 234
Princess Maha Chakri Sirindhorn Anthropology Centre (SAC), 177–78, 180, 181, 182n1, 183n6
psychiatric hospital, 29

realist social ontology, 15n3
reflexivity, 2, 6, 9, 11, 14, 240
re-Islamization, 13
relics, 56, 141–42, 190, 195–96, 203, 205, 207
religious experience, 188, 198–99, 204–5. See also under identity
religious form, 13, 198, 208
religious practice, 198, 203–4, 206–7
revolution of 1973, 170

ritual, 9, 38, 40n7, 65, 130, 136–37, 140, 145

*sadharanabhoki* (communal property
    system), 150, 158–59, 161n1
Salween, 46–48, 60n8
*samaneri* (female novice), 189
*samatha. See under* meditation
Samma Sikkha School, 11, 150, 156, 159
sangha (ordained community), 11, 44, 53,
    194, 198, 208
    community, 194
    Thai, 11
Santi Asoke, 11–12, 14, 234–35, 238
    community, 234–35, 244–45
self-organization, 4, 5
self-reflection, 11, 197
sexuality, 13, 192, 206–207. *See also under*
    identity
sharing, 72, 94, 207, 234, 238, 244. See also
    *dana*
signless liberation (*animitta-vimokkha*), 27
*sila* (ethical precept), 149, 156–57. *Also see*
    precept.
Sisa Asoke Community, 150, 232, 234–35,
    239, 240–44
site, 4, 8, 10, 14, 22, 36, 39, 47, 51–52,
    60n10, 71, 93, 136–37, 195–96
social movements, 2, 5–6, 13, 187, 231–32.
    *See also* movements.
spaces
    between, 10
    communicative, 8, 13, 92, 102
    public, 90, 92, 98, 144
    organization of, 22, 23, 33, 34, 38, 130,
        168
    sacred/religious, 13, 58, 119, 187, 193,
        194, 205, 208
    social, 73, 231, 237
    strategies/tactics for negotiating, 187–
        88, 192, 194–96, 198, 208
spell (*khatha*), 25–26, 29–30, 36–37
spirit
    cult, 2, 8, 10, 13–14
    mediums, 26, 29–32, 39n2, 132–40,
        142–43
    local, 138, 145

malevolent, 37
    possession, 37–38, 130
    power of, 129–30, 132, 143, 145–46
    town, 9, 130
    worship, 29, 142
state apparatus, 35
Strathern, Marylin, 15n4
subjectivity, 2, 13, 14
*suep chata khon* (extending lifespan sutra),
    30
Swe Kabin, 47
symbiosis, 4, 10, 35–36
sympathy, 4, 10, 13, 85, 203

Tablighi Jama'at, 108–12, 114, 125n1,
    126n7, 126n9
Tai Yai (Shan), 28, 213, 225n5
Tamo Mountain, 43–45, 48, 50–53, 54,
    55–58
Tanabe, Shigeharu, 137
Tantric Theravada, 39n2
teacher. See *khu*
Tha Song Yang District, 45, 52
Thai (Tai) Lue, 172–73
Thai people, 48
Thai traditional medicine, 63, 65–67,
    69–70, 72–76, 78–81, 82n10
Thailand-Myanmar border, 7, 10, 14, 43,
    45–46, 50, 54, 57, 59, 107
Thammaya, 48, 59n6
Theary Seng, 88, 95, 98–102
*ton bun* (holy man), 132
totality, 3–4, 107–8, 222
tourism, 170–72, 176, 179
transcendence
    experience of, 194, 202, 204
    faculties associated with, 194–95, 202
    as a goal, 197
    mental, 206
transitional justice, 88
Turner, Victor, 9, 27, 38

U Tuzana (Thuzana), 43, 50
    *See also* Phue Khaw Taw; Myaing Gyi
    Ngu
UN, 98